BIBLICAL INTERPRETATION IN THE GNOSTIC GOSPEL OF TRUTH FROM NAG HAMMADI

SOCIETY OF BIBLICAL LITERATURE

DISSERTATION SERIES

J. J. M. Roberts, Old Testament Editor
Charles Talbert, New Testament Editor

Number 79

BIBLICAL INTERPRETATION IN THE
GNOSTIC GOSPEL OF TRUTH
FROM NAG HAMMADI

by
Jacqueline A. Williams

Jacqueline A. Williams

BIBLICAL INTERPRETATION IN THE GNOSTIC GOSPEL OF TRUTH FROM NAG HAMMADI

Scholars Press
Atlanta, Georgia

BIBLICAL INTERPRETATION IN THE GNOSTIC GOSPEL OF TRUTH FROM NAG HAMMADI

Jacqueline A. Williams

Ph.D., 1983
Yale University

Advisor:
Bentley Layton

© 1988
Society of Biblical Literature

Library of Congress Cataloging-in-Publication Data

Williams, Jacqueline A.
  Biblical interpretation in the Gnostic Gospel of truth from Nag Hammadi

  (Dissertation series)
  Bibliography: p.
  1. Gospel of truth—Criticism, interpretation, etc.
  2. Valentinus, 2nd cent. 3. Gnosticism. I. Title.
  II. Series: Dissertation series (Society of Biblical Literature)
  BT1390.W46 1988   229'.8   85-18483
  ISBN: 0-89130-876-8
  ISBN: 0-89130-877-6 (pbk.)

Printed in the United States of America

Contents

PREFACE vii

Chapter

1. THE TEXT AND THE PROBLEM 1
2. COMMENTARIES 15
3. EVALUATION OF VALENTINUS' USE OF TEXTS 175
4. VALENTINUS' INTERPRETATION:
   HIS PRESUPPOSITIONS AND METHOD 189

APPENDIX: VALENTINUS IN A LETTER (frg. 2)
   PRESERVED IN CLEMENT OF ALEXANDRIA,
   STROM. II 114.6 ~MATT 5:8 205

BIBLIOGRAPHY 209

INDEX OF MODERN AUTHORS 219

Preface

This book was originally presented as a dissertation to the faculty of Yale University in December 1983, for the degree of Ph.D., under the title, "The Interpretation of Texts and Traditions in the Gospel of Truth." It has not been revised in any substantial way.

My interest in Valentinian Gnosticism began during my undergraduate days at Duke. Through the encouragement of Professor Orval Wintermute, I began to study Greek and Coptic. At the same time, I developed an interest in New Testament studies and later became intrigued with the interpretations given to biblical texts by Valentinian Gnostics. While at Yale, I learned many things from people too numerous to name, but I would like to thank in particular those people whose thought has most influenced my own: Professors Nils Dahl (now retired), Bentley Layton, and Wayne Meeks. Professor Layton directed the dissertation and was unfailing in his advice and constructive criticism. Professor Meeks also commented on my ideas and was helpful throughout the research and writing. Of course, the imperfections are my own responsibility. Abbreviations follow the guidelines for contributors to the *Journal of Biblical Literature* (*JBL*) 95 (1976) 335-346, except for abbreviations for Nag Hammadi texts, which are taken from the table in *IDBSup* 615-616.

Finally, I would like to thank my spouse, Peter Niculescu, and my father, Charles Esmond Williams. This book is dedicated in gratitude to my father and to the memory of my mother, Jessie Cox Williams, whose love was an unfailing source of strength throughout the years.

1
The Text and the Problem

THE TEXT

The Gospel of Truth (GTr) is one of the Gnostic texts attested in a hoard of manuscripts found near Nag Hammadi in Upper Egypt.[1] It now survives only in Coptic, although it was almost certainly composed in Greek.[2] Two copies of the text were found among the Nag Hammadi manuscripts, one in NHC XII, a translation in the Sahidic dialect, and the other in NHC I, a translation in the Subachmimic dialect. Both of these manuscripts date from the early fourth century, as evidence from the cartonnage indicates.[3] The manuscript in Codex XII is extremely

---

[1] J. M. Robinson, "The Discovery of the Nag Hammadi Codices," *BA* 42 (1979) 206-224 tries to reconstruct the history of the discovery through interviews with persons involved at various stages of the history of the library until it finally was housed in the Coptic Museum in Cairo; details of the discovery, which took place in 1945, remain obscure and contradictory.

[2] For a summary of the arguments regarding the original language, see J.-E. Ménard, *L'Evangile de Vérité*, NHS 2 (Leiden: Brill, 1972), pp. 9-17. For a Greek retroversion (and French translation), see J.-E. Menard, *L'Evangile de Vérité: Rétroversion Grecque et Commentaire* (Paris: Letouzey & Ané, 1962), pp. 31-71. The likelihood of recovering the original Greek is slim, however, due to a lack of control in several areas, for example, a dearth of witnesses and ignorance of the circumstances of transmission, including the ability of the translator(s). These factors are observed and described more completely by B. Layton in "The Recovery of Gnosticism," *Second Century* 1 (1981) 85-89.

[3] Only Codex I can be dated from the cartonnage, although presumably all the codices date from roughly the same time; paleographical evidence supports a mid-fourth century date for both codices as well. The most

fragmentary; examination of the Coptic in the fragments that are extant suggests that the grammatical constructions in the Sahidic version may have been more straightforward than those in the Subachmimic translation of Codex I, but the fragmentary state of the Sahidic version precludes detailed examination or extensive use by scholars today. Because the Subachmimic version is preserved with only a few lacunae, it has been the basis of all of the scholarly work on GTr. At present only one critical edition of the text has been published,[4] but another is forthcoming.[5] Photographic facsimiles of the two manuscripts have also been published.[6]

The title, authorship, place of composition, and date of composition of GTr are all uncertain. These questions are closely related in that knowledge of one might lead to discovery of the others. The internal evidence is not explicit on any of these points. The incipit of GTr, when coupled with a *testimonium*, does give some clue as to its title. Irenaeus, *Adv. Haer.* III

---

thorough discussion can be found in J. W. B. Barns, G. M. Browne, and J. C. Shelton, eds., *Nag Hammadi Codices: Greek and Coptic Papyri from the Cartonnage of the Covers*, NHS 16 (Leiden: Brill, 1981). See also *The Facsimile Edition of the Nag Hammadi Codices: Cartonnage* (Leiden: Brill, 1979). B. Layton reviews these two works in *JAOS* 102 (1982) 397-398. He draws particular attention to the date of the cartonnage (c. 340's) and underlines that the publication of the cartonnage shows that the Nag Hammadi manuscripts probably had no connection with a Pachomian monastery which was nearby.

[4]*Evangelium Veritatis: Codex Jung f.VIIIv-XVIv,XIXr-XXIIr*, ed. and trans. M. Malinine, H. C. Puech, G. Quispel (Zurich: Rascher, 1956) and ed. and trans. M. Malinine, H. C. Puech, G. Quispel, W. Till *Evangelium Veritatis (Supplementum): Codex Jung f.-XVIr-XVIIIv* (Zurich and Stuttgart: Rascher, 1961). Strictly speaking, this is not a critical edition but rather a transcription of the manuscript in Codex I together with some conjectural emendations based on the editors' understanding of Coptic and Gnosticism. This edition has been recollated against the manuscript under ultra-violet light by S. Emmel, and I have used his collation in this study with his kind permission.

[5]H. Attridge, ed., *Nag Hammadi Codex I (The Jung Codex)*, NHS 22-23 (Leiden: Brill, 1985). I have not had access to this edition during the preparation of the present study.

[6]Department of Antiquities of the Arab Republic of Egypt in conjunction with the United Nations Educational, Scientific and Cultural Organization, *The Facsimile Edition of the Nag Hammadi Codices*, Codex I (Leiden: Brill, 1977); Codices XI, XII XIII (Leiden: Brill, 1973).

11.9 asserts that the Valentinians used a "Gospel of Truth."[7] The manuscript in Codex I does not include a title,[8] but the incipit of the text in Codex I reads "The Gospel of Truth...," which suggests that this may have been the title of the work.[9] On balance, there is no reason not to accept the suggestion that "Gospel of Truth" is the title of our document; it is likely that this document is to be identified with the one mentioned by Irenaeus (Irenaeus does not mention the author's name).

An uncertain *testimonium* is found in pseudo-Tertullian, who says in *Adv. Omnes Haer.* 4.6,[10] that Valentinus "has" his own gospel, although he does not say that Valentinus wrote it. On the basis of this statement, some scholars have maintained that Valentinus was the author of GTr.[11] The external evidence obtained from heresiological sources is inconclusive and thus cannot verify Valentinus' authorship; it is not clear whether any

---

[7]Hi vero qui sunt a Valentino, iterum existentes extra omnem timorem, suas conscriptiones preferentes, plura habere gloriantur, quam sint ipsa Evangelia. Siquidem in tantum processerunt audaciae, uti quod ab his non olim conscriptum est, veritatis Evangelium, titulent, in nihilo conveniens Apostolorum Evangeliis. . . .

[8]It is not possible to determine whether the manuscript of Codex XII had a title because the manuscript is so fragmentary.

[9]K. Grobel, *The Gospel of Truth: A Valentinian Meditation on the Gospel* (New York: Abingdon, 1960), p. 21, was content to understand "gospel" in the sense of "good news" and to conclude that the work has no title (cf. the discussion of the confusion of title and genre below). J. Munck, "Evangelium Veritatis and Greek Usage as to Book Titles," *ST* 17 (1963) 133-138, explains that in common practice there was often no differentiation between the title and the contents of ancient Greek writings. When titles did become used, they were primarily a means of identification and were not an expression of the contents; thus, the opening lines of a work were often used. GTr may in fact have not had a title originally, but the opening lines may have come to be regarded as the title. More recently, B. Standaert, "'Evangelium Veritatis' et 'Veritatis Evangelium': La question du titre et les témoins patristiques," *VC* 30 (1976) 138-150, has argued that the absence of a distinct title for GTr can be attributed to the habit of the scribe. Although the author (i.e., Valentinus) may not have intended the opening words to be the title, when "gospel" came to be used as a designation for many written works rather than its first use as simply "good news," the opening words may have been taken as the title.

[10]Evangelium habet etiam suum praeter haec nostra.

[11]E.g., Grobel, p. 19. Van Unnik, *Jung Codex*, pp. 99-104, was the first to make a reasoned case for Valentinus' authorship.

of the heresiologists had actually seen a copy of GTr. Nine fragments of Valentinus' own work, however, are extant.[12] A detailed literary and stylistic comparison of GTr with these fragments has indicated that Valentinus was probably the author of GTr. The first scholar to make a convincing case on this basis was B. Standaert.[13] Through a rhetorical and stylistic comparison of frgs. 1, 2, 5, and 8 with GTr 17:5-18:10, Standaert shows that the fragments of Valentinus share with GTr a supple use of language and its evocative force through such features as a mixing of abstract vocabulary with idiomatic expressions.

Although certainty of authorship is impossible to determine, the present study accepts the conclusions of Standaert. In the Appendix to the present study, a sample of Valentinus' use of texts in the extant fragments is analyzed; the way the text is incorporated into this fragment is almost identical to that of the texts analyzed in Chapter 2 and thus supports Standaert's arguments. Even if GTr is eventually shown not to have been written by Valentinus, the results of the present study will not be affected since this study concerns questions whose meaning and solution are independent of the question of authorship of GTr. For the sake of convenience and because my own preliminary work indicates Valentinus' probable authorship of GTr, I will refer to the author as Valentinus throughout this study. The weight of internal and external evidence suggests that GTr is the work mentioned by Irenaeus and that Valentinus was its author.

The place and date of composition are even more difficult to

---

[12]The fragments have been collected by W. Voelker in *Quellen zur Geschichte der christlichen Gnosis* (Tübingen: Mohr, 1932), pp. 57-60. G. C. Stead, "In Search of Valentinus," *The Rediscovery of Gnosticism*, I, ed. B. Layton (Leiden: Brill, 1980), 78-90, discusses the fragments and concludes that Valentinus was a biblical Platonist, a conclusion with which this study concurs.

[13]"'L'Evangile de Vérité': Critique et Lecture," *NTS*, 22 (1976) 243-275; his discussion of the fragments of Valentinus is on pp. 259-265. In addition to his analysis of the fragments of Valentinus, Standaert discusses the rhetorical structure of the prologue (GTr 16:31-17:4) and epilogue (GTr 42:37-43:24), explaining that both exhibit a concentric arrangement. The prologue may be compared formally with the opening of Rom, Heb, or even Mark. The epilogue may be compared formally with the end of Matt. Moreover, Standaert outlines the rhetorical structure of the remaining portion of GTr and concludes that the entire work exhibits a concentric arrangement. Finally, he discusses the religious language of GTr and the themes (e.g., Name, Son) which are developed in the latter part of GTr.

The Text and the Problem 5

determine, but identification of the author enables us to get an idea of the possible place and date of composition. Irenaeus reports that Valentinus "came to Rome under Hyginus [c. 136-140], flourished under Pius [c. 140-154], and remained until Anicetus [c. 154-(?)]," *Adv. Haer.* III 4.2.[14] Because most of Valentinus' career was spent in Rome, it is likely that he composed GTr in Rome. Rome was, moreover, a center of Christian scholastic activity throughout the second century and would have been likely to attract creative thinkers such as Valentinus.[15] Because there is little indication in GTr of an elaborate myth involving a system of aeons underlying GTr,[16] the work probably was written at a relatively early stage in the development of Valentinus' thought. There is no indication that figures which would be viewed as emanations in later Valentinianism are anything but attributes of the Father; this accords with Tertullian's report in *Adv. Val.* 4.2.[17] Thus, if GTr were written by Valentinus in Rome before he concentrated on more speculative views about the locus of activities of the divine realm, then one might suggest that GTr was composed in the early years (c. 136-140's) of his stay in Rome.

---

[14] Valentinus enim venit Roman sub Hygino; increvit vero sub Pio, et prorogavit tempus usque ad Anicetum. The Greek is preserved in Eusebius, *H. E.* IV 11: Οὐαλεντῖνος μὲν γὰρ ἦλθεν εἰς 'Ρώμην ἐπὶ 'Υγίνου· ἤκμασε δὲ ἐπὶ Πίου, καὶ παρέμεινεν ἕως 'Ανικήτου.

[15] The evidence for Christianity in Rome in the mid-second century is presented and discussed by G. Lüdemann in "Zur Geschichte des ältesten Christentums in Rom. I. Valentin und Marcion. II. Ptolemäus und Justin," *ZNW* 70 (1979) 86-114. Lüdemann's evaluation of the evidence is often directly to the point, although Christian "schools" in Rome may not have been as unified under the umbrella of an organized church as he seems to assume.

[16] Despite the objections of H. Jonas, "Evangelium Veritatis and the Valentinian Speculation," *Studia Patristica* 6 (ed. F. L. Cross; TU 81; Berlin: Akademie, 1962) 96-111.

[17] Eam postmodum Ptolomaeus intrauit, nominibus et numeris Aeonum distinctis in personales substantias sed extra deum determinatas, quas Valentinus in ipsa summa diuinitatis ut sensus et affectus <et> motus incluserat. One figure, namely, error, may be hypostatized, but no one has yet identified error with one of the Valentinian aeons in a way that allows the Valentinian system of aeons to remain intact. B. Pearson, "Did the Gnostics Curse Jesus?" *JBL* 86 (1967) 304 and H. Jonas, *The Gnostic Religion*, 2d ed., rev. (Boston: Beacon, 1963) p. 316, n. 48 see in the use of "error" a veiled reference to the creator, but they do not give evidence for further elements of this supposed myth.

Along with the questions of title, authorship, place of composition, and date of composition has frequently come the question of genre of GTr. If one knew only the title, "Gospel" of Truth, one might assume that the genre is "gospel," but just a cursory glance at the contents indicates that GTr does not share the form of the canonical gospels. This issue generated a large body of literature in the early days after the publication of GTr,[18] probably because the question of the genre of GTr was confused with the question of its title. Obviously GTr is not a gospel of the Markan type.[19] After all, GTr shows little interest in recounting words or activities of Jesus, except for occasional summary accounts (e.g., 18:15-26; 19:17-34; 20:22-21:1), which are highly stylized. GTr is not a "passion narrative with a biographical introduction."[20] Thus, the title of GTr gives no indication of its genre. The genre of GTr, in fact, has not yet been adequately described. Certain suggestions which have been made, for example, that GTr seems to be a "meditation on the gospel,"[21] function only as stopgaps. Until the question of genre is resolved,[22] scholars cannot adequately

---

[18] E.g., J. W. Dunn, "What does 'Gospel of Truth' Mean?" *VC* 15 (1961) 160-164; O. A. Piper, "Change of Perspective: Gnostic and Canonical Gospels," *Int* 16 (1962) 402-417.

[19] H. Koester has argued in "One Jesus and Four Primitive Gospels," *Trajectories through Early Christianity*, by J. M. Robinson and H. Koester (Philadelphia: Fortress, 1971), pp. 161-166, that only the canonical gospels, i.e., those that "developed out of the passion narrative (Mark and John), and the gospels dependent upon Mark (Matthew and Luke), have a genuine claim to the title 'gospel'" (p. 162). By this, he does not mean to discredit other writings which bear the title 'gospel'; rather such a designation is entirely legitimate because many of them continue genres, such as sayings, that predate the canonical gospels. Nevertheless, these gospels do not represent a unique Christian genre because they have prototypes in other ancient literature. Koester's point is that non-canonical gospels are not distortions of one kerygma (i.e., the earliest Christian preaching about Jesus' passion, death, and resurrection) upon which the canonical gospels were based.

[20] Koester, p. 162.

[21] This is Grobel's expression, p. 21 (and the subtitle of his commentary).

[22] No attempt is made to do so in this study; further research is hindered by our ignorance of the aim of GTr. H. Attridge, "The Gospel of Truth as an Exoteric Text," to be published in the proceedings of a conference on Gnosticism held at Southwestern Missouri State University in March 1983, has suggested that GTr was directed toward people who did not share the author's basic theological presuppositions. The internal evidence, however, remains inconclusive.

comment on why GTr is entitled "gospel." The most that one can say is that the word "gospel" in GTr may be intended in its earliest Christian sense ("good news"), as Paul especially uses the word.[23]

THE PROBLEM

The present study is occasioned by the absence of any systematic examination of Valentinus' use of texts and traditions.[24] The problem of determining which texts Valentinus used and how he interpreted them has been discussed; it was first broached by van Unnik,[25] who examined a few key passages in detail. For example, he asserted that in the passage on the living book of the living (GTr 19:35-20:7), Valentinus used a throne vision from Rev 5, transposing certain conceptions therein with the result that the eschatological context of the passage in Rev has been transformed in GTr into a metaphysical context in which no hint of an eschatological expectation is retained. Van Unnik implies that Valentinus has

---

[23]L. Cerfaux, "De Saint Paul à 'L'Evangile de Vérité,'" *NTS* 5 (1958-59) 103-112; also W. C. Van Unnik, "The 'Gospel of Truth' and the New Testament," in *The Jung Codex*, F. L. Cross, trans. and ed. (London: Mowbray, 1955), pp. 79-129.

[24]Certain passages have been discussed often, especially those regarding (a) a book (GTr 19:34-20:27); (b) sheep (GTr 31:35-32:17; 32:17-30); and (c) the divine name (GTr 38:4-41:3). The following examples are illustrative of the type of treatment these passages have received in the secondary literature: (a) J. Daniélou, *The Theology of Jewish Christianity* (London: Darton, Longman & Todd, 1964), pp. 203-204: Piper, p. 405; C. I. K. Story, *The Nature of Truth in the Gospel of Truth and the Writings of Justin Martyr* (Leiden: Brill, 1970), pp. 126-131; and van Unnik, pp. 108-112; (b) H. I. Marrou, "'L'Evangile de Vérité et la diffusion du comput digital dans l'antiquité,'" *VC* 12 (1958) 98-103; Ménard, 1972, p. 152; P. H. Poirier, "*L'Evangile de Vérité*, Ephrem le Syrien et le comput digital," *RevEtudAug* 25 (1979) 27-34; Story, p. 21; and van Unnik, pp. 112-113; and (c) Daniélou, pp. 147-160; J. D. Dubois, "Le contexte judaïque du 'nom' dans l'Evangile de Vérité," *RThPh*, ser. 3, 24 (1974) 198-216; Standaert, *NTS*, pp. 269-274; and van Unnik, pp. 113-114. In general, these works do not focus on detailed analysis of Valentinus' use of texts in an effort to determine the interpretation he gives to the texts; the works do, however, provide valuable information on other aspects of GTr.

[25]Pp. 107-108, 115. He gives a list of parallels on pp. 115-121; GTr 33-36 was not available when he wrote.

deliberately obscured the text of Rev in order to achieve this end.[26] In fact, van Unnik was able to determine one result of Valentinus' interpretation of Rev 5 here and also to sketch the process whereby the text was interpreted, but he did not go into detail about the specific interpretive changes that Valentinus made in using the text of Rev 5. He concluded from his study that at least the gospels, the Pauline epistles, Heb, and Rev were used and that there are traces of use of Acts, 1 John, and 1 Peter.[27]

Van Unnik's chief interest in GTr was history of the canon. For this reason he was eager to find attestation for as many New Testament books as possible. Moreover, he located GTr in Rome and stressed that GTr provides attestation for virtually all of the writings which were eventually accepted into the New Testament canon. Thus, he implied that the closing of the canon (at least in Rome) can be pushed back to a much earlier date than is commonly accepted, that is, to the middle of the second century.[28] Recent scholarship on the history of the canon has shown the problem to be much more complex than van Unnik supposed,[29] even more so if one takes account of the wide variety of Christian groups attested in early Christianity rather than concentrating only on those groups that can in retrospect be considered centrist.

The present study demonstrates conclusively that Valentinus did in fact use many of the writings that would form the New Testament, but the mere fact that he used them does not settle the question of their canonicity for him. There are no verbatim quotations or quotation formulae.[30] While the texts used in GTr must have been familiar to Valentinus and his readers, in fact GTr itself gives no clear indication of the status of the books used. A need for a Christian Scripture apart from the Jewish Scripture was just beginning to be perceived at the time GTr was written.[31]

---

[26]Van Unnik, pp. 108-110.
[27]Van Unnik, p. 122.
[28]Van Unnik, pp. 123-125.
[29]See especially H. von Campenhausen, *The Formation of the Christian Bible* (Philadelphia: Fortress, 1972).
[30]Quotation formulae are discussed at greater length in Chap. 3, where reference is made to H. Koester, *Synoptische Überlieferung bei den apostolischen Vätern*, TU 65 (Berlin: Akademie, 1957).
[31]As Campenhausen's work has made so clear. On pp. 148-165, he argues that Marcion's denigration of Jewish Scriptures in his *Antitheses* and his publication of a Christian "Gospel" and "Apostle" (i.e., a new canon of Scripture) forced other Christians to reevaluate the importance

What is intriguing about Valentinus' use of certain books is that, with the exception of Gen, they do not form part of the Jewish Scriptures. That he chose to interpret texts from books that were not part of the Jewish Scripture represented a radical departure from current Christian practice of interpreting Jewish Scriptures through allegory and typology.[32]

Even though no one has undertaken a detailed analysis of textual interpretations in GTr, some scholars have addressed the question of Valentinus' interpretation of specific portions of the New Testament. C. K. Barrett, for example, examined Valentinus' interpretation of John in GTr through a word study. He examined two categories of theological terms: words which occur frequently in John but infrequently in GTr and words which exhibit a less marked difference in relative frequency of usage. In both categories, he attributed the theological differences that GTr exhibits when compared with John to two factors: the absence in GTr of a primitive eschatological motif that runs throughout John and an assessment in GTr of the human situation in terms of ignorance rather than sin.[33] Although Barrett's discussion is hampered by his underlying assumption that the author of GTr has perverted John through a wrong understanding of its central theological issues, his work illustrates the extent to which Valentinus has used Johannine motifs. The present study shows that Valentinus has developed certain Johannine motifs in GTr and has been influenced by other motifs. The result is not that he has misunderstood central Johannine motifs but that he has chosen to develop certain motifs which are central to the theology of GTr.

Other scholars have investigated the influence of Paul upon GTr,

---

of Jewish Scripture for them. In fact, a studied response to Marcion's canon did not come until Irenaeus' four-gospel canon (*Adv. Haer.* III 11.9), and the limits of the canon still were not fixed for almost another century. Although Christian gospels and writings of Paul were already attested by the time of Marcion, attestation is not the same as canonicity. Moreover, attestation of a particular writing is no guarantee of its authority. This observation should be underscored because the present study discusses GTr as an early example of interpretation of Christian writings (GTr is not the earliest attestation of these writings). Whether these works were considered canonical is a question that is left open for the time being, although Chapter 4 reopens the question of whether the writings were scriptural for Valentinus.

[32]These subjects are discussed more fully in Chapter 4.

[33]"The Theological Vocabulary of the Fourth Gospel and the Gospel of Truth," *Current Issues in New Testament Interpretation*, W. Klassen and E. F. Snyder, eds. (New York: Harper & Row, 1961), pp. 210-223, 297-298.

among them being E. H. Pagels.[34] She postulated the existence of two Pauline traditions in the second century, one Gnostic and the other anti-Gnostic, based on her interpretation of Clement of Alexandria, *Strom.* VII 106.4, which relates the Valentinian assertion that their tradition could be traced back from Valentinus through a certain Theudas (otherwise unknown) to Paul. The evidence for an actual clash of different versions of an apostolic succession is sketchy.[35] Pagels apparently assumed that Valentinians carried on their Pauline tradition rather than developing it. By basing her work on a hypothetical, unified Valentinian tradition, she presented a Valentinian exegesis of numerous Pauline passages even if no examples survive from antiquity.[36] Although her treatment of the interpretation of Paul in GTr[37] was influenced by presuppositions about Valentinianism in general that may not be valid of GTr in particular, she nevertheless has provided insights into Valentinus' interpretation of certain Pauline theological passages, such as Col 2:13-15, where she demonstrated that the crucifixion is used as a metaphor of revelation.[38]

While earlier scholars' research on the interpretation of texts and traditions in GTr has yielded some valuable results, more work of an analytical nature needs to be done beyond that which has been undertaken in commentaries.[39] The present study provides detailed analyses of portions of GTr in which a reasonable case can be made for Valentinus' use of a particular text. The goal is not to recover the text that Valentinus used but rather to gain insight into his own thought. Recovery of the text used

---

[34] *The Gnostic Paul* (Philadelphia: Fortress, 1975).

[35] Indeed, Gnostics may have been the first to think of the idea of tracing their tradition back to Paul (cf. the report in Clement, *Strom.* VII 106.4 that Basilides traced his tradition back to Peter). Irenaeus, *Adv. Haer.* III 3.1, gives his interpretation of apostolic tradition (as a succession of bishops instituted by the apostles) which may be in response to Valentinian claims.

[36] This is observed by R. M. Grant in his appreciative review of Pagels's book in *RelSRev* 34 (1977) 33; Grant calls her result a "Valentinianesque gloss on the Pauline texts."

[37] She arranged her material in the biblical order of the Pauline epistles and hence did not include a separate section on GTr.

[38] Pagels, p. 139. She did not, however, discuss the background of this exegesis.

[39] See especially Grobel and J. Ménard (1972). Grobel's commentary is especially useful because of his command of the Coptic language; Ménard's commentary is particurly sensitive to similarities between GTr and other Gnostic literature.

The Text and the Problem   11

by Valentinus would in any case be extremely difficult, if not impossible.[40] In the first place, the original Greek text of GTr apparently has not survived; the original text would be absolutely necessary, for example, in order to study connective particles. In the second place, even if the Greek of GTr were available the particular method of interpretation that Valentinus used would preclude recovery of the biblical text, owing to Valentinus' interpretive process of allusion to the biblical text. Valentinus never quotes or cites a text in GTr but rather incorporates allusions so that no seams are visible; in other words, his interpretations are interwoven with his allusions. In the process of incorporating allusions into GTr, Valentinus retains enough of the text that he is interpreting so that it can be recognized, but at the same time he adds, deletes, or substitutes some words or phrases with the result that his own theological views are conveyed.

The analytical procedure used in the present study can identify the degree of similarity or difference between a given passage of GTr and its proposed literary source.[41] The procedure used in this study comprises four parts. First, the contexts of both the proposed source and the passage of GTr are summarized. Here the task is to bring out common elements which are present in the contexts. In some cases the contexts are quite different; this may affect the evaluation of probability which is assigned later.

Second, those portions of the reference that are similar in both the proposed source and in GTr are discussed. Here a philological approach is adopted, in order to show whether there are any unusual or striking words or figures in the source. If such items are carried over into GTr, it is important evidence that Valentinus has intentionally alluded to the source. In addition, technical observations regarding changes which

---

[40]See the Greek retroversion by Ménard, 1962; cf. discussion of retroversions above.
[41]To select the references that would be included in the corpus, I first read carefully through GTr many times, making notations of possible references. I then noted biblical passages that were cited in the secondary literature as possible sources. By collating suggestions in the secondary literature with my own suggestions, I was able to see at a glance who first proposed the reference; that person is given credit at the beginning of each analysis. Finally, I followed an abbreviated form of the method described below in order to eliminate proposals for which a reasonable case could not be made. Out of approximately four hundred suggestions, I chose to consider seventy-three.

Valentinus has made in the proposed source are also given; those observations include: identification of unusual or unique diction, commentary on grammatical difficulties, and precise description of the ways in which the Coptic text does or does not correspond to the biblical source.

Third, the overall likelihood that Valentinus used the proposed source is evaluated, and the probability is assigned to one of three classes (probable, possible, dubious). Here the task is to evaluate evidence that has already been adduced, such as similarity or difference in contexts and the frequency with which words and images occurred in literature of Valentinus' day. For example, if a specific word occurs only in the proposed source and GTr, this evidence is excellent.

Fourth, Valentinus' interpretation of the proposed source is discussed. Here the task is not simply to expound GTr but to show how the interpretation of each text fits into the context of the passage in GTr. This last section is omitted when the proposed reference is shown to be dubious.

This procedure is followed for each of the seventy-three passages in which a possible reference to a text occurs. Moreover, for each passage a synopsis is included, in which the proposed source and the passage of GTr are quoted side-by-side so that similarities can be seen at a glance.[42] Words and phrases that constitute verbatim parallels have solid underlining whereas parallel words and phrases in which small differences, such as tense or person, occur have broken underlining. The Coptic is given beneath this portion of the synopsis.

The aim of the procedure is first to demonstrate the ways in which Valentinus has altered a text that he has used and then to explain how he has interpreted the text. The results are twofold: determination of which writings were used and understanding of Valentinus' interpretive method. Discussion of these results is reserved for Chapters 3 and 4. The present study demonstrates the complexity of the interpretive technique used by Valentinus in presenting his understanding of the gospel. It also shows the degree of sophistication with which Christians were already capable of treating originally Christian texts. Thus, even though the issue of canonicity is not central to this study, the fact that Valentinus interprets portions

---

[42]Such a manner of presentation is not original. H. Koester used a similar construction of synopses in his book, *Synoptische Überlieferung bei den apostolischen Vätern*, as also did E. Massaux in *Influence de l'Evangile de saint Matthieu sur la littérature chrétienne avant saint Irénée* (Gembloux, Duculot, 1950).

of works that would soon be canonical is important for a better understanding of the history of Christian interpretation of Scripture. GTr provides an excellent example of the depth of insight that Christians in the second century could bring to their interpretation of Christian texts.

2
Commentaries

This technical chapter contains analyses of seventy-three passages where Valentinus may have interpreted a biblical text. The chapter can be understood and used without a knowledge of Coptic. The arrangement of the individual analyses is as follows:

    Synopsis: GTr in English | Biblical parallel
    Coptic text of GTr passage, for reference
    A. Context: summary of context of proposed source and passage in GTr
    B. Elements of Comparison: philological analysis
    C. Evaluation of the Parallel: explanation of the degree of certainty (probable, possible, dubious) ascribed to the parallel
    D. Interpretation: discussion of Valentinus' interpretation of the passage in light of changes made in the proposed source
    Selections considered dubious do not have a D section.

English translations of GTr are my own, for CG I from the Coptic of Malinine et al., as recollated by S. Emmel, and for CG XII from the facsimile edition; biblical texts are taken from Rahlfs (LXX) and Nestle-Aland, 26th ed. (NT).

Sigla

_____ (Solid underlining)	indicates verbatim parallel
_ _ _ _ _(Dotted underlining)	indicates nearly verbatim parallel
=	indicates "is the same as"
≅	indicates "is nearly the same as"

Sigla (continued)

≠ indicates "is not the same as"

≟ indicates "may be the same as"

~ indicates "should be compared with"

A² indicates Subachmimic ˙(dialect of Coptic)

S indicates Sahidic (dialect of Coptic)

1. GTr 17:11-21 (A²) ~ Rom 1:21, 23, 25, 27

Postulated by Williams.[1] Possible.

And the agitation condensed like fog so that no one could see.	²¹καὶ ἐσκοτίσθη ἡ ἀσύνετος αὐτῶν καρδία.
Thus, error found power	(cf. τῆς πλάνης vs. 27) ²³καὶ ἤλλαξαν τὴν δόξαν τοῦ ἀφθάρτου θεοῦ
and worked at her matter in emptiness, without having known the truth.	(cf. τὴν ἀλήθειαν below) ἐν ὁμοιώματι εἰκόνος
She came to be in a molded form (πλασμα), preparing (it) through power	φθαρτοῦ ἀνθρώπου . . .

---

[1]Others have noted similarities between the beginning of GTr and the beginning of Rom, most notably, L. Cerfaux, "De saint Paul à 'L'Evangile de la Vérité,'" *NTS* 5 (1958-59) 103-112, but his interpretation is wooden and unconvincing. R. McL. Wilson, *Gnostic Problem* (London: Mowbray, 1958), p. 168, n. 62, also broaches in passing the question of the use of Rom here; he notes that the theme of ignorance of God can be traced back to Wis 13:1-9.

Commentaries   17

in beauty the substitute for the truth.	(cf. ἐν τῷ ψεύδει) ²⁵οἵτινες μετήλλαξαν τὴν ἀλήθειαν τοῦ θεοῦ ἐν τῷ ψεύδει . . .

¹¹ⲡⲛⲟⲩϣⲏ ⲇⲉ· ⲁϥ¹²ⲱⲣⲝ̄ ⲙ̄ⲡⲣⲏⲧⲉ ⲛ̄ⲟⲩ²ⲁⲁⲥⲧⲛ̄ ¹³ⲕⲁⲁⲥⲉ· ϫⲉ ⲛⲉϣⲁⲁⲅⲉ
ⲛⲉⲩ ¹⁴ⲁⲃⲁⲗ ⲉⲧⲃⲉ ⲡⲉⲉⲓ ⲁⲥⲉⲁⲙⲉⲁⲙ ¹⁵ⲛ̄ϭⲓ ⲧⲡⲗⲁⲛⲏ· ⲁⲥⲣ̄ ²ⲱⲃ ⲁϯ²ⲩⲁⲏ ¹⁶ⲛ̄ⲧⲉⲥ
²ⲛ̄ⲛ ⲟⲩⲡⲉⲧϣⲟⲩⲉⲓⲧ· ¹⁷ⲉⲙⲡⲉⲥⲥⲟⲩⲱⲛ ⲛ̄ϯⲧⲙⲛ̄ⲧ¹⁸ⲙⲏⲉ· ⲁⲥϣⲱⲡⲉ ²ⲛⲛ ⲟⲩⲡⲗⲁⲥⲙⲁ
¹⁹ⲉⲥⲥⲁⲃⲧⲉ ²ⲛ ⲧⲉⲁⲙ· ²ⲛ̄ ⲟⲩⲙⲛ̄ⲧ²⁰ⲥⲁⲉⲓⲉ ⲛ̄ⲧⲝ̄ⲃ̄ⲃⲓⲱ ⲛ̄ϯⲧⲙⲛ̄ⲧ²¹ⲙⲏⲉ

A. Context

Rom 1:18-32 (disregard of God and its result). Although God can be known even through his creation, pagans have lost sight of natural theology. Their intellect has become "darkened," and they have substituted idols, some in human form, for God's truth.

GTr 17:4-30 (ignorance of the Father and its result). Since God is intrinsically unknowable except through the Son's coming, humanity had no knowledge of God. Their intellect had become "darkened," and they had created a beautiful "modeled form" and substituted this for God's truth.

B. Elements of Comparison

And the agitation condensed like fog so that no one could see.	καὶ ἐσκοτίσθη ἡ ἀσύνετος αὐτῶν καρδία

(1) and = καί —verbatim.

(2) condensed like fog so that no one could see ≅ ἐσκοτίσθη —Paul uses σκοτίζειν in the figurative sense of darkening someone's religious and moral perception; this sense occurs sometimes in literature of the period, e.g. Plutarch, *Adv. Colotem* 1120 E, Testament of Reuben 3:8, 2 Clem 19:2, Eph 4:18. Valentinus develops the image into one of dense fog, a rather uncommon image. It is not entirely certain which Greek word is behind the Coptic: ὁμίχλη is likely and occurs in this figurative sense also in Plutarch, *De cohibenda ira* 460^2 as well as in the LXX (e.g.,

Job 24:20; Wis 2:4; Sir 24:3). Valentinus' particular development of the image may, however, be unique.

Thus error found power	(cf. τῆς πλάνης vs. 27)
	²³καὶ ἤλλαξαν
	τὴν δόξαν τοῦ ἀφθάρτου θεοῦ
and worked at her matter	
in emptiness, without having	
known the truth.	(cf. τὴν ἀλήθειαν below)

(3) error ≅ τῆς πλάνης —nearly verbatim, except for case and use of article.

(4) the truth ≅ τὴν ἀλήθειαν —verbatim, except for case.

	ἐν ὁμοιώματι εἰκόνος
She came to be in	
a molded form (πλάσμα)	φθαρτοῦ ἀνθρώπου

(5) a molded form (πλάσμα) ≅ εἰκόνος φθαρτοῦ ἀνθρώπου —Both Paul and Valentinus refer to the mortal nature of the human being, although their purpose is rather different. Paul contrasts the immortal God's glory with idols, some of whom have been fashioned after mortal human beings. Valentinus refers to the mortal nature outright in his use of πλάσμα, which had become a technical term for the corruptible body of Adam; in Philo, for example, its use is virtually restricted to this sense (see, e.g., De Opif. Mundi 137 for πλάσσειν).[3] In contexts of truth and falsehood, however, it can also mean "fiction" or "delusion" (e.g., Sextus Empiricus, Adv. Math. 1.263). Valentinus may have both of these senses in mind.

in beauty	(cf. ἐν τῷ ψεύδει)
the substitute for	οἵτινες μετήλλαξαν
the truth	τὴν ἀλήθειαν τοῦ θεοῦ
	ἐν τῷ ψεύδει

---

[2] ’Ὡς γὰρ δι’ ὀμίχλης τὰ σώματα, καὶ δι’ ὀργῆς τὰ πράγματα μείζονα φαίνεται.
[3] See also TDNT, s.v.

(6) in beauty ≅ ἐν τῷ ψεύδει —Valentinus has identified "lie" with "beauty." According to Paul, idols are deceitful, whereas for Valentinus, the modeled form is beautiful. This passage, however, shows that Valentinus understands the word "beauty" in a negative sense; thus we are prepared for the assertion in 17:27 that truth cannot be beautified.

(7) the substitute for ≅ μετήλλαξαν —Each of these expressions sets up the contrast between "beauty" and "lie" and their respective opposite.

(8) the truth = τὴν ἀλήθειαν —verbatim.

C. Evaluation of the Parallel

The contexts are similar in that both refer to the result of disregard or ignorance of God. Of the eight elements of comparison, four are verbatim (1, 8) or nearly so (3, 4). Inexact parallels include the notion of intellectual darkening, the idea that falsehood has been substituted for truth, and reference to a crafted object in human form. While individually unimpressive, these elements are important parts of a strong passage of Rom, a book known to be used elsewhere in GTr (e.g., Nos. 45, 73). For these reasons, a deliberate reference to Rom is possible here.

D. Interpretation

Paul's God is knowable and known, but Valentinus does not use this theme since his God is inconceivable and unknown, except through Jesus Christ.[4] Like Paul, however, he is concerned with the presence of evil and asserts that ignorance on the part of all became powerful, as error. The former (i.e., ignorance) must be seen as an ethical category and state. The latter (i.e., error) may be hypostatized: she is said to have created a πλάσμα and in so doing to have taken beauty, which is a deception, rather than truth, which is unchangeable, as her model. Valentinus may, therefore, shift the topic of discussion simultaneously to the creation of humanity, as suggested by πλάσμα (17:18, 24), an implicit allusion to Gen 1:26, and to a residual inherent error or evil present in human beings.[5]

---

[4]Compare No. 48, where this theme of the unknowable Father reappears.

[5]In frg. 1 of Valentinus (Clement of Alexandria, *Strom.* II. 36.2-4), angels are said to have formed the first human being. Mythological lan-

This is quite different from the ethics of ignorance in Rom in which ignorance is viewed as voluntary. The passage in GTr might even be considered an implicit exegesis of Paul's phrase, ἐν ὁμοιώματι εἰκόνος φθαρτοῦ ἀνθρώπου, and "truth" must refer in some sense to God himself both in Rom and GTr.

2. GTr 18:11-18 (A²) ~ Col 1:25-27

Identified by van Unnik, p. 116. Probable.

	(²⁴ . . . ἡ ἐκκλησία)
	²⁵ ἧς ἐγενόμην ἐγὼ διάκονος . . .
It is to the perfect	(cf. τοῖς ἁγίοις αὐτοῦ below)
that this,	
the gospel (εὐαγγέλιον)	τὸν λόγον
of the one who is sought,	τοῦ θεοῦ
has made itself known,	(cf. ἐφανερώθη below)
through the mercies of the	
Father.	(cf. τοῦ θεοῦ above)
By this (gospel),	
the hidden	²⁶τὸ μυστήριον
mystery (μυστήριον)	τὸ ἀποκεκρυμμένον
	ἀπὸ τῶν αἰώνων καὶ
	ἀπὸ τῶν γενεῶν —
	νῦν δὲ ἐφανερώθη
	τοῖς ἁγίοις αὐτοῦ
Jesus Christ	²⁷ . . . ὅ ἐστιν Χριστός
shed light upon those in	
darkness	ἐν ὑμῖν

---

¹¹ⲡⲉⲉⲓ ⲡⲉⲩ¹²ⲁⲅⲅⲉⲗⲓⲟⲛ ⲙ̄ⲡⲉⲧⲟⲩⲕⲱⲧⲉ ⲛ̄¹³ⲥⲱϥ ⲛ̄ⲧⲁϥⲟⲩⲁⲛ̄ϩϥ ⲛ̄ⲛⲉⲧ¹⁴ϫⲏⲕ
ⲁⲃⲁⲗ ϩⲓⲧⲛ̄ ⲛⲓⲙⲛ̄ⲧϣⲁⲛ̄ϩⲧⲏϥ ¹⁵ⲛ̄ⲧⲉ ⲡⲓⲱⲧ ⲡⲓⲙⲩⲥⲧⲏⲣⲓⲟⲛ ⲉⲑⲏⲧ
¹⁶ⲓⲏ̅ⲥ̅ ⲡⲉⲭⲣ̅ⲥ̅ ⲡⲉⲉⲓ ⲁⲃⲁⲗ ϩⲓⲧⲟⲟⲧϥ ¹⁷ⲁϥⲣ̄ ⲟⲩⲁⲉⲓⲛ ⲁⲛⲉⲧϩ̄ⲙ̄ ⲡⲕⲉⲕⲉⲓ
¹⁸ⲁⲃⲁⲗ

---

guage is flexible by nature, however, and here GTr is concerned with the presence of ignorance in the world. Hence, creation is described in terms of "error."

Commentaries

A. Context

Col 1:24-29 (Paul's office and ministry). Ps-Paul reminds his readers of his own mission to preach the account about God to the Gentiles and God's activity through Christ. The content of this account is God's "hidden mystery": it concerns the coming of Christ, who was made known to God's "saints."

GTr 18:11-18 (Jesus Christ and the gospel). Valentinus refers to Jesus Christ's mission to teach by means of the gospel about the Father, who thereby showed mercy. The content of this gospel is ambiguous: it is both knowledge about the Father and the agent of knowledge, the "hidden mystery," Jesus Christ. Jesus' mission is his coming to shed light upon those in darkness, or, in other words, it is the self-revelation of the gospel to the "perfect."

B. Elements of Comparison

the gospel	τὸν λόγον
of the one who is sought . . .	τοῦ θεοῦ
through the mercies of the Father.	(cf. τοῦ θεοῦ)

(1) gospel ≅ τὸν λόγον —Valentinus has already equated "gospel" and "word" in the opening sentence of GTr (16:31-35): "The gospel of truth is a joy for those who have received grace from the Father of truth that they should know him through the power of the Word which came forth from the fullness. . . ."

(2) of the one who is sought ≅ τοῦ θεοῦ —"The one who is sought" is the deity, but Valentinus characteristically calls the deity "Father" rather than "God" in GTr. He has already stated (17:4-6) that all were *searching for* the Father from whom they had come forth and who contained them within himself.

(3) the Father ≅ τοῦ θεοῦ —typical change from "God" to "Father."

to the perfect . . .	(cf. τοῖς ἁγίοις αὐτοῦ)
has made itself known	(cf. ἐφανερώθη)

(4) to the perfect ≡ τοῖς ἁγίοις αὐτοῦ — Ἅγιος had become part of the Christian ingroup vocabulary at an early stage, particularly, it seems, in the Pauline churches, where it was used as a self-designation for members. Similarly, "the perfect" in GTr is also part of the distinctive vocabulary for readers of the text, and it too refers to insiders, to Gnostics.

(5) made itself known ≡ ἐφανερώθη —The two are virtually equivalent in meaning, but ps-Paul uses the passive voice, whereas Valentinus apparently did not, although it is impossible to be certain of the original voice of the Greek underlying the Coptic.

the hidden	τὸ μυστήριον
mystery,	τὸ ἀποκεκρυμμένον
Jesus Christ	. . . Χριστός
shed light upon those	
who were in darkness	ἐν ὑμῖν

(6) the hidden mystery = τὸ μυστήριον τὸ ἀποκεκρυμμένον —verbatim. This esoteric jargon (found also in Corp. Herm. 1:16, σοφίαν ἐν μυστηρίῳ τὴν ἀποκεκρυμμένον) was used by the deutero-Pauline school but not, apparently, by Paul himself,[6] though μυστήριον alone is a characteristic part of his vocabulary. In ps-Paul, the phrase is used in reference to the Gentiles' participation in God's plan of salvation. It is attested in this passage of Col and, in a similar context, Eph 3:4-9. Both passages, as also GTr, use it to speak of Christ's preordained coming as part of the message of salvation, but Valentinus makes no reference to a distinction of Gentiles and Jews.

(7) Jesus Christ ≡ Χριστός —This difference is probably trivial. It is possible, however, that the text--in which we find not the full word "Christ" but merely the Greek compendium χρς —does not in fact refer to "the Christ" but rather to "the good one," ὁ χρηστός. Some Valentinian texts apparently avoid reference to Christ altogether, substituting its homonym χρηστός, e.g., OnRes 43:37.[7]

---

[6]The collocation of μυστήριον and ἀποκεκρυμμένον at 1 Cor 2:7 is accidental.

[7]See B. Layton, The Gnostic Treatise on Resurrection from Nag Hammadi, HDR 12 (Missoula: Scholars Press, 1979), p. 44, who also refers to the Manichaeans according to Alexander of Lycopolis, C. Manich. 24, p. 34,18 sq. Brinkm.

(8) on those who were in darkness ≅ ἐν ὑμῖν —These are practically equivalent. Ps-Paul says that Christ is "in" or "among" his readers, who are insiders, believers. Valentinus says that Jesus gave light to those who were in darkness; once enlightened, these, of course, were also insiders, Gnostics.

C. Evaluation of the Parallel

The context of GTr is more directly concerned with Jesus Christ, whereas Col is concerned with Paul's office as an apostle. Yet, both passages use the striking phrase, "hidden mystery." This is the only element of comparison (6) that is verbatim; it is characteristic of Col and Eph, although not peculiar to them. Other differences in the elements of comparison can largely be understood as characteristic alterations made by Valentinus, such as the change from "God" to "Father" and from "saints" to "perfect." Use of Col is virtually certain elsewhere in GTr (e.g., No. 14), and Valentinus' use of it here is probable as well.

D. Interpretation

The immediate topic has been changed, from Paul's preaching mission among the Gentiles to Jesus' preaching mission to all humanity. Ps-Paul's striking phrase, "hidden mystery," which referred to God's plan to admit Jews and Gentiles to salvation and also, apparently, to Christ's presence among the community has become, in GTr, merely an epithet of Jesus. As Paul preached by means of his gospel, so Jesus Christ is said to have preached ("gave light") by means of the gospel about the Father. The content of the Valentinian gospel is thus not Christ (as in Paul) but knowledge of the Father, and the work of Christ is to disseminate that knowledge.

3. GTr 18:18-21 (A²) ~ John 14:6

Identified by Malinine et al., p. 51. Probable.

(Jesus Christ)	⁶λέγει αὐτῷ [ὁ] ᾽Ιησοῦς·
he en̲li̲g̲h̲t̲e̲n̲e̲d̲ them;	(cf. ἡ ζωή below)
he_	ἐγώ
gave them	εἰμι_
a way	ἡ ὁδός

24   Biblical Interpretation in the Gospel of Truth

and the way is the truth about which he taught them.	καὶ	ἡ ἀλήθεια
	καὶ	ἡ ζωή.

¹⁸ⲁϥ ⲟⲩⲁ¹⁹ⲉⲓⲛ ⲁⲣⲁⲩ ⲁϥϯ ⲛⲟⲩⲙⲁⲉⲓⲧ ⲡⲓ²⁰ⲙⲁⲉⲓⲧ ⲛⲁⲉ ⲡⲉ ϯⲙⲛⲧⲙⲏⲉ
ⲉⲛ²¹ⲧⲁϥⲧⲁⲙⲁⲩ ⲁⲣⲁⲥ·

A. Context

John 14:1-7 (opening of Jesus' farewell discourse). For those who want knowledge of the Father, Jesus ambiguously "is" a true way of life that is or imparts salvation.

GTr 18:16-24 (Jesus Christ's teaching provokes his crucifixion). Unto those who want knowledge of the Father, Jesus bestows a true way of life and imparts such knowledge.

B. Elements of Comparison

he enlightened them;	(cf. ἡ ζωή below)	
he	ἐγώ	
gave them	εἰμι	
a way ...	ἡ ὁδός ...	
the truth	ἡ ἀλήθεια	
	καὶ	ἡ ζωή

(1) enlightened ≠ ἡ ζωή —Valentinus' expression "enlightened, gave light" is not the same as John's "life" (ζωή), although Valentinus may have presupposed the equation "light = life" found in the prologue of the gospel he is using here (John 1:4). There are also other places where light and life are associated: for example, *Corp. Herm.* 1:9 (ὁ δὲ **Νοῦς** ὁ θεός, ἀρρενόθηλυς ὤν, ζωὴ καὶ φῶς ὑπάρχων) may attest to an esoteric tradition which associated life and light. Elsewhere in GTr, "enlighten" means "impart knowledge," as 32:31-37 may suggest. Also, in 32:21 "give life" (rescue) has the allegorical meaning of "impart knowledge"; cf. No. 48.

(2) he gave ≅ ἐγώ εἰμι —In John, Jesus *is* the way, whereas in GTr Jesus gave others a way. The Johannine metonymy is enigmatic;

Commentaries 25

Valentinus has resolved the trope in a narrative description of Jesus' work as savior.

(3) a way ≅ ἡ ὁδός —nearly verbatim. This is a striking metaphor, both in John and in GTr. An early and influential example of the figurative use concerned two ways ("paths," "streets") open to Heracles; Xenophon (*Memorabilia* 2,1,21ff.) attributes the story to Prodicus the Sophist (b. cir. 470-460 B.C.E.). There are similar instances throughout the hellenistic era. Examples in early Christian literature include *Barn.* 19, *Didache* 1-4. Sometimes it is qualified by "life" (*Didache* 1:2, ἡ ὁδὸς τῆς ζωῆς) or "light" (*Barn.* 19:1, ἡ ὁδὸς τοῦ φωτός).

(4) the truth = ἡ ἀλήθεια —verbatim. "Truth" occurs frequently in John (e.g. 1:14,17; 17:17) and in GTr (e.g. 16:31,33; 17:17-18; 26:28). The expression, "way of truth," occurs in Ode of Solomon 11:3.[8]

C. *Evaluation of the Parallel*

The contexts of the two passages are similar in their proximity to a description of events leading up to Jesus' crucifixion and to the description of the crucifixion itself. One of the four elements of comparison (4) is verbatim and another one (3) nearly so. Of the two inexact elements, one involves a change from the typically Johannine self-predication form to narrative form, but the other involves an actual difference in thematic material used. The latter element is given prominence through the rearrangement of elements. Even though element (1) introduces a different theme ("life"), such material can be found elsewhere in John. John is used frequently in GTr, and its use here is likely also.

D. *Interpretation*

In his interpretation of the passage, Valentinus resolves two rhetorical obscurities. First, he resolves the notion that Jesus "is" a way in a narrative description of Jesus' teaching activity which observes that Jesus bestows a way. Second, he resolves "life," which may have been considered ambiguous (eternal life vs. continuation of ψυχή) in a different

---

[8]J. H. Charlesworth, *The Odes of Solomon* (Missoula: Scholars Press, 1977), p. 52; he also gives other references to this expression, especially in the Qumran literature.

image, "light," which is the equivalent of knowledge (γνῶσις). Other changes, such as the change from first person to third person, are trivial and are dictated by the more important changes. In rearranging the order of elements, "light" is given prominence. Further, Valentinus has identified "way" and "truth." The latter is apparently the content of Jesus' teaching (18:20-21). The Johannine statement about Jesus' person has been transformed into a narrative description, therefore, of Jesus' role as the illuminator.

4. GTr 18:24-27 (A²) ~ Gen 2:17, 3:7

Identified by Grobel, p. 53, n. 66. Probable.

nailed to a tree	2:17ἀπὸ δὲ τοῦ ξύλου
	τοῦ γινώσκειν
	καλὸν καὶ πονηρὸν
	οὐ φάγεσθε ἀπ' αὐτοῦ·
	ᾗ δ' ἂν ἡμέρᾳ
	φάγετε ἀπ' αὐτοῦ
	θανάτῳ ἀποθανεῖσθε.
	3:7καὶ εἶδεν ἡ γυνὴ,
	ὅτι καλὸν τὸ ξύλον ...
He (Jesus Christ) became	καὶ λαβοῦσα
a fruit	ἀπὸ τοῦ καρποῦ αὐτοῦ,
of the knowledge	(cf. τοῦ ξύλου)
of the Father.	
Now it did not cause ruin	(cf. θανάτῳ ἀποθανεῖσθε)
because it was eaten	ἔφαγεν

---

²⁴ⲁⲩⲁϥⲧϥ ⲁⲩⲱϩⲉ· ⲁϥ²⁵ϣⲱⲡⲉ ⲛ̄ⲛⲟⲩⲧⲁϩ ⲙ̄ⲡⲓⲥⲁⲩⲛⲉ ⲛ̄²⁶ⲧⲉ ⲡⲓⲱⲧ· ⲛ̄ⲧⲁϥⲧⲉⲕⲟ
ⲉⲉ ⲉⲛ ⲭⲉ ²⁷ⲁⲃⲟⲩⲁⲙϥ

A. Context

Gen 2:15-17, 3:1-7 (the forbidden fruit and the temptation). Knowledge of good and evil brought death to the first woman and man and was conveyed by fruit of a tree in paradise.

Commentaries

GTr 18:21-34 (the crucifixion of Jesus and its result). Knowledge of the Father brought salvation and joy to all and was conveyed by fruit of the tree of Jesus' crucifixion.

B. Elements of Comparison

(1) [Formal structure] a fruit, (scil. of the tree), of the knowledge, of the Father ≅ τοῦ καρποῦ, τοῦ ξύλου, τοῦ γινώσκειν, καλὸν καὶ πονηρόν —The entire passage is a set of contrasts: the two fruits are not identical, just as the persons eating the respective fruits are not the same, and so forth. Some elements are retained and others altered, as the following comparison shows.

He (Jesus Christ) became a fruit (scil. of the tree) of the knowledge of the Father	καὶ λαβοῦσα . . . τοῦ καρποῦ (scil. τοῦ ξύλου) (scil. τοῦ γινώσκειν) καλὸν καὶ πονηρόν

(2) a fruit ≅ τοῦ καρποῦ —With the words τοῦ καρποῦ, Gen 3:6 makes an abbreviated cross-reference to Gen 2:17. This in turn leads to a contrast between (knowledge of) the Father in GTr and (knowledge of) good and evil in Gen. Fruit of knowledge of the Father is thus parallel to fruit of the tree of knowledge of good and evil. Although Valentinus does not use "tree," which appears in Gen 3:3 here, he must have it in mind, as its use in 18:24 indicates ("he was nailed to a tree"). In Gen, "fruit" refers to fruit on the tree of knowledge of good and evil, but in GTr, the "fruit" is on a different tree, the cross. Fruit was produced through the nailing of Jesus on the tree; that fruit was knowledge of the Father. Reference to the fruit of the tree of knowledge is not common in early Christian literature, although there is occasional reference to the tree of knowledge in Gnosticism (e.g., ApocryJn 23:28), usually as a correction to Gen 3. *Diognetus* 12 has a long exposition which centers on the tree of knowledge and the tree of life. The passage states, concerning the former, that disobedience, rather than the tree of knowledge, causes death. The word "fruit" appears in this passage, but it probably has a figurative sense, i.e., "result, outcome, product," although undoubtedly this author also alludes to Gen.

Now it did not cause ruin because it was eaten	(cf. θανάτῳ ἀποθανεῖσθε) ἔφαγεν

(3) Now it did not cause ruin ≅ θανάτῳ ἀποθανεῖσθε —The rhetorical structure differs in that the narration of God's warning in Gen has become in GTr, a narration of past event and, by extension, general fact. More important is the difference in meaning between the two. In Gen, eating of the fruit brought expulsion, misery, and death; in GTr, eating of the fruit brought discovery of the Father.

(4) it was eaten ≅ ἔφαγεν —The passages differ in voice and in subject. In Gen, Eve eats of the fruit, whereas in GTr, the Gnostics eat of it. Because the fruit is different in each case (see [2]), the result of eating of it is also different (ruin and discovery, respectively; see [3]).

C. Evaluation of the Parallel

The sketchiness of the verbal contact might raise the question of whether the text of Gen 2:17; 3:7 was in fact used, but the shared imagery of "fruit," "[tree of] knowledge," and eating this particular fruit is not common in early Christian literature. The evidence for Valentinus' use of Gen elsewhere in GTr is ambiguous, but here, as usually in the other proposed references to Gen, a typological interpretation is indicated.

D. Interpretation

Valentinus has formulated a typological pendant to the Gen story, tacitly expositing 1 Cor 15:20-22. The typological points of contrast are: forbidden knowledge versus shared knowledge; knowledge of good and evil versus knowledge of the Father; death versus salvation; Eve/Adam versus Jesus; primordial time versus the time of Jesus. Thus, Valentinus does not "correct" the Gen 2-3 story in that he does not deny that eating of the fruit of the tree of knowledge of good and evil brought ruin. Whereas the fruit of the tree of knowledge of good and evil brought ruin, the fruit of the tree of knowledge of the Father brought the opposite of ruin— discovery of Jesus Christ.[9] Whereas the first woman and man ate the fruit of the tree of knowledge of good and evil and died, Christ became a fruit of the Father's knowledge in his death and so brought discovery that some

---

[9] See 18:27-30. The lack of differentiation between Jesus and the Father in GTr is particularly clear in these lines because 18:32-33 mentions the Father as the one who is discovered within those who eat of the fruit.

Commentaries

people belong to the Father (18:31-34). In so doing, the contrast between the time of ignorance which Adam and Eve initiated and the time of knowledge which Jesus' death initiated is apparent to those who now have that knowledge.

5. GTr 18:33-35 (A²) ~ Col 1:16-17

Identified by van Unnik, p. 116. Probable. Cf. No. 6.

(They found the Father
   in themselves . . .)
this one who
made all,

for all
  were
    within him

and all
  were
    in need of him.

^{16}ὅτι
ἐν αὐτῷ (sc. τῷ υἱῷ)
ἐκτίσθη τὰ πάντα . . .
^{17}καὶ αὐτός
ἐστιν πρὸ πάντων
καὶ τὰ πάντα
(cf. συνέστηκεν below)
ἐν αὐτῷ
    συνέστηκεν

---

^{33}ⲛⲉⲉⲓ ⲛ̄ⲧⲁ²³⁴ⲧⲉⲛⲟ ⲙ̄ⲡⲧⲏⲣϥ̄ ⲉⲣⲉⲡⲧⲏⲣϥ̄ ⲛ̄³⁵²ϩⲏⲧϥ̄ ⲁⲩⲱ ⲡⲧⲏⲣϥ̄
ⲉϥϣⲁⲁⲧ· ⲙ̄ⲙⲁϥ

A. Context

Col 1:15-20 (early christological hymn). Ps-Paul has adapted an earlier hymn which says that God's image, the pre-existent Christ, made the universe, and the universe came into existence by (or in) "him."

GTr 18:31-35 (the Father's creation). God (called the Father) made all (or the entirety), and all were in him and yet needed him.

30   Biblical Interpretation in the Gospel of Truth

B. *Elements of Comparison*

| this one (Father) who | ἐν αὐτῷ (sc. τῷ υἱῷ) |
| made all | ἐκτίσθη τὰ πάντα |

(1) Father ≅ ὁ υἱός —Col specifies an agent of creation, namely, the Son. GTr says outright that the Father created all.

(2) made ≅ ἐκτίσθη —Only the voice differs. Both Greek κτίζειν and the Coptic verb (ⲧⲉⲛⲟ, S ⲧⲁⲛⲟ) can mean "create" or "make" without necessary reference to the creation account in Gen. Neither ps-Paul nor Valentinus necessarily refers to a *creatio ex nihilo*, although for that matter, the Gen text does not state this explicitly either.

(3) all = τὰ πάντα —verbatim. This expression is a commonplace for "the universe" in the hellenistic world, and ps-Paul also uses τὰ πάντα in a cosmological sense, which is further explicated in Col 1:20c (i.e., all things that are in heaven or on earth). Valentinus too uses "all" in a cosmological sense, but he probably means the entirety of those who belong to the Father, as 21:8-14 shows.[10]

for all	καὶ τὰ πάντα
were	(cf. συνέστηκεν)
within him	ἐν αὐτῷ
	συνέστηκεν

(4) were within him ≅ ἐν αὐτῷ συνέστηκεν —The idea that all are in God was a commonplace (*Corp. Herm.* 5:10, πάντα δὲ ἐν σοὶ, πάντα ἀπὸ σοῦ; Paris magical papyrus, PGM 4,2838, ἐκ σέο γὰρ πάντ' ἐστὶ καὶ εἰς <σ'>, αἰώνιιε, πάντα τελευτᾷ). The background is Stoic,[11] especially those passages in which συνέστηκεν is used (e.g., ps.-Aristotle, *Mund.* 6 [379b], ἐκ θεοῦ πάντα καὶ διὰ θεοῦ συνέστηκεν). In using this

---

[10]In this passage and, indeed, on the entire page, Valentinus speaks of the perfection of "all," but it is clear that individuals comprise "all." The individuals that comprise "all" are those who have knowledge. He does not refer to a future resurrection but rather, as each person gains knowledge, this one takes a place within the all-encompassing Father.

[11]E. Lohse, *Colossians and Philemon* (Philadelphia: Fortress, 1971) pp. 41-61 provides the most complete discussion of the background and meaning of the Col passage; my discussion relies heavily on this.

Commentaries 31

verb, the Col passage retains some contact with its Stoic background, but ps-Paul seems to have used the preposition ἐν in an instrumental sense. Valentinus apparently understood the preposition in a locative sense and hence retained more contact with the Stoic background of the all-encompassing God.[12]

C. *Evaluation of the Parallel*

The contexts of the two passages are quite similar. Of the four elements of comparison, one is verbatim and the others nearly so. Although two of these elements of comparison (3 and 4) are commonplaces, and no one is strong enough in itself to determine use of Col, the combination of these two with element (2) considerably strengthens the evidence. Valentinus also uses Col elsewhere (e.g., No. 14).

D. *Interpretation*

Valentinus does not keep ps-Paul's idea of the pre-existent Christ as the agent of creation, although nothing in the passages specifically says this. He also reinterprets τὰ πάντα so it refers not to material reality but to spiritual reality. Moreover, he takes ps-Paul's ἐν locatively and takes ps-Paul's "him" to refer to the Father rather than to Christ. Effectively, this eliminates the reality of the creation of the material universe from consideration and introduces the Stoic cosmic model of the all-encompassing deity. This is not to say that Valentinus denies a material universe but rather that the Father's creation was the creation of that which is within him, in a spiritual and metaphysical sense. The clause, "and all were in need of him," makes the passage into a paradox: though the Father contains all, the latter also need him. This underlines the importance of the message of salvation brought by Jesus Christ, namely, the knowledge of the Father that causes one to discover him within oneself and thus to realize that one is oneself within the Father.

---

[12]W. R. Schoedel, "Gnostic Monism and the Gospel of Truth," in B. Layton, ed., *The Rediscovery of Gnosticism*, I (Leiden: Brill, 1980) 380-381, discusses the background of the idea of the all-encompassing God. Among his examples are Hermas, *Mand.* 1:1 and *Corp. Herm.* 11:18-20; 16:12.

6. GTr 19:7-10 (A²) ~ Col 1:16-17

Identified by Williams.[13] Probable. Cf. No. 5.

It is he (the Father) who made all	¹⁶ὅτι ἐν αὐτῷ (sc. τῷ υἱῷ) ἐκτίσθη τὰ πάντα . . . ¹⁷καὶ αὐτός ἐστιν πρὸ πάντων
and all are within him	καὶ τὰ πάντα (cf. συνέστηκεν below) ἐν αὐτῷ
and all had need of him.	συνέστηκεν

⁷ⲚⲦⲀϤ ⲠⲈⲚⲦⲀϤⲦⲤⲈⲚⲞ ⁸ⲘⲠⲦⲎⲢϤ ⲀⲨⲰ ⲠⲦⲎⲢϤ ⲈϤⲚ2Ⲏ⁹Ⲧϥ· ⲀⲨⲰ
ⲚⲈⲢⲈⲠⲦⲎⲢϤ ϢⲀⲀⲦ· ¹⁰ⲘⲘⲀϤ ⲠⲈ·

A. Context

Col 1:15-20 (early christological hymn). Ps-Paul has adapted an earlier hymn which says that God's image, the pre-existent Christ, made the universe, and the universe came into existence by (or in) "him."

GTr 19:1-10 (perfection of all). Although two lacunae at 19:1, 2 make the context unclear, it apparently concerns the perfection of all, which is understood as a return to the Father of all who have knowledge. The passage itself is much like No. 5.

B. Elements of Comparison

This passage is almost exactly like No. 5; only the Coptic syntax differs (for which cf. synopsis above).

---

[13]Obviously similar to No. 5 and probably for that reason not mentioned by other commentators.

C. Evaluation of the Parallel

The use of the Col passage is probable for the reasons given in No. 5.

D. Interpretation

This passage also reinterprets τὰ πάντα, takes the ἐν locatively, and uses the model of the all-encompassing deity. Moreover, the clause "and all had need of him" makes this into a paradox, as in No. 5.

7. GTr 19:17-27 (A²)   Luke 2:46-47

Postulated, with hesitation, by Malinine et al., p. 52. Dubious.

He (Jesus) became a quiet and leisurely guide at school He came into public view. He spoke the word as a teacher. The self-appointed wise men came up to him, testing him, but he humiliated them, because they were empty. And they despised him because they were not truly intelligent.	⁴⁶καὶ ἐγένετο μετὰ ἡμέρας τρεῖς εὗρον αὐτὸν (᾽Ιησοῦς) ἐν τῷ ἱερῷ καθεζόμενον ἐν μέσῳ (cf. ἐπερωτῶντα below) (cf. τῶν διδασκάλων below) τῶν διδασκάλων καὶ ἀκούοντα αὐτῶν καὶ ἐπερωτῶντα αὐτούς. ⁴⁷ἐξίσταντο δὲ πάντες οἱ ἀκούοντες αὐτοῦ ἐπὶ τῇ συνέσει . . . αὐτου.

---

¹⁷ⲁϥϣⲱⲡⲉ ⲛ̄ⲭⲁⲅⲙⲁⲓⲧ· ¹⁸ⲉϥⲥⲉⲣⲁ̄ⲥ̄ⲧ ⲁⲩⲱ ⲉϥⲥⲣⲁϥⲧ· ⲙⲙⲁ ¹⁹ⲛ̄ⲭⲓ
ⲥⲃⲱ ⲁϥⲓ ⲁⲧⲙⲏⲧⲉ ⲁϥⲭⲉ ²⁰ⲡⲓⲱϫⲭⲉ· ⲉϥⲟⲉⲓ ⲛⲟⲩⲥⲁ²· ²¹ⲁⲩⲉⲓ
ϣⲁⲣⲁⲉⲓ ⲛ̄ϭⲓ ⲛ̄ⲥⲟⲫⲟⲥ ²²ⲛ̄²ⲣⲏⲓ̈ 2ⲙ̄ ⲡⲟⲩ²ⲏⲧ· ⲟⲩⲁⲉⲉ²³ⲧⲟⲩ
ⲉⲩⲡⲓⲣⲁⲍⲉ ⲙ̄ⲙⲁϥ ⲛ̄ⲧⲁϥ ²⁴ⲁⲉ ⲛⲉϥⲭⲡⲓⲟ ⲙ̄ⲙⲁⲩ ϫⲉ ⲛⲉ· ²⁵²ⲛ̄ⲡⲉⲧϣⲟⲩⲉⲓⲧ
ⲛⲉ· ⲁⲩⲙⲉⲥ²⁶ⲧⲱϥ ϫⲉ ⲛⲉ²ⲛ̄ⲡ̄ⲙ̄ⲛ̄²ⲏⲧ ⲉⲛ ²⁷ⲛⲉ ⲙⲁⲙⲏⲉ

34 Biblical Interpretation in the Gospel of Truth

A. Context

Luke 2:41-51 (the boy Jesus in the temple). At the age of twelve, Jesus sits in the temple debating with the teachers, who are amazed at his understanding.

GTr 19:17-30 (Jesus' public [19-27] and private [27-30] ministry). To satisfy the need of all for knowledge of the Father, Jesus undertakes a dual career of private "guide" (perhaps παιδαγωγός) and public teacher. In his public capacity he debates with, and refutes, so-called "wise men," who despise him because they have no understanding.

B. *Elements of Comparison*

at school | ἐν τῷ ἱερῷ

(1) at school ≠ ἐν τῷ ἱερῷ —There is little resemblance between school and temple here, although Luke does present teaching activity as occurring there. If Valentinus has used Luke 2:46-47, he has seized upon one of the activities that might occur in the temple and, in so doing, has substituted Luke's signified (place of teaching, school) for the signifier (temple in Jerusalem).

He came into pubic view. | καθεζόμενον ἐν μέσῳ
He spoke the word | (cf. ἐπερωτῶντα)
as a teacher. | (cf. τῶν διδασκάλων)

(2) into public view ≠ ἐν μέσῳ —These expressions could be translated in an overliteral fashion as "to the midst" (GTr) and "in the midst" (Luke). A supposed parallel would have to be explained as follows: (a) Luke's ἐν μέσῳ (abs.) is taken for ἐν μέσῳ αὐτῶν, "in their midst"; (b) the Coptic phrase (ⲉⲧⲙⲏⲧⲉ) stands for the Greek εἰς τὸ μέσον (abs.), a koine idiom meaning "into public view" or simply "forward"; (c) although these phrases have entirely different meanings, the only formal difference is in the choice of preposition (and concomitant case endings); and (d) Valentinus (if he used Luke) has altered the preposition and has removed all details of the setting.

(3) he spoke the word ≠ ἐπερωτῶντα —If Valentinus has used this, he has removed any suggestion that Jesus himself may have learned from others and has stressed Jesus' proclamation as a teacher.

Commentaries

(4) as a teacher ≅ τῶν διδασκάλων —Luke has the boy Jesus sitting among the teachers and only by implication teaching (2:47). Valentinus has no reference to such circumstances and setting and calls Jesus a teacher outright.

The self-appointed wise men came up to him, testing him, but he humiliated them	. . . τῶν διδασκάλων καὶ ἀκούοντα αὐτῶν καὶ ἐπερωτῶντα αὐτούς

(5) self-appointed wise men ≅ τῶν διδασκάλων —If Valentinus has used Luke, he has introduced the notion that those with whom Jesus discussed were not actually wise.

(6) testing him, humiliated them ≅ ἀκούοντα αὐτῶν, ἐπερωτῶντα αὐτούς —Both Luke and Valentinus present some interchange as occurring between Jesus and those with whom he discussed.

And they despised him because they were not truly intelligent.	ἐξίσταντο δὲ πάντες οἱ ἀκούοντες αὐτοῦ ἐπὶ τῇ συνέσει . . . αὐτοῦ

(7) they despised him ≅ ἐξίσταντο . . . πάντας —In Luke, Jesus' teaching evokes astonishment, which is not necessarily positive or negative. The emotion evoked by Jesus in GTr, however, is negative: the socalled wise men despised him.

(8) they were not truly intelligent ≅ ἐπὶ τῇ συνέσει . . . αὐτοῦ — The statement in Luke is about Jesus' precocity and understanding; the statement in GTr is about the lack of intelligence of the so-called wise men.

C. Evaluation of the Parallel

Although a number of elements of comparison may be proposed, not one is truly convincing. Moreover, details used in the Lukan story are absent, and there is no other evidence that Valentinus used Luke in GTr. The passage in GTr is apparently a summary account of Jesus' ministry and shows no relationship to any specific event as portrayed in Luke or any other known gospel.

8. GTr 19:32-34 (A²) ~ 1 Cor 13:12

Postulated by Malinine et al., p. 52. Dubious.

They knew, and they were known; they received glory and they gave glory.	¹². . . ἄρτι γινώσκω ἐκ μέρους, τότε δὲ ἐπιγνώσομαι καθὼς καὶ ἐπεγνώσθην.

³²ⲀⲨⲤⲀⲨⲚⲈ ³³ⲀⲨⲤⲀⲞⲰⲚⲞⲨ ⲀⲨⲬⲒ ⲀⲨ† ³⁴ⲈⲀⲨ

A. Context

1 Cor 13:8-13 (love chapter). Love is eternal, but knowledge is temporal. Knowledge is only imperfect and partial, but when the perfect comes, those with partial knowledge will have complete understanding and will themselves be completely understood.

GTr 19:27-34 (the private ministry of Jesus). Jesus' disciples learn about the Father's outward manifestations, probably meaning themselves as "ways" of the Father. They are able to know and be known because knowledge of the Father is tantamount to knowledge of themselves.

B. Element of Comparison

They knew, and they were known	τότε δὲ ἐπιγνώσομαι καθὼς καὶ ἐπεγνώσθην

they knew, they were known ≅ ἐπιγνώσομαι, ἐπεγνώσθην —Both Paul and Valentinus speak of reciprocal knowledge. In addition, both omit the object of knowledge with the first of the two verbs, but presumably in both cases it is God or the Father. If Valentinus has used this passage, he has changed the tense from future to past, and he has changed the person and number from first singular to third plural. Moreover, he has omitted the temporal contrast, i.e., "now" and "then." The contrast between "know" (γινώσκειν) and "know completely" (ἐπιγινώσκειν) goes along with this and is also omitted. It is uncertain which of these two words stood behind the Coptic translation of GTr.

C. Evaluation of the Parallel

The contexts of the two passages are quite different, and the passages themselves share only one common element, the idea of reciprocal knowledge. The evidence for its similarity in GTr to 1 Cor is simply not strong enough to outweigh the changes that would have to have been made, as well as the brevity of the reference. Thus, the use of 1 Cor here is dubious, even though there is some evidence that Valentinus uses 1 Cor elsewhere (e.g., No. 16).

9. GTr 19:34-20:3 (A²) ~ Rev 13:8

Identified by van Unnik, pp. 109-110. Probable.

	⁸(πάντες οἱ κατοικοῦντες
	ἐπὶ τῆς γῆς,)
	οὗ οὐ γέγραπται
	τὸ ὄνομα αὐτοῦ
The living book	ἐν τῷ βιβλίῳ
of the living (pl.)	τῆς ζωῆς
appeared in their heart,	
that (book) which is written	(cf. οὐ γέγραπται above)
in the thought and mind (νοῦς)	
[of the] Father.	τοῦ ἀρνίου τοῦ ἐσφαγμένου
And from before	ἀπὸ
the foundation (καταβολή)	καταβολῆς
of all things	κόσμου.
it has lain in his	
incomprehensible parts.	

---

³⁴ⲀϤⲞⲨⲰⲚϨ ⲀⲂⲀⲖ 2ⲘⲠⲞⲨ³⁵2ⲎⲦ Ⲛ̄ϬⲒ ⲠⲒⲬⲰⲰⲘⲈ ⲈⲦⲀⲚϨ ³⁶Ⲛ̄ⲦⲈ
ⲚⲈⲦⲀⲚϨ ⲠⲈⲈⲒ ⲈⲦⲤⲎϨ 2ⲢⲎ³⁷ⲈⲒ˙ 2Ⲙ̄ ⲠⲒⲘⲈⲈⲨⲈ˙ ⲞⲨⲀ2Ⲙ̄ ⲠⲒⲚⲞⲨⲤ
¹[Ⲛ̄ⲦⲈ Ⲡ]ⲒⲰⲦ˙ ⲀⲨⲰ Ⲝ̄ⲒⲚ̄ 2ⲀⲐⲎ Ⲛ̄ⲦⲔⲀ²[ⲦⲀ]ⲂⲞⲖⲎ Ⲙ̄ⲠⲦⲎⲢϤ ⲈϤⲚ̄2ⲢⲎⲒ̈
2Ⲛ̄ ³ⲚⲒⲀⲦⲦⲈ2ⲀⲨ Ⲛ̄ⲦⲞⲞⲦϤ

38   Biblical Interpretation in the Gospel of Truth

A. Context

Rev 13:1-10 (vision of the beast from the sea). John the Seer relates a vision in which a beast was allowed to blaspheme and to make war on the believers for forty-two months and had authority over all the earth. Only those who had been foreordained in the pre-existent Christ's book of life did not worship it.

GTr 19:27-20:3 (the appearance of the living book of the living). After his description of the private ministry of Jesus, Valentinus describes the appearance of a book, which is responsible for the reception of knowledge by the believers or Gnostics. The book appears within them, but it also pre-existed in the Father's mind.

B. Elements of Comparison

| The living book | ἐν τῷ βιβλίῳ |
| of the living (pl.) | τῆς ζωῆς |

(1) the living book of the living ≅ τῷ βιβλίῳ τῆς ζωῆς —Valentinus has expanded the image, "book of life," by making it clear that (a) it is the book containing the names of those who are living (i.e., are saved) and (b) the book itself is living.

(a) The Jewish and Christian tradition of a book in which the names of members of a community are inscribed may have resulted from study of passages like Exod 32:32 and Ps 69:28. John the Seer has associated the idea with that of heavenly tablets, as did other writers of apocalyptic literature (e.g., 1 Enoch 47:3; 104:1; 108:7; Jubilees 30:22ff., 2 Baruch 24:1); names or deeds were held to be recorded on such tablets.[14] As John uses the expression, the names of those who will be saved

---

[14] See the discussion of the "book" image in A. Y. Collins, *The Combat Myth in the Book of Revelation* (Missoula: Scholars Press, 1976) pp. 24-25. She notes on p. 24 that there are three major types of heavenly books: (1) 'the roster of the elect kept in heaven'; (2) 'books of judgment in which deeds are recorded'; and (3) 'books of destiny in which future events are inscribed'. She demonstrates that the suggestion that the scroll of Rev 5 is identified in Rev with the book of life is not tenable due to the latter's explicit connection with the last judgment (see Rev 3:5; 20:15; and 21:27, whereas Rev 5 is not a judgment scene. For additional information on the

Commentaries

are recorded in the book. Even though it seems clear that Valentinus develops the imagery of Rev 13:8 on his own initiative, it should be noted that some fluctuation in the traditional image "book of life" occurs even within Rev (βιβλίον τῆς ζωῆς in Rev 13:8; 17:8; 20:12; 21:27; but βίβλος τῆς ζωῆς in Rev 3:5; 13:8 v.l.; 20:15) and that there is evidence of an expression "book of the living" [pl.] (rather than "life") known to others besides Valentinus, e.g., 1 Clem 53:4, βιβλίον ζώντων.

(b) The addition of "living" to modify "book" (the *living* book) does not seem to be attested elsewhere.

that (book) which is written in the thought and mind(νοῦς) [of the] Father	οὐ γέγραπται τοῦ ἀρνίου τοῦ ἐσφαγμένου

(2) that (book) which is written ≅ οὐ γέγραπται [τὸ ὄνομα αὐτοῦ ἐν τῷ βιβλίῳ] —In Rev, names are written in the book of life (v. 8 asserts that those who worship the beast are those whose names are *not* written in the book of life). In this passage, the contents written in the book are not specified, but because Jesus is later (20:24) said to clothe himself with the book, the book is, in a sense, living.

(3) [of the] Father ≅ τοῦ ἀρνίου τοῦ ἐσφαγμένου —Rev describes the book of life as belonging to the slain Lamb. By making a characteristic change from one aspect of deity to another (Son to Father), Valentinus is able to locate the book within the thought and mind of the Father. In this sense, the book belongs to the Father.

from before the foundation (καταβολή) of all things	ἀπὸ καταβολῆς κόσμου

(4) from before the foundation = ἀπὸ καταβολῆς —verbatim. In Greek, this expression could be formulated with any of three prepositions: outside the New Testament, the preposition ἐκ predominates (as in Polybius, 1.36.8; 24.8.9, and Diodorus Siculus 12.32.2); ἀπό (Rev 13:8; 17:8;

---

image of a "book," see the monograph by L. Koep, *Das himmlische Buch in Antike und Christentum* (Bonn: Peter Hanstein, 1952).

Matt 25:34; Luke 11:50; Heb 4:3; 9:26) and πρό are common in the New Testament. Strictly speaking, any of these prepositions could be the Greek original of GTr.[15]

(5) foundation of all ≡ καταβολῆς κόσμου —Valentinus has changed the reference point from "world" to "all," apparently using τὰ πάντα rather than κόσμος. In this context, the phrase τὰ πάντα is ambiguous, referring to either ὁ κόσμος (everything here and now; the orderly universe) or "the entirety" (of those belonging to the Father, of those in the heavenly realm).

C. Evaluation of the Parallel

The contexts of the two passages are not similar; John envisages a future time, whereas Valentinus discusses the appearance of Jesus on earth. Yet, of the five elements of comparison, one (4) is verbatim, and the other four are nearly so, if one takes account of typical changes made by Valentinus and his neglect of certain images (such as "slain Lamb") peculiar to Rev which do not further his point. The elements of comparison occur roughly in the same order also. Valentinus knows and uses Rev elsewhere (as in No. 10), and his use of it here is likely.

D. Interpretation

Valentinus takes the imagery of the book of life from Rev 13:8 and also the implication that names were written in the book. In his interpretation of the image of the book, he stresses that it is a living book (because Jesus brings it and envelops himself in it) and that it is related to living persons. It may be said to belong to those in whose hearts it appeared (19:34-35), much as it belongs to the Father by virtue of its being in the Father's thought and mind (19:37-20:1). Jesus took the book because it was predestined for him to take it and thus initiate the time of salvation (20:3-9,11-12). Both Rev and GTr express the notion that some were foreordained to salvation because of the book's contents. In GTr, the book itself is pre-existent, whereas in Rev all of the events which were to happen have already occurred proleptically in heaven before creation—especially the slaying of the Lamb, Christ. Thus, the phrase, "from the

---

[15]The translation "from before" reflects a nuance peculiar to Coptic; in all likelihood a single Greek preposition stood behind the Coptic phrase.

foundation . . ." applies to Christ in Rev and to the book in GTr. By changing κόσμος to "all," Valentinus exhibits an unwillingness to retain spatial categories. Moreover, he implicitly underscores the Father's predetermination that all those who are within him and so belong to him will be saved.

10. GTr 20:3-6, 11-13 (A²) ~ Rev 5:3, 6-7

Identified by van Unnik, p. 109. Probable.

(the living book of the living) this which	(cf. τὸ βιβλίον below)
no one was able (literally, is able)	³καὶ οὐδεὶς ἐδύνατο
to take	ἐν τῷ οὐρανῷ οὐδὲ ἐπὶ τῆς γῆς οὐδε ὑποκάτω τῆς γῆς ἀνοῖξαι τὸ βιβλίον οὔτε βλέπειν αὐτό . . . ⁶καὶ εἶδον . . . ἀρνίον ἑστηκὸς ὡς ἐσφαγμένον
since it is set down (literally, was set down) for the one who will take it and be slain.	(cf. above ἀρνίον ἑστηκὸς ὡς ἐσφαγμένον)
. . . Jesus became long-suffering, accepting suffering	(cf. ἀρνίον above)
until he took that book	⁷καὶ ἦλθεν καὶ εἴληφεν (scil. τὸ βιβλίον) ἐκ τῆς δεξιᾶς τοῦ καθημένου ἐπὶ τοῦ θρόνου.

---

³ⲡⲉⲉⲓ ⁴ⲉⲧⲉ ⲙ̄ⲛ ⲟⲁⲙ ⲛ̄ⲗⲁⲩⲉ ⲁϥⲓⲧϥ̄ ⲉⲡⲓ⁵ⲇⲏ ⲉⲥⲕⲏ ⲙ̄ⲡⲉⲧⲛⲁϥⲓⲧϥ̄ ⲛ̄ⲥⲉⲍⲗ̄⁶ⲍⲱⲗϥ̄...¹¹ⲓⲏ̄ⲥ̄ ⲁϥⲣ̄ ⲱⲁⲣϣ̄ϩⲏⲧ ⲉϥϣⲱⲡ ⲛ̄ⲛⲓⲙⲕⲟⲩⲁ
¹²ϣⲁⲛ̄ⲧⲉϥϥⲓ ⲙ̄ⲡⲓⲭⲱⲱⲙⲉ ⲉⲧⲙ̄¹³ⲙⲉⲩ

A. Context

Rev 5:1-10 (throne vision). Using metaphorical language and imagery appropriate to a vision, John the Seer tells of a book (scroll) which is in God's right hand. No one was able or worthy to open it until a Lamb, who was standing as though slain, took the book. The Lamb is invested with Messianic titles. John associates salvation with his taking the book.

GTr 20:3-14 (the book). Using metaphorical language and imagery, Valentinus describes a pre-existent book that no one was able to take until Jesus did because he was predestined to take it and be slain. The appearance of the book has made salvation possible.

B. Elements of Comparison

| the living book of the living | τὸ βιβλίον |

(1) the living book of the living ≅ τὸ βιβλίον —Valentinus clearly identifies the book which is "set down for the one who will take it and be slain" (20:4-6) with the living book of the living (20:3; cf. No. 9). John the Seer, however, does not make this identification. The book (little book, scroll: βιβλίον) of Rev 5 is subsequently (in Rev 6 and 8:1-5) said to be opened and is not identified with the book of life. John does mention, however, the "Lamb's book of life" in 21:27, and though he surely did not identify this book with the book of Rev 5, Valentinus may have made such an identification.

| no one was able to take | οὐδεὶς ἐδύνατο . . . ἀνοῖξαι |

(2) no one was able to take ≅ οὐδεὶς ἐδύνατο . . . ἀνοῖξαι —Valentinus' assertion that only Jesus had been able to take the book may be compared with John's vision of the Lamb taking the book in 5:7 and with the earlier statements that no one in heaven or on earth was able to open the book (5:3) and that no one was found worthy to open the book (5:4). Valentinus takes the phrase "no one was able"[16] (οὐδεὶς ἐδύνατο) from Rev 5:3 and completes it with a verb (λαμβάνειν) from Rev 5:7.

---

[16] Literally, is able, but this is apparently just a Copticism.

the one who will take it	ἀρνίον
and be slain	ἑστηκὸς ὡς ἐσφαγμένον
... Jesus	(cf. ἀρνίον
... took	... εἴληφεν
that book	(scil. τὸ βιβλίον)
	(... ἔλαβεν τὸ βιβλίον, vs. 8)

(3) the one who will take it ≅ ἀρνίον —In Rev, the Lamb who was slain is a metaphor for Jesus (so Rev 14:1; 21:22; 22:1). In using the passage, Valentinus substitutes the signified (Jesus) for the signifier (the Lamb).

(4) and be slain ≅ ἑστηκὸς ὡς ἐσφαγμένον —Valentinus takes the description of the Lamb in heaven (i.e., ἑστηκὸς ὡς ἐσφαγμένον) and applies it to the role of Jesus on earth; in so doing, he connects the phrase "and be slain" directly to Jesus' action of taking the book.

(5) took = εἴληφεν —verbatim.

C. Evaluation of the Parallel

The contexts of the two passages are different in that Rev describes a vision and GTr describes the appearance of a pre-existent book, but both passages use highly metaphorical language to express the idea that Jesus' death effected salvation. Although only one of the elements of comparison (5) is verbatim, the others are quite close if one takes account of factors such as imagery that has been resolved into a simpler form. Moreover, the elements occur in the same order. Valentinus uses Rev elsewhere, and he has almost certainly done so here.

D. Interpretation

By identifying the book of life (Rev 13:8) with the book which the Lamb was said to take (Rev 5:7) and then by identifying the Lamb with Jesus, Valentinus changes the focus of the passage in two ways. First, he builds on the allusion to Rev 13:8 from the previous lines and sees the pre-existent book as awaiting the arrival of Jesus alone to take it so that those who had already been predetermined to be saved could have salvation. Second, he shifts the emphasis to the role of Jesus himself in taking the book. Thus, Jesus took the book in death (... "and be slain") in order to effect salvation, whereas in Rev the Lamb was depicted proleptically as slain before it took the book.

11. GTr 20:10-13 (A²) ~ Heb 2:17-18

Identified by van Unnik, p. 110. Probable.

For this reason,	¹⁷ὅθεν ὤφειλεν κατὰ πάντα τοῖς ἀδελφοῖς ὁμοιωθῆναι,
the merciful,	ἵνα ἐλεήμων γένηται
the faithful, Jesus,	καὶ πιστὸς ἀρχιερεὺς . . .
became long-suffering	
accepting suffering	¹⁸ἐν ᾧ γὰρ πέπονθεν
until he took that book.	αὐτὸς πειρασθείς . . .

---

¹⁰ετβε πεει πιϣανϩητ πιπιστος ¹¹ιηc αϥⲣ ϣαⲣϣϩητ ⲉϥϣⲱπ ⲛ̄ⲛⲓ̈ⲥⲉ ¹²ϣⲁⲛⲧⲉϥϥⲓ ⲙ̄ⲡⲓϫⲱⲱⲙⲉ ⲉⲧⲙ̄¹³ⲙⲉⲩ

A. Context

Heb 2:10-18 (the suffering of Jesus). The author uses the image of Jesus as a "merciful" and "faithful" high priest whose function was to make expiation for the sins of the people. Not only did he suffer, but also, as any human being, he was subject to temptation. His death was salvific.

GTr 20:3-14 (the suffering of Jesus). After discussing the significance of the living book of the living (20:3-9), Valentinus develops this image and describes the suffering and taking of the book (i.e., dying) by Jesus, who is given the epithets "merciful" and "faithful." His death was salvific.

B. Elements of Comparison

For this reason . . .	ὅθεν . . .
the merciful,	ἐλεήμων . . .
the faithful, Jesus	πιστὸς ἀρχιερεύς

(1) for this reason = ὅθεν —verbatim.

Commentaries

(2) merciful = ἐλεήμων —verbatim. 'Ελεήμων is used throughout the LXX and other Jewish literature (Philo, Somn. 1,93) as well as occasionally in early Christian literature (Justin, Dial. 107.2) as an epithet of God but is only infrequently used of Christ in early Christian literature (as Heb 2:17). It could also be used to describe believers (Matt 5:7; Didache 3:8), but in general the word was not common in religious or secular literature of the period.

(3) faithful = πιστός —verbatim. Πιστός is much more common, especially as an epithet of God (Isa 49:7; Philo, Rer. Div. Her. 93; Leg. All. 3, 204; 1 Cor 1:9; 2 Cor 1:18; Heb 10:23; 11:11), but also of the Lord (= Christ, 2 Thess 3:3; 2 Tim 2:13) and of the Lamb (also = Christ, Rev 19:11). In the New Testament and early Christian literature, only Heb 2:17 and GTr 20:10 combine these two epithets in speaking of Jesus.

(Jesus) became long-suffering . . .	
accepting suffering	πέπονθεν
	αὐτοὺς πειρασθείς

(4) accepting suffering ≅ πέπονθεν —Valentinus retains the emphasis on Jesus' suffering from Heb 2:18 and gives it a different nuance by adding that Jesus became long-suffering. The latter is reminiscent of Heb 5:8, ἔμαθεν ἀφ' ὧν ἔπαθεν τὴν ὑπακοήν, although references to Jesus' sufferings are fairly common in early Christian literature (e.g. Luke 22:15; 1 Pet 2:28; Ignatius, Smyrn. 2:1; Barn. 5:13).

C. Evaluation of the Parallel

The contexts of the passages are similar in that both speak of the suffering of Jesus Christ. Three of the four elements of comparison are verbatim. One is merely an adverbial expression, but the other two (2, 3) are striking and relatively rare epithets. The inexact element of comparison is quite close. Moreover, the elements of comparison occur in the same order in both passages. Since the combination of "merciful" and "faithful" applied to Jesus in Heb has been considered unique,[17] it is extremely probable that Valentinus drew the imagery from Heb.

---

[17]Van Unnik, p. 110; his observation still stands, in light of the evidence adduced here.

D. Interpretation

Valentinus' use of Heb here is more striking theologically for what it omits than for what it takes. He does not refer to "high priest" here (or elsewhere in GTr), a motif which is especially characteristic of Heb, nor does he discuss the temptation of Jesus. Rather, he uses imagery which, in Heb, recalled Israel's portion of the covenant with God as shown by the high priest ("merciful" and "faithful") with no obvious reference to a covenant, unless one understands the illustration of a "will" (διαθήκη) which follows (20:14-19) as retaining the "covenant" motif. There is in any event no contrast between the old and new covenants. Moreover, by omitting the reference of the temptation of Jesus, Valentinus stresses the predestined, fateful nature of Jesus' life and death.

12. GTr 20:13-14 (A²) ~ Mark 10:45 = Matt 20:28

Identified by van Unnik, p. 112, n. 1, 119.[18] Probable.

Since he (Jesus) knows that his death is life for many.	⁴⁵καὶ γὰρ ²⁸(ὥσπερ) ὁ υἱὸς τοῦ ἀνθρώπου οὐκ ἦλθεν διακονηθῆναι ἀλλὰ διακονῆσαι καὶ δοῦναι τὴν ψυχὴν αὐτοῦ (cf. τὴν ψυχὴν αὐτοῦ) λύτρον ἀντὶ πολλῶν.

---

¹³ⲉⲡⲓⲇⲏ ϥⲥⲁⲩⲛⲉ ϫⲉ ⲡⲓⲙⲟⲩ ¹⁴ⲛ̄ⲧⲟⲟⲧϥ̄ ⲟⲩⲱⲛϩ̄ ⲛ̄ϩⲁϩ ⲡⲉ

A. Context

Mark 10:43-45 (Son of Man serves and dies). The larger context centers around the request of James and John for preferential treatment when Jesus returns to earth (10:35ff.), but the story concludes with a Son of

---

[18]Van Unnik preferred Mark 14:24 as the parallel, but the points of contact in it are not as clear as those in Mark 10:45 = Matt 20:28.

Commentaries 47

Man saying which stresses Jesus' role as servant and his voluntary death to benefit many.

Matt 20:26-28 (Son of Man serves and dies). The Son of Man saying differs only slightly in Matt from the Markan parallel.

GTr 20:11-14 (Jesus suffers and dies). Jesus has accepted suffering because he knows that he will eventually take up a book which will result in his death but which will benefit many.

B. Elements of Comparison

... his death	δοῦναι τὴν ψυχὴν αὐτοῦ
is life	(cf. τὴν ψυχὴν αὐτοῦ)
for many	λύτρον ἀντὶ πολλῶν

(1) his death ≅ δοῦναι τὴν ψυχὴν αὐτοῦ —Mark and Matt do not mention the word "death," but it is clear that they refer to Jesus' death; Valentinus mentions Jesus' death outright and stresses Jesus' knowledge of his death and its effects.

(2) life ≅ τὴν ψυχὴν —Mark and Matt speak of Jesus' death as a ransom, but Valentinus draws attention to its life-giving qualities. The idea of Jesus' death as a ransom appears also in *Diog.* 9:2, and Valentinian Gnostics also use ransom language, e.g. On Res 46:26; 47:25; GPh 52:35-53:11. Ransom language is not common in early Christian literature which is contemporary with GTr.

(3) for many = ἀντὶ πολλῶν —verbatim in all three.

C. Evaluation of the Parallel

The contexts of the two passages are not similar. Only one of the elements of comparison (3) is verbatim, and the order of those in GTr differs from their order in Mark and Matt. The inexact elements express similar thoughts. Because Valentinus nowhere else uses Mark, but frequently uses Matt, the latter is more likely to be the source of this reference.

D. Interpretation

Valentinus draws the reader's attention to the life-giving quality of

Jesus' death. In so doing, he changes the emphasis from the voluntary nature of the death (indeed, the death as a service to humanity) as Matt had it, which was connected to the pericope on serving, to Jesus' own knowledge of the salvific effects of his death. His omission of "ransom" is more problematic; perhaps its use would have detracted from the contrast between death and life. Because Jesus' death is connected to his taking the book (20:12-13), "many" should apparently be understood as those who were written in the book, whereas the synoptic passage leaves open the meaning of "many."

13. GTr 20:15-19 (A²) ∼ Heb 9:17

Postulated by van Unnik, p. 110. Possible.

Just as	
in the manner of a will,	¹⁷διαθήκη γὰρ
not yet opened,	(cf. μήποτε ἰσχύει below)
with the substance of	ἐπὶ νεκροῖς βεβαία,
the late master of the house	(cf. ὁ διαθέμενος below)
lying hidden,	(cf. ἐπὶ νεκροῖς βεβαία)
so it is with all	
which were hidden	
	ἐπεὶ μήποτε ἰσχύει ὅτε
	ζῇ ὁ διαθέμενος.

¹⁵ⲡⲣⲏⲧⲉ ⲛ̄ⲛⲟⲩⲇⲓⲁⲑⲏⲕⲏ ⲉⲙ̄ⲡⲁ¹⁶ⲧⲟⲩⲏⲛ ⲁⲣⲁⲥ ⲉⲥϩⲏⲧ ⲛ̄ϭⲓ ⲧⲟⲩⲥⲓⲁ
¹⁷ⲙ̄ⲡⲛⲉⲡ ⲙ̄ⲡⲏⲉⲓ ⲉⲛⲧⲁϩⲙⲟⲩ ¹⁸ⲙ̄ⲡⲣⲏⲧⲉ ⲇⲉ ⲙ̄ⲡⲧⲏⲣϥ̄ ⲉⲧⲉ ¹⁹ⲛⲉϥϩⲏⲡ·

A. Context

Heb 9:15-22 (Christ the high priest mediates a new covenant). The author of Heb uses the illustration of a will, which takes effect only at the death of the one who made it, to show that Christ's death brought a new "covenant" into effect. He is playing on the ambiguity of διαθήκη, which means both the legal instrument "will" and God's "covenant" with his people.

Commentaries   49

GTr 20:10-27 (Jesus' death is compared to putting a will into effect). Valentinus uses the illustration of a will, which takes effect only at the death of the one who made it, to show that Jesus' death revealed all (the all). He is playing on the imagery of διαθήκη, which literally means the legal instrument "will" but which also suggests "document" or "book" in general, continuing the imagery of the "living book of the living" (Nos. 9, 10).

B. Elements of Comparison

in the manner of a will | διαθήκη γάρ

(1) will = διαθήκη —verbatim. This is the usual Greek word for the legal instrument "will."

not yet opened, | (cf. μήποτε ἰσχύει below)
with the substance . . . | ἐπὶ νεκροῖς βεβαία,
lying hidden, | (cf. ἐπὶ νεκροῖς βεβαία)

(2) not yet opened ≅ μήποτε ἰσχύει —The ideas expressed by the phrases are the same, namely, that a will is not valid until it is unsealed at the death of the one who made it.

(3) with the substance lying hidden ≅ ἐπὶ νεκροῖς βεβαία —Heb is explicit: only at death can a will be established or take effect. Valentinus makes the same point more circuitously.

the late master of the house | ὁ διαθέμενος

(4) the late master of the house ≅ ὁ διαθέμενος —Heb's "testator" (ὁ διαθέμενος) is in this context roughly equivalent to GTr's "late master of the house." The latter also occurs in GTr 25:31 and 2 Tim 2:21.

C. Evaluation of the Parallel

The contexts of the two passages are similar insofar as both center around the death of Jesus Christ. GTr, however, seems not to have retained the ambiguity of διαθήκη as "will" or "covenant" which is integral to the Heb passage, although it is only implicit in the Greek, of course. Only one of the elements of comparison is verbatim; it is a common word, although its use as an image does not seem to be common. The other three are inexact, although each expresses much the same idea in GTr as in Heb. Valentinus uses Heb elsewhere, but here the illustration which both GTr and Heb have is a statement of the obvious (a will is of no regard while the one who made it is alive) which both Valentinus and the author of Heb could have arrived at independently.

D. Interpretation

If Valentinus has used Heb 9:17, he has omitted the argument that Jesus' death in any way has mediated a new covenant. Jesus' death in GTr has nothing to do with redeeming persons from the first covenant (Heb 9:15) but rather reveals all, which had been concealed. This alteration may have been facilitated by changing "testator" (ὁ διαθέμενος) of Heb to "master of the house." Jesus appeared because all had been concealed. This may indicate that before Jesus' coming, all those who were to be saved, all those who comprise the Father or the fullness of the deity, in effect, were legatees of the will but could not collect until Jesus opened the will in his death. The Father is invisible and could only be made known by Jesus, who brought the book with the names of those who would receive knowledge. Those who receive knowledge are "all," a cosmological technical term in GTr.[19] Jesus' death, then, could be seen as a mediation of sorts in that he brought knowledge of the invisible Father to earth.

14. GTr 20:23-27 (A²) ~ Col 2:14

Identified by van Unnik, pp. 110-111. Probable.

Jesus appeared; he clothed himself with that book;	¹⁴ἐξαλείψας τὸ καθ' ἡμῶν χειρόγραφον τοῖς δόγμασιν ὃ ἦν ὑπεναντίον ἡμῖν, καὶ αὐτὸ ἦρκεν ἐκ τοῦ μέσου
He was nailed to a beam; he published the edict (διάταγμα) of the Father on the cross.	προσηλώσας αὐτὸ (cf. τῷ σταυρῷ below) (cf. χειρόγραφον . . . δόγμασιν) τῷ σταυρῷ·

---

[19]Cf. discussion of No. 5.

²³ⲁϥⲟⲩⲁⲛϩ̄ ⲁⲃⲁⲗ ⲛ̄ϭⲓ ²⁴ⲓⲏ̄ⲥ̄ ⲁϥⲉⲁⲗⲉϥ ⲙ̄ⲡⲓⲭⲱⲱⲙⲉ· ⲉ²⁵ⲧⲙ̄ⲙⲉⲩ
ⲁⲩⲁϥⲧϥ̄ ⲁⲩϣⲉ· ⲁϥ²⁶ⲧⲱϭⲉ ⲙ̄ⲡⲇⲓⲁⲧⲁⲅⲙⲁ ⲁⲃⲁⲗ ⲛ̄²⁷ⲧⲉ ⲡⲓⲱⲧ· ⲉⲓ
ⲡⲉϥⲣⲟⲥ·

A. Context

Col 2:13-15 (the crucifixion of Christ). The crucifixion of Christ has effected forgiveness of sins and also victory over powers and principalities. Life and salvation are brought thereby. The passage uses language which had already become traditional in early Christianity by the time ps-Paul wrote.[20]

GTr 20:18-27 (the crucifixion of Jesus). The crucifixion of Jesus has effected the salvation of those who were predestined for it by being written in the living book of the living. This is expressed with imagery that is capable of several resolutions: his crucifixion while wrapped in an edict of the Father.

B. Elements of Comparison

He was nailed	προσηλώσας αὐτὸ
to a beam	(cf. τῷ σταυρῷ)
on the cross	τῷ σταυρῷ

(1) he was nailed ≅ προσηλώσας αὐτό —The word προσηλώσας occurs only in Col 2:14 in the New Testament and is infrequent in other religious and secular literature of the early Christian period. It can be used with τῷ σταυρῷ to mean "crucify" (e.g., Josephus, *Bell.* 2,308). Although these two phrases contain shared vocabulary, their constructions are different. In GTr, Jesus is the thing crucified, whereas in Col, he is the one who crucifies (i.e., the "bond which stood against us with its legal demands" [χειρόγραφον τοῖς δόγμασιν ὅ ἦν ὑπεναντίον ἡμῖν]; this happens, of course, while Jesus himself is being crucified!).

(2) to a beam ≅ τῷ σταυρῷ —GTr contains two expressions, beam and

---

[20]See Lohse, pp. 106-107 for a fuller explanation of this; the most obvious clue is the large number of participles in these verses of Col.

cross, as compared to one, σταυρός, in Col. Valentinus also uses "beam" in 18:24. Both instances probably translate Greek ξύλος, which in early Christian literature often refers to the cross (*Barn.* 5:13; 1 Pet 2:24; *Poly. to Phil.* 8:1; Melito, *Peri Pascha* [ed. Bonner] 12:28; 13:16), particularly in the prophetic-christological or typological exegesis of Deut 21:22-23 (see Acts 5:30, 10:39; Gal 3:13).

(3) on the cross = τῷ σταυρῷ —verbatim. The word "cross" is frequently used in references fo Jesus' crucifixion, especially in the Pauline writings, where the motif of the "crucified Messiah" plays a central role (e.g., 1 Cor 1:18; Gal 5:11).

a will	(cf. No. 13, διαθήκη)
(Jesus) . . . clothed himself with that book (document)	χειρόγραφον τοῖς δόγμασιν
. . . he published the edict (διάταγμα) of the Father	(cf. χειρόγραφον . . . δόγμασιν)

(4) will, book, edict ≅ χειρόγραφον τοῖς δόγμασιν —By edict (20:26), Valentinus means the "will" of 20:15, in which Jesus wraps himself. Ps-Paul speaks of a χειρόγραφον, "handwritten document," more specifically, a bond or certificate of indebtedness. Modern interpretation is divided on just what ps-Paul means by the cheirograph. The cheirograph could refer to the Mosaic Law but is probably more general, a record of human transgressions, written either by God or by human beings collectively in their sins. The cheirograph is said to be accumulated by "our trespasses" (Col 2:13) and is further modified by another legal term, δόγμα. Valentinus takes χειρόγραφον in the less specific sense of "written document" and offers three resolutions of the ambiguity: "living book of the living," "will," and "edict" (cf. Nos. 9, 13, and the present passage). Jesus may not actually be identified with the written document here, but he is closely associated with it in that he is said to wrap himself in it. The identification of Jesus with a written document is thought by some[21] to have become a traditional exegesis of Col 2:14 in the early years of Christianity, particularly in those strands with continuing Jewish influence. A

---

[21] For a summary of opinions and an exegesis of this passage, see O. Blanchette, "Does the Cheirographon of Col 2,14 Represent Christ Himself?" *CBQ* 23 (1961) 306-312.

Commentaries 53

comparison with Ode of Solomon 23 may support this,[22] but one should also bear in mind that the Col passage itself shows the marks of using traditional language. Another explanation might be that an interpretation of Jesus' crucifixion such as this may have arisen early, before ps-Paul, and might have flourished in those same circles.

C. Evaluation of the Parallel

The context of both Col and GTr is the crucifixion of Jesus. Of the four elements of comparison, one (3) is verbatim. Shared vocabulary occurs in two of the others; in the remaining element (4), the difference can be explained as the replacement of the ambiguous term χειρόγραφον with a more general legal term διάταγμα. Reference to "nailing" in the context of crucifixion (1) is sufficiently distinctive to support the hypothesis that Valentinus has used Col in this case. Moreoever, the elements of comparison occur in almost the same order in GTr as in Col. Valentinus knows and uses Col elsewhere, so it is likely that he has used it here, even though he may also have known the early Christian tradition which identified Jesus with a book.

D. Interpretation

By explaining that Jesus was clothed in the living book of the living, which is also compared to the Father's legal will, the significance of the crucifixion is underlined. Since Jesus' appearance on earth has made the contents of the pre-existent book known, his crucifixion with the Father's "edict" puts salvation into effect. Valentinus identifies Jesus with the χειρόγραφον of Col 2:14, but because he has made Jesus the thing that was crucified rather than the one who crucifies as in Col (see [1]), he uses another term, διάταγμα. In other words, because Jesus' crucifixion cannot be seen as "against us," Valentinus uses the legal term διάταγμα with

---

[22]There Jesus is identified with a letter. See, on this, J. Daniélou, *The Theology of Jewish Christianity*, pp. 203-204, and Blanchette, pp. 308-312. Daniélou notes certain elements common to the Ode and GTr which do not occur in Rev, in specific, the connection of the document and the cross together with the revelation of the Father. Blanchette argues that it is exegetically possible to identify "the cheirograph against us" in Col 2:14 with Christ in much the same way as Christ is said to have come in the likeness of sinful flesh in Rom 8:3. Thus, Col 2:14 is able to retain both the apocalyptic image of the celestial book and the Pauline category of the "body."

which Jesus and his work can be identified. In Col 2:14, the bond which is "against us" is nailed to the cross when Jesus is crucified in order to effect forgiveness and life, but in GTr, Jesus, wrapped with the Father's edict, is nailed to a beam, the cross, in order to effect salvation for those whose names are written in the pre-existent book.

15. GTr 20:28-29 (A²) ~ Phil 2:8

Postulated by Grobel, p. 67, nn. 119, 121. Possible.

(O such magnificent teaching!)	(Χριστός ' Ιησοῦς)
Drawing himself (Jesus) down	⁸ἐταπείνωσεν ἑαυτὸν
	γενόμενος ὑπήκοος
to death ...	μέχρι θανάτου

---

²⁸ⲈϤⲤⲰⲔ ²⁹ⲘⲘⲀϤ ⲀⲠⲒⲦⲚ̄ ⲀⲠⲘⲞⲨ

A. Context

Phil 2:6-11 (an early christological hymn). The hymn speaks of Christ Jesus' pre-existence, his voluntary humiliation, his service, obedience, death, and exaltation.

GTr 20:27-34 (Jesus' death is a lesson). The death of Jesus is considered "magnificent teaching" (20:28) because it was voluntary and resulted in his eternal imperishability.

B. Elements of Comparison

| Drawing himself (Jesus) down | ἐταπείνωσεν ἑαυτόν ... |
| to death ... | μέχρι θανάτου |

(1) drawing himself down ≅ ἐταπείνωσιν ἑαυτον —Both GTr and Phil emphasize Jesus' voluntary action in bringing about his own death. Of course, by "voluntary" Paul and Valentinus mean different things. Paul includes the notion of humiliation, i.e., that Christ Jesus exposed himself to shame; Valentinus understands that Jesus was predestined to take the book and die but nevertheless speaks as if the death were voluntary.

(2) to death ⁀ μέχρι θανάτου —verbatim (?). It is not clear from the Coptic whether Valentinus retained the preposition μέχρι, "unto, to such a degree as," or (somewhat more likely) substituted εἰς.

C. Evaluation of the Parallel

The contexts are similar in their mention of Jesus' voluntary death, although Paul and Valentinus in fact mean different things by it. One element of comparison (2) is probably verbatim; the other is inexact but makes much the same point in both passages. There is no clear evidence that Valentinus used Phil elsewhere, and his use of it here is no more than possible.

D. Interpretation

If Valentinus has used the Phil passage, he has imposed upon in his own interpretation of the voluntary nature of Jesus' death and has omitted any reference to the motifs of humiliation, obedience, and service from Phil. Thus, Valentinus considers Jesus' voluntary death to be "magnificent teaching" (20:28).

16. GTr 20:28-32 (A²) ~ 1 Cor 15:53-54

Identified by van Unnik, p. 117. Probable.

| (Jesus) Drawing himself down to death, clothed in eternal life, having put off the perishable rags, he put on imperishability. | ⁵³(Δεῖ γὰρ) (cf. vs. 54 ὁ θάνατος) (cf. vs. 54 ἀθανασίαν) τὸ φθαρτὸν τοῦτο ἐνδύσασθαι ἀφθαρσίαν . . . ⁵⁴ὅταν δὲ τὸ φθαρτὸν τοῦτο ἐνδύσηται ἀφθαρσίαν καὶ τὸ θνητὸν τοῦτο ἐνδύσηται ἀθανασίαν, τότε γενήσεται ὁ λόγος ὁ γεγραμμέος. κατεπόθη ὁ θάνατος εἰς νῖκος. |

²⁸ⲉϥⲥⲱⲕ ²⁹ⲙ̄ⲙⲁϥ ⲁⲡⲓⲧⲛ̄ ⲁⲡⲙⲟⲩ ⲉⲣⲉⲡⲓⲱⲛϩ̄ ³⁰ⲛ̄ⲁⲛⲏ2ⲉ ⲧⲟ 2ⲓⲱⲱϥ
ⲉⲁϥⲃⲱϣ ³¹ⲙ̄ⲙⲁϥ ⲛ̄ⲛⲓⲡⲗⲁϭⲉ ⲉⲧⲧⲉⲕⲁⲓⲧ· ³²ⲁϥϯ 2ⲓⲱⲱϥ ⲛ̄ⲧⲙⲛ̄ⲧⲁⲧ· ⲧⲉⲕⲟ

A. Context

1 Cor 15:51-57 (the mystery of the resurrection). Paul says that all will be changed at the eschaton. Those who are dead will be raised in a form that will not perish, and those who are still alive will be transformed. In both cases, the resurrection and eschaton will demonstrate the conquest of death by life.

GTr 20:27-34 (Jesus' death and eternal life). Valentinus says that Jesus voluntarily died but had eternal life. He shed his body at death and donned, as it were, imperishability. His death demonstrated the conquest of death by life.

B. Elements of Comparison

... death,	(cf. ὁ θάνατος)
clothed in eternal life	(cf. ἀθανασίαν)
	κατεπόθη εἰς νῖκος

(1) death = ὁ θάνατος —verbatim. Here Paul uses "death" in a general sense, whereas Valentinus restricts himself to the death of Jesus.

(2) eternal life ≅ ἀθανασίαν —These two expressions are roughly equivalent. Paul's use of ἀθανασίαν is probably dictated by parallelism since ἀφθαρσίαν immediately precedes this reference (see [4]).

(3) clothed in eternal life ≅ κατεπόθη εἰς νῖκος —For Paul, the opposite of death in its general sense is "victory" over it. For Valentinus, Jesus already has the opposite of his death, namely, eternal life. The notions of death being *swallowed up* in victory and of Jesus being *clothed in* eternal life are different ways of expressing the same point, that death is *enveloped* by its opposite and transformed into it.

having put off	
the perishable rags	τὸ φθαρτὸν τοῦτο
he put on imperishability	ἐνδύσασθαι ἀφθαρσίαν

Commentaries

> τὸ θνητὸν τοῦτο
> ἐνδύσηται ἀθανασίαν

(4) perishable rags, imperishability ≅ τὸ φθαρτόν, ἀφθαρσίαν; τὸ θνητόν, ἀθανασίαν —Both passages show the antithesis, "perishability versus imperishability." Paul elaborates this antithesis with a parallel opposition, "mortality versus immortality." Valentinus omits the latter, but elements (1) and (2) show that he may have incorporated it in another form. Valentinus' mention of "rags" may recall a common notion that the body is to be held in low esteem.[23] This is expressed by use of garment imagery.

(5) put off, put on ≅ ἐνδύσασθαι —Paul's mention of "putting on" is a clear allusion to the baptismal ritual of early Christians (cf. especially Gal 3:27, where he makes this explicit). Valentinus balances this expression with its opposite, thus extending the rhetorical antithesis of "perishability versus imperishability." The motif of "putting off"[24] does not happen to occur in the undisputed letters of Paul, although contemporaneous baptismal liturgy[25] probably referred to both dying and rising with Christ, and thus putting off and putting on; such terminology is attested in ps-Pauline texts, e.g., Col 3:9-10, Eph 4:22, 24. In 1 Cor, Paul may also allude to the heavenly garment imagery, although he does not make this explicit.[26]

C. Evaluation of the Parallel

The contexts are similar insofar as both speak of eternal life or resurrection, but they differ in emphasis. One element of comparison (1) is exact; moreover, the other four, though inexact, can be understood as

---

[23] See Plato, Phaedo 114c; Corp. Herm. 1:24-26; GTh 37; see also J. Z. Smith, "The Garments of Shame," HR 5 (1965-66) 217-239, who discusses this notion in GTh. The most thorough discussion of the many nuances given to the image "garment" in the ancient world is found in RAC 10, col. 945-1025 ("Gewand [der Seele]").
[24] Cf. Corp. Herm. 1:26, where the souls are said to cast off their garments in their ascent to God.
[25] The classic work on this topic is by W. A. Meeks, "The Image of the Androgyne: Some Uses of a Symbol in Earliest Christianity," HR 13 (1974) 165-208.
[26] This is the view of H. Conzelmann, 1 Corinthians (Philadelphia: Fortress, 1975), p. 291. In n. 27, Conzelmann gives references to other examples of this, e.g., Ode of Solomon 15:2; Asc Isa 4:17.

modifications of Pauline imagery or terminology or as alterations in the rhetorical structure. Although the evidence for Valentinus' use of 1 Cor is not particularly strong elsewhere in GTr, his use of it here seems clear.

D. Interpretation

Paul's statement emphasizes the transformation that the eschaton and resurrection are expected to bring. Because he makes the allusion to baptism more specific by adding "put off" and because he applies the passage to Jesus, Valentinus modifies the import of the passage from eschatology to soteriology. By applying Paul's statement specifically to Jesus and removing the eschatological element, Valentinus has cleared the way for seeing the antithesis of "perishable, imperishable" as a substitution which each person makes at the moment of conversion rather than simply as a transformation from one state to another at the eschaton. In place of his perishable rags (the body), Jesus is said to put on imperishability, which could in turn be generalized and applied to the Gnostic while still in the body (as GPh 56:18-19 does). Valentinus does not go this far, however, and the passage remains essentially Pauline, with the possible exception of the reference to "perishable *rags*," which might refer to the Platonic motif of the body as a garment (e.g., *Crat.* 403b, which speaks of the soul as denuded of the body after death). The motif of putting on garments in the context of resurrection is developed in Valentinian Gnosticism, e.g. GPh 57:19-22.

17. GTr 20:32-34 (A^2) ~ John 10:17-18

Identified by Grobel, p. 69, n. 124. Probable.

he put on imperishability,	^{17}ἐγὼ τίθημι τὴν ψυχήν μου ...
a thing that no one	^{18}οὐδεὶς
can take	αἴρει (v.l.) αὐτὴν
from him	ἀπ' ἐμοῦ

---

^{32}ⲁϥϯ ϩⲓⲱⲱϥ ⲛ̄ⲧⲙⲛ̄ⲧⲁⲧ· ⲧⲉⲕⲟ ^{33}ⲡⲉⲉⲓ ⲉⲧⲉ ⲙⲛ̄ ϣϭⲁⲙ ⲛ̄ⲗⲁⲁⲩⲉ
^{34}ⲁⲩ ϥⲓⲧϥ ⲛ̄ⲧⲟⲟⲧϥ̄

A. Context

John 10:7-18 (the good shepherd). In a series of sayings, Jesus explains the meaning of a figure (παροιμία) that he has told about a shepherd. He himself is the good shepherd, who voluntarily dies for the sheep, that is, the believers, and then resurrects himself.

GTr 20:28-34 (resurrection of Jesus). Jesus' voluntary death led to his resurrection in an imperishable or incorruptible state.

B. Elements of Comparison

... imperishability,	... τὴν ψυχήν μου
... no one	οὐδεὶς
can take	αἴρει ...
from him	ἀπ' ἐμοῦ

(1) imperishability ≅ τὴν ψυχήν μου —John uses ψυχή here to mean the state of being alive on earth, but it also means, on another level, the transcendent life force, as Jesus' allusion to the resurrection suggests. Valentinus has resolved this ambiguity by understanding ψυχή as an imperishable entity, hence "imperishability."

(2) no one can take from him ≅ οὐδεὶς αἴρει ... ἀπ' ἐμοῦ — Valentinus has paraphrased this by making the grammatical changes necessary to incorporate a saying of Jesus into GTr in past narrative form.

C. Evaluation of the Parallel

The contexts of both passages speak of Jesus' death and resurrection. Although neither of the elements of comparison is verbatim, one resolves an ambiguity in John, and the other paraphrases a saying of Jesus. Valentinus frequently uses John elsewhere, and he has probably used John here as well.

D. Interpretation

Valentinus' reference to "imperishability" is the key to his interpretation. Because the phrase, "he put on imperishability" refers to Jesus' resurrection, Valentinus' statement that no one can take it away from Jesus must refer to the resurrected state. Thus, Jesus in his resurrected state is imperishable or incorruptible. Strictly speaking, however, there is no description of the actual event of the resurrection in GTr but rather the donning of imperishability apparently occurs at the crucifixion itself. The resolution of ψυχή into imperishability shifts the focus away from the voluntary nature of Jesus' death to the eternal nature of the imperishability obtained thereby.

18. GTr 21:10-14,20-23 (A^2) ~ John 12:32

Identified by Williams. Probable.

all must go to him (the Father). Then, as <each> person gains knowledge, he receives his own, and he draws them to himself. . . . and all must go to him and each person receive his own	^{32}κἀγὼ [' Ἰησοῦς] ἐὰν ὑψωθῶ ἐκ τῆς γῆς, πάντας (v.l. πάντα) ἑλκύσω πρὸς ἐμαυτόν. (cf. πάντας, v.l. πάντα)

---

^{10}ⲁⲛⲁⲅⲕⲏ ⲁⲧⲣⲉⲡⲧⲏⲣϥ ⲱⲉ ⲁ^{11}ⲡⲣⲏⲓ ϣⲁⲣⲁϥ ⲧⲟⲧⲉ ⲉⲣⲉⲡⲟⲩ ^{12}ⲉⲉⲓ ⟨ⲡⲟⲩⲉⲉⲓ⟩ ⲥⲁⲩⲛⲉ ϣⲁϥϫⲓ ⲛ̄ⲛⲉⲧⲉ ^{13}ⲛⲟⲩϥ ⲛⲉ ⲁⲩⲱ ϣⲁϥⲥⲱⲕ ⲙ^{14}ⲙⲁⲩ ϣⲁⲣⲁϥ—^{19}ⲁⲛⲁⲅ^{20}ⲕⲏ ⲛ̄ⲇⲉ ⲁⲡⲣⲉⲡⲧⲏⲣϥ ϣⲉ ^{21}ⲁⲡⲣⲏⲓ ϣⲁⲣⲁϥ ⲛ̄ⲧⲉ ⲡⲟⲩⲉⲉⲓ ⲡⲟⲩ^{22}ⲉⲉⲓ (ⲡⲟⲩⲉⲉⲓ) ϫⲓ ⲛⲛⲉⲧⲉⲛⲟⲩϥ ^{23}ⲛⲉ·

A. Context

John 12:27-33 (the judgment has come). At the end of his public ministry, a voice from heaven is heard by the crowd; this introduces Jesus' proclamation of judgment. After his crucifixion, Jesus will cause all persons to ascend to him (6:44).

GTr 21:8-25 (the perfection of all). The Father has the perfection of all within him, and he causes all to ascend to him as they gain knowledge.

Commentaries   61

B. *Elements of Comparison*

(the Father)	(᾽Ιησοῦς)
all . . .	πάντας (v.l. πάντα)
he draws them to himself	ἑλκύσω πρὸς ἐμαυτόν

(1) Father ≅ ᾽Ιησοῦς —Valentinus makes a typical change in the aspect of deity from Son (Jesus) to Father.

(2) all = πάντα = πάντας —The manuscripts of John preserve two different readings at this point. Some early manuscripts, including p66, read πάντα. The neuter is ambiguous here because, although it should refer to all things, the context requires that it refer to people. Valentinus' "all" is similarly ambiguous; it may refer to all people, but it may refer to all people with knowledge to the degree that they comprise the entirety of those who belong to the Father, i.e., have a true, metaphysical existence.

(3) he draws . . . to himself ≅ ἑλκύσω πρὸς ἐμαυτόν —Valentinus has paraphrased what John gives as words of Jesus and has incorporated them into a statement about the Father.

C. *Evaluation of the Parallel*

Although the contexts are not particularly similar, the three elements of comparison show close parallels in the two passages. One point of comparison (2) is verbatim; another represents a change typical of GTr; the third is a paraphrase of part of John 12:32. This paraphrase is so close, once the typical change from Jesus to Father is recognized, that Valentinus' use of John 12:32 can hardly be doubted, especially since John is often interpreted in GTr.

D. *Interpretation*

Because the context of GTr does not refer to the death of Jesus as did John, the emphasis of the passage has been changed considerably. This is also true because the passage refers to the Father rather than to Jesus. Thus, the Father is presented as drawing all to himself as each gains knowledge, much as a magnet draws iron. In John, belief in Jesus (12:36) means that one will eventually ascend to where Jesus is but only after Jesus' resurrection and, in fact, at the last day (6:44). In GTr, the reception or acquisition of knowledge initiates the action of drawing, but there is no indication that a lapse in time occurs. Moreover, no resolution is offered of the ambiguous word "all," but the meaning is apparently that all who have knowledge (which comes from Jesus, 20:34-21:8) return to their origin within the Father. The ambiguous sense of "all" is thus well-suited for its use in a metaphysical concept.

19. GTr 21:25-28 (A²) ~ Rom 8:29-30

Identified by van Unnik, p. 118. Probable.

(the Father)	(ὁ θεός)
Those whose names he foreknew	²⁹ὅτι οὓς προέγνω, καὶ προώρισεν συμμόρφους τῆς εἰκόνος τοῦ υἱοῦ αὐτοῦ, εἰς τὸ εἶναι αὐτὸν πρωτότοκον ἐκ πολλοῖς ἀδελφοῖς.
were called at the end as persons having knowledge.	³⁰οὓς δὲ προώρισεν, τούτους καὶ ἐκάλεσεν . . . (cf. συμμόρφους τῆς εἰκόνος τοῦ υἱοῦ αὐτοῦ above)

²⁵ⲚⲈⲈⲒ Ⲛ̄²⁶ⲦⲀϤⲢ̄ϢⲀⲢⲠ̄ Ⲛ̄ⲤⲀⲨⲚⲈ ⲘⲠⲞⲨ²⁷ⲢⲈⲚ ⲀⲐⲀⲎ ⲀⲨⲘⲞⲨⲦⲈ ⲀⲢⲀⲨ
²⁸ϨⲰⲤ ⲞⲨⲈⲈⲒ ⲈϤⲤⲀⲨⲚⲈ

A. Context

Rom 8:28-30 (God's purpose). God predestines (calls) certain people to salvation, i.e., those who love him. Salvation consists in being made like the image of God's Son.

GTr 21:18-31 (the perfection of all). God predestines (calls) certain people to salvation, i.e., those whose names are written in the living book of the living (21:4-5). Salvation consists in possession of knowledge.

B. Elements of Comparison

(the Father)   (ὁ θεός)

Commentaries 63

| those whose names he foreknew | οὓς προέγνω |
| | καὶ προώρισεν |

(1) Father ≅ ὁ θεός —typical change from God to Father.

(2) he foreknew = πρόεγνω = προώρισεν —Paul uses two closely related words, προγινώσκειν ("know beforehand," "have foreknowledge of") and προορίζειν ("decide upon beforehand," "predestine") to express God's role in choosing those who are to be saved. Valentinus keeps only one of Paul's terms.

those ... were called	τούτους καὶ ἐκάλεσεν
at the end	
as persons having knowledge	(cf. συμμόρφους τῆς εἰκόνος τοῦ
	υἱοῦ αὐτοῦ)

(3) were called ≅ ἐκάλεσεν —Both Paul and Valentinus make it clear that the deity has called certain persons. GTr suggests that these were called by name (21:26-27), but "name" is also implicit in the meaning of the verb Paul uses, καλεῖν, i.e., "call by name." Valentinus puts the verb in the passive.

(4) as persons having knowledge ≅ συμμόρφους τῆς εἰκόνος τοῦ υἱοῦ αὐτοῦ —Although these two phrases are literally quite different, Valentinus' phrase may be an interpretation of Paul at this point (see part D).

C. Evaluation of the Parallel

The theological concept of predestination to salvation forms the context of both passages. Of the four elements of comparison, one (2) is verbatim. Two of the inexact elements represent either a change typical of Valentinus or a grammatical change dictated by incorporation of the passage into GTr. A fourth element is a paraphrasing interpretation of one of Paul's phrases. No single point of comparison is strong enough to demonstrate that Valentinus has used Rom here, but the cumulative weight of the four elements of comparison indicates that his use of Rom is likely. This is all the more so because several passages in GTr (e.g., Nos. 45, 71, and 73) show almost certain use of Rom.

D. Interpretation

The passage in Rom has two points of emphasis: a christological one, that the Son is the first-born among many brothers and sisters; and a soteriological one, that those who are predestined are made like the image of God's Son. Valentinus has eliminated much of Paul's text in the course of interpreting it, and in so doing, simplifies the rhetoric. More important, he has retained only the soteriological emphasis of the passage. By putting Paul's "called" in the passive, Valentinus may avoid reference to the Father's activity in calling, thus enabling the impassive Father to remain distant from the affairs of the world. By adding the phrase "at the end" he may suggest that the eschaton has been initiated for those who have knowledge because only with the taking of the book by Jesus could those who were to be saved be known and called. The phrase "as persons having knowledge" apparently interprets Paul's phrase "conformed to the image of his Son." Those who have knowledge in GTr are those who have eaten of the fruit of the Father's knowledge which was brought by Christ in his crucifixion (18:24-28). Thus, they might be seen as "conformed to the image of his Son" (Rom 8:29). If error is to be regarded as the demiurge in GTr 17:14-36, then those who have eaten of the fruit of the Father's knowledge may be seen to have the image of Christ (or the Son) rather than the image of error.

20. GTr 21:32-34 (A²) ~ John 10:3

Postulated by van Unnik, p. 118. Possible.

| (For he whose name has not been spoken is ignorant.) How else will one hear if his name has not been called? | (. . . ὁ θυρωρός) . . . καὶ τὰ πρόβατα τῆς φωνῆς αὐτοῦ ἀκούει καὶ τὰ ἴδια πρόβατα φωνεῖ κατ' ὄνομα . . . |

---

[32]ⲘⲘⲀⲚ ⲈⲰ ⲚⲢⲎⲦⲈ ⲈⲢⲈⲞⲨ [33]ⲈⲈⲒ ⲚⲀⲤⲰⲦⲘ ⲈⲘⲠⲞⲨⲰⲰ Ⲙ[34]ⲠⲈϤⲢⲈⲚ

A. Context

John 10:1-6 (the shepherd and his sheep). John attributes a story (παροιμία, "figure") to Jesus; it is about a shepherd who calls his own sheep by name in herding them. The sheep follow the shepherd, but they will not follow a stranger. Jesus later explains that the figure is about himself (10:7ff.).

GTr 21:28-37 (realization of predestination). Only those whose names have been called have knowledge, which is what quickens them. Others have a human body but are empty of what would quicken them because they are ignorant.

B. Elements of Comparison

(1) [Rhetorical structure] How else will one hear if his name has not been called? ≠ ἀκούει . . . φωνεῖ κατ' ὄνομα —By transforming the passage into a rhetorical question, Valentinus has made certain necessary changes in tense and voice and has used the negative.

| How else will one hear | πρόβατα . . . ἀκούει |

(2) will . . . hear ≅ ἀκούει —In both passages, the one called is said to hear.

(3) one ≠ πρόβατα —In John, the sheep are said to hear the shepherd's voice; in GTr, the one whom the Father foreknew hears (cf. 31:35-32:4, where Jesus is identified with a shepherd). "One" in GTr may be a resolution of John's image of "sheep."

| if his name has not been called | φωνεῖ κατ' ὄνομα |

(4) name has . . . been called ≅ φωνεῖ κατ' ὄνομα —Both passages share the idea of calling one by name.

C. Evaluation of the Parallel

The contexts of the two passages are dissimilar, unless one considers GTr to be an interpretation of Jesus' παροιμία in John (see part D). Such an interpretation would, of course, have to be textually based, and there is only a little evidence therein. John's imagery may be resolved in one of the elements of comparison (3), but this is not certain. The other elements of comparison are also inexact, but this can be explained by understanding that the rhetorical structure of John has been changed in the process of incorporation into GTr. Because Valentinus uses John frequently (and in fact uses John 10 in No. 17), however, his use of John here is possible also.

D. Interpretation

If Valentinus has interpreted John 10:3 here, he may have understood his own rhetorical question as an interpretation of Jesus' παροιμία. In other words, he may have identified Jesus with the shepherd (cf. 31:35) and the believers as the sheep (whose names the shepherd calls) as John intended (John 10:7-18); and then further identified the Father as the shepherd (the one who calls; cf. 32:17-19) and those who have knowledge with those whose names are called. This, of course, requires that no distinction be made between the Father and Jesus. It is just possible that Valentinus has understood Jesus' statement that he is the door of the sheep (John 10:7) to mean that someone else is the shepherd, i.e., the Father, and that he sees no tension between this and Jesus' statement that he is the shepherd (John 10:11). Such an interpretation is not at all clear, however, from the sketchy points of contact with the Johannine text.

21. GTr 21:32-34 (A²) ~ Rom 10:14

Postulated by Grobel, p. 75, n. 144. Dubious.

| How else will one hear if his name has not been called? | ¹⁴Πῶς οὖν ἐπικαλέσωνται εἰς ὃν οὐκ ἐπίστευσαν; |

³²MMAN ЄѠ ΝΡΗΤЄ ЄΡЄΟΥ³³ЄЄΙ ΝΑⲤѠΤΜ ЄΜΠΟΥѠѠ Μ³⁴ΠЄϤΡЄΝ

A. Context

Rom 10:5-17 (righteousness comes by faith). By using christological proofs from prophecy, Paul shows that those who call upon Jesus will be saved. People can only believe (have faith), however, if they have heard the good news, but not all respond to the Christian proclamation.

GTr 21:28-37 (realization of predestination). Only those whose names have been called have knowledge, which is what quickens them. Others

Commentaries 67

have a human body but are empty of what would quicken them because they are ignorant.

B. *Elements of Comparison*

How else | Πῶς οὖν

(1) how else ≅ πῶς οὖν —Both passages contain a rhetorical question. Although Valentinus does not begin the question in exactly the same way as Paul, the form and phrasing are quite similar.

his name has not been called | ἐπικαλέσωνται

(2) his name has not been called ≅ ἐπικαλέσωνται —Valentinus makes "name" explicit, whereas Paul does not, although ἐπικαλεῖν sometimes has the implicit object, "name." In the active and passive the verb can actually mean "name," although the passive sometimes uses ὄνομα also. Ἐπικαλέσωνται in Rom 10:14 is unambiguously in the middle voice, however, as its construction with εἰς shows: it therefore means "call upon." In Rom, the one who is called upon is ὃν οὐκ ἐπίστευσαν. In GTr, the passive must be used since no object is supplied: it therefore means "has [not] been called."

C. *Evaluation of the Parallel*

The contexts of the two passages are different; Paul writes of belief, whereas Valentinus writes of predestination. Predestination is a Pauline concept, however, and both passages may be seen as concerning salvation, in a loose sense. Nevertheless, the difference in voice completely changes the meaning of the passage, and only the rhetorical question (1) in GTr reminds the reader of Rom. Moreover, shared distinctive imagery is lacking. Even though Valentinus knows and uses Rom elsewhere, it is unlikely that he used it here.

22. GTr 22:2-4 (A[2]) ~ John 3:31

Postulated by Malinine et al., p. 54. Possible.

Thus, if one knows, he is from above. | [31]ὁ ἄνωθεν ἐρχόμενος ἐπάνω πάντων ἐστίν.

²ⲍⲱⲥⲧⲉ ⲟⲩ³ⲉⲉⲓ ⲉϥⲱⲁⲥⲁⲩⲛⲉ· ⲟⲩⲁⲃⲁⲗ ⲡⲉ ⁴ⲍⲙ̄ ⲡⲥⲁⲛ2ⲣⲉ·

A. Context

John 3:31-36 (the one from above). Jesus' origin is above; he is from heaven and so is above all (i.e., all earthly things). He is sent by God to proclaim God's message and to bestow eternal life on those who believe in God's Son.

GTr 22:2-7 (one from above). The origin of one who has knowledge is above. As soon as one recognizes one's origin (through a predestined call), one may return there.

B. Elements of Comparison

he is from above | ὁ ἄνωθεν ἐρχόμενος

(1) he is ≅ ὁ . . . ἐρχόμενος —This generalization in John undoubtedly refers to Jesus; the readers would have recognized here the common Johannine motif of Jesus' being (sent) from heaven. The participial expression, ὁ ἐρχόμενος is a christological epithet (6:14; 11:27). It is not clear whether GTr in its Greek original retained John's participle. Ἐρχέσθαι can have the very attenuated meaning of "is"; the Coptic of GTr also has "is." Thus, it is impossible to determine from the Coptic whether Valentinus retained John's christological image.

(2) from above = ἄνωθεν —verbatim. Ἄνωθεν is frequently used in the sense of "from above," e.g. Philo, *Mos.* 2.69; Hermas, *Mand.* 9:11; 11:8,20,21; Jas 1:17; 3:17.

C. Evaluation of the Parallel

The contexts of the two passages are similar. The element of comparison (2) that is verbatim is common outside of John, but it is especially characteristic of John. Moreover, the inexact element is nearly verbatim as well. Yet, because it is impossible to determine if the Greek of GTr had ἐρχέσθαι, the evidence for Valentinus' use of John here is too scant

Commentaries 69

to be certain whether he used it. He does, however, frequently use John, and so a prominent motif from that gospel which also appears in GTr may well have been taken from John.

D. Interpretation

Valentinus has taken a reference to Jesus as one from above and has applied it to persons with knowledge, if he has used John here. He may have intended the reader to recognize that the original context referred to Jesus and so to understand that those with knowledge share a common origin with Jesus. Those who have knowledge are predestined to be called and to return to their origin from above, i.e., in the Father.

23. GTr 22:13-15 (A^2) ~ John 3:8

Identified by Williams. Probable.

Whoever knows in this manner	^{8}τὸ πνεῦμα . . .
understands	ἀλλ' οὐκ οἶδας
where he came from	πόθεν ἔρχεται
and where he is going.	καὶ ποῦ ὑπάγει.
	οὕτως ἐστὶν πᾶς
	ὁ γεγεννημένος
	ἐκ τοῦ πνεύματος.

---

^{13}ⲡⲉⲧⲛⲁⲥⲁⲩⲛⲉ ⲙ̄^{14}ⲡⲓⲣⲏⲧⲉ ϣⲁϥⲙ̄ⲙⲉ ϫⲉ ⲛ̄ⲧⲁϥⲓ ⲛ̄^{15}ⲧⲟⲛ·
ⲁⲩⲱ ϫⲉ ⲉϥⲛ̄ⲛⲁ ⲁⲧⲟⲛ

A. Context

John 3:1-15 (Jesus and Nicodemus). Jesus explains to Nicodemus that only those born anew through water and the Spirit can see the kingdom of God. Because this concept is difficult to grasp he compares the mysterious origin and destiny of those born of the spirit with the mysterious coming and going of the wind. In so doing, two word plays, πνεῦμα, "wind," "spirit," and possibly ἄνωθεν, "anew," "from above," occur.

GTr 22:2-15 (knowledge: its content and its result). The origin of those with knowledge is from above, as is their destiny. Moreover, the content of their knowledge is an understanding of their origin and destiny. Because those who have been predestined respond to the Father's call to return to him, they act on this knowledge and understand that their origin is in the Father.

B. Elements of Comparison

(1) [Rhetorical structure] whoever knows . . . understands, where he came from, and where he is going ≅ ἀλλ' οὐκ οἶδας, πόθεν ἔρχεται, καὶ ποῦ ὑπάγει —In John, the reference is part of an illustration used by Jesus about the wind, which is then applied to the Spirit. In GTr, the reference is a generalization that applies to those with knowledge. This accounts for the slight differences in verb forms and syntax.

| whoever knows . . . | |
| understands | . . . οἶδας |

(2) (he) understands ≅ οἶδας —Except for the difference in person (due to the change in rhetorical structure), the Coptic is an acceptable rendering of the Greek.

| where he came from | πόθεν ἔρχεται |
| and where he is going | καὶ ποῦ ὑπάγει |

(3) where he came from and where he is going ≅ πόθεν ἔρχεται καὶ ποῦ ὑπάγει —The similarity between these passages is striking. In the first phrase (he came, ἔρχεται), it is not clear whether Valentinus changed the tense from present to past because the evidence of the Coptic is ambiguous. The subjects, however, are different. In John, the subject is "wind/spirit," whereas in GTr, the subject is "whoever." This passage in GTr has been cited as an example of a so-called "Gnostic formula"[27] which is tantamount to a Gnostic creedal statement about

---

[27] This can also be found in *Exc. Theod.* 78,2; Irenaeus, *Adv. Haer.* I 21. 5; Acts of Thomas 15; TriTrac 53:24-26; *Corp. Herm.* 4:4-5; 11:21; the Manichaean Fortunatus according to Augustine, *c. Fortunatum* 20; and Porphyry, *De abstinentia* I, 27. See also Malinine et al., p. 54, which lists most of these references.

Commentaries   71

origin and destiny. Although this "formula" may have been a popular saying in Gnosticism, it may have arisen independently in various circles (cf. Pirke Aboth 3, 1 also). Moreover, it is also found elsewhere in John; in 8:14, it appears on the lips of Jesus and is related to the Johannine motif of Jesus as the man from heaven who will ascend there again.

C. *Evaluation of the Parallel*

In form, the contexts are different: John contains an illustration, put into the mouth of Jesus, whereas GTr is a generalization. Both passages speak of one's origin and destiny, however. The difference in rhetorical structure (1), therefore, accounts for most of the differences between the two passages. Of the other two elements of comparison, both are almost verbatim, although one is a common verb and the other (3) an expression that occurs frequently outside of John. John is apparently the earliest attestation of the common phrase used in (3), and, given Valentinus' frequent use of John, it is probable that he drew the phrase from John. In consequence, Valentinus' use of the proposed passage is likely also.

D. *Interpretation*

Contrary to Nicodemus' lack of understanding about the Spirit, those with knowledge (in GTr) understand whence they themselves came and whither they go. Their origin is from above, and their destiny is from above as well. They came from the Father, and they return to the Father, who calls them, when they gain knowledge. Valentinus may have understood John's analogy of the origin and destiny of one born of the Spirit with the origin and destiny of the wind as applying to the Gnostics, whose origin and destiny are in the Father.

24. GTr 22:18-20 (A²) ~ Luke 15:17

Postulated by van Unnik, p. 118. Dubious.

| (The one who will know understands in the manner of one who has become drunk and has turned away from his drunkenness;) when he returned to himself, | (ὁ νεώτερος υἱός, "the prodigal son") ¹⁷εἰς ἑαυτὸν δὲ ἐλθὼν |

72   Biblical Interpretation in the Gospel of Truth

he set up those that   ἔφη.
were his own.
                                πόσοι μίσθιοι τοῦ πατρός
                                μου περισσεύονται ἄρτων,
                                ἐγὼ δὲ λιμῷ ὧδε ἀπόλλυμαι.

---

[18]ⲉⲁϥⲛⲁⲩ2ϥ ⲁⲣⲁϥ ⲟⲩ[19]ⲁⲉⲉⲧϥ ⲁϥⲧⲉ2ⲟ ⲛ̄ⲛⲉⲧⲉⲛⲟⲩϥ [20]ⲁⲣⲉⲧⲟⲩ ⲛⲉ·

A. Context

Luke 15:11-24 (parable of the prodigal son). Jesus tells a parable about a son who requests his inheritance early, only to spend it on a dissolute life. One day he realizes that he has wasted his life, returns to his Father, and is received joyfully by him.

GTr 22:16-20 (illustration about a drunken person who becomes sober). Those who know their origin and destiny know it with the same kind of understanding that someone who was formerly drunk has about the folly of drunkenness. When such realization occurs, the Father (or Jesus) is able to establish what is his own.

B. Elements of Comparison

when he returned to himself | εἰς ἑαυτὸν δὲ ἐλθών

(1) returned = ἐλθών —"Returned" is a possible translation of the participle ἐλθών (constructed with εἰς) in Luke, but this particular word did not necessarily stand behind the Coptic of GTr.

(2) to himself = εἰς ἑαυτόν —verbatim.

C. Evaluation of the Parallel

Despite one phrase which is identical in both passages, the two passages have nothing in common. The contexts are completely different. One would have to assume that an allegory of the parable of the prodigal son (prodigal son = drunken person) underlies the passage in order to see any relationship between the contexts at all, but there is no further indication

Commentaries 73

that such an allegorization had occurred. Moreover, the parable of the prodigal son is unique to Luke, but there is nothing particularly Lukan in the phrase, "when he returned to himself." Finally, Valentinus uses Luke nowhere else in GTr. All of these factors make Valentinus' use of Luke dubious here.

25. GTr 22:19-23 (A²) ~ John 10:4

Postulated by van Unnik, p. 118. Possible.

He set up those that are his own. He has caused many to turn away from error. He has gone before them to their ways.	⁴ὅταν τὰ ἴδια πάντα ἐκβάλῃ ἔμπροσθεν αὐτῶν πορεύεται καὶ τὰ πρόβατα αὐτῷ ἀκολουθεῖ . . .

¹⁹ⲀϤⲦⲈ2Ⲟ ⲚⲚⲈⲦⲈⲚⲞⲨϤ ²⁰ⲀⲢⲈⲦⲞⲨ ⲚⲈ· ⲀϤⲤⲦⲞ Ⲛ̄2Ⲁ2 ²¹ⲀⲂⲀⲖ 2Ⲛ̄ ⲦⲈⲠⲖⲀⲚⲎ ⲀϤⲤⲰⲔ ²²2ⲒⲐⲎ Ⲙ̄ⲘⲀⲨ ⲰⲀⲚⲒⲘⲀⲈⲒⲦ ²³Ⲛ̄ⲦⲞⲞⲦⲞⲨ

A. Context

John 10:1-6 (the shepherd and his sheep). John attributes a story (παροιμία, "figure") to Jesus; it is about a shepherd who calls his own sheep by name in herding them. The sheep follow the shepherd, but they will not follow a stranger. Jesus later explains that the figure is about himself (10:7ff.)

GTr 22:16-27 (illustration of drunkenness). Although the context is obscure at points, an illustration about returning to oneself from drunkenness is given (22:16-19). This is apparently applied to someone, perhaps Jesus, who is said to establish those who belong to him, to cause them to desist from error, and to be their leader or pioneer on their return to the Father.

B. Elements of Comparison

Those that are his own | . . . τὰ ἴδια . . .

(1) those that are his own = τὰ ἴδια —verbatim. The expression τὰ ἴδια is the usual Greek expression to refer to something that belongs to someone, such as private property. In John 10:4, it is used of sheep, when a shepherd (later identified with Jesus, 10:11) calls "his own." The possessor referred to in the word "his" in GTr 22:19-20 is unclear but may refer to the one who has turned away from his drunkenness, to the Father, or to Jesus (who has not been mentioned since p. 20 but whose role seems to be suggested in 22:21-23).

he has gone before them | ἔμπροσθεν αὐτῶν πορεύεται

(2) he has gone before them ≅ ἔμπροσθεν αὐτῶν πορεύεται —Only the tense is different in the two passages. In John, the subject is the shepherd, i.e., Jesus (10:11); it may be Jesus in GTr.

C. Evaluation of the Parallel

The contexts of the two passages are dissimilar, unless one considers GTr to be an interpretation of Jesus' παροιμία in John (see D). As in No. 20, where another suggested parallel to John 10 is discussed, there is little grounding for such an interpretation in the text. Nevertheless, the first of the two elements of comparison is verbatim, although it is a common expression. The second element is quite similar but is not distinctively Johannine. Despite the absence of Johannine terminology or imagery, Valentinus may have used John here since he almost certainly used John 10 elsewhere (No. 17).

D. Interpretation

Valentinus may interpret Jesus' παροιμία by identifying τὰ ἴδια with Jesus' own (= those Gnostics who are no longer ignorant) and the subject of "he has gone before them" with Jesus (as John later identifies the shepherd with Jesus, 10:11, 14). Thus, Jesus may be understood as the one who has established his own, has caused many to turn away from error, that is, their former state of ignorance, and has gone before them to their ways. The last expression may indicate Jesus' role as a leader, pioneer, or guide and thereby demonstrate Valentinus' interpretation of the Johannine imagery of the shepherd.

26. GTr 24:9-14 (A²) ~ John 1:18

Identified by Malinine et al., p. 55. Probable.

While the Father uncovers his bosom— and his bosom is the Holy Spirit— manifesting what is hidden of him— what is hidden of him is his son	(cf. τοῦ πατρός below) (cf. τοῦ κόλπον below) ¹⁸θεὸν οὐδεὶς ἑώρακεν πώποτε. ὁ μονογενὴς υἱός (v.l.) ὁ ὢν εἰς τὸν κόλπον τοῦ πατρὸς ἐκεῖνος ἐξηγήσατο.

⁹ⲉϥϭⲱⲗⲡ̄ ⲙ̄ⲡⲉϥⲧⲁⲡ ¹⁰ⲁⲃⲁⲗ· ⲛ̄ϭⲓ ⲡⲓⲱⲧ ⲡⲉϥⲧⲁⲡ ⲇⲉ ¹¹ⲡⲉ
ⲡⲓⲡⲛ̄ⲁ̄ ⲉⲧⲟⲩⲁⲁⲃ ⲉϥⲟⲩ¹²ⲱⲛϩ̄ ⲁⲃⲁⲗ· ⲙ̄ⲡⲓⲡⲉⲑⲏⲡ ⲛ̄ⲧⲟ¹³ⲟⲧϥ̄
ⲡⲓⲡⲉⲑⲏⲡ ⲛ̄ⲧⲟⲟⲧϥ̄ ⲡⲉ ¹⁴ⲡⲉϥϣⲏⲣⲉ·

A. Context

John 1:14-18 (prologue). John describes the appearance of the Word (Jesus) on earth. He was human, and yet he imparted grace from the Father's fullness. Although God is invisible, the Son, who is depicted metaphorically as residing in the Father's bosom, has made God known.

GTr 24:9-24 (revelation of the Father's secret). Valentinus uses the imagery of uncovering the Father's bosom to indicate the manifestation of the Son, who had been hidden from people as the Father's secret. The manifestation occurred so that all who seek might gain knowledge of the Father and rest in him who is rest itself.

B. Elements of Comparison

While the Father uncovers | (cf. τοῦ πατρός)
his bosom | (cf. τὸν κόλπον)

(1) the Father ≅ τοῦ πατρός —In GTr, the Father is the actor, whereas in John, "Father" is a reference point in describing the Son's location (in the Father's bosom).

(2) his bosom ≅ τὸν κόλπον —Practically verbatim. Greek habitually omits personal possessives with parts of the body, while Coptic regularly requires them. In early Christian literature, the Father's bosom is referred to only, it appears, in John 1:18 and this passage of GTr.

his Son | ὁ μονογενὴς υἱός

(3) his Son ≅ ὁ μονογενὴς υἱός —Practically verbatim. Greek can omit the possessive if the definite article is included, but Coptic regularly requires personal possessives. There is no mention of "only-begotten" (μονογενής) in GTr. According to John, the Son makes the Father known, while in GTr what is hidden of the Father is the Son.

C. Evaluation of the Parallel

The contexts are similar insofar as they mention the appearance or revelation of the Son, but they differ in emphasis. The prologue to John centers on the Word (Jesus, the Son), but GTr focuses on the Father. Two of the three elements of comparison (1, 3) are simply common terminology in early Christian literature, but the third element contains a reference to the Father's bosom, which in literature prior to GTr is apparently peculiar to John. Its presence in GTr makes Valentinus' use of this passage from John probable.

D. Interpretation

The import of the two passages is quite different. GTr does not state that the Son makes the Father (or God) known, as John does, but that the Father manifests the Son. Moreover, the role of the Father's bosom is different. The Son is (metaphorically) located there in John, but GTr identifies "bosom" with the Holy Spirit. "Bosom" in GTr may be understood metaphorically as an aspect or expression of deity (Holy Spirit) which is

27. GTr 24:11-17 (A²) ~ Eph 3:9-10

Postulated by Williams.[29] Possible.

(the Father) manifesting	⁹καὶ φωτίσαι [πάντας] τίς ἡ οἰκονομία τοῦ μυστηρίου
what is hidden of him—what is hidden of him is his son—	τοῦ ἀποκεκρυμμένου . . .
in order that	¹⁰ἵνα
	γνωρισθῇ [νῦν]
through the bowels of the Father, the aeons	(cf. διὰ τῆς ἐκκλησίας below) ταῖς ἀρχαῖς καὶ ταῖς ἐξουσίαις ἐν τοῖς ἐπουρανίοις διὰ τῆς ἐκκλησίας
may know him	(cf. γνωρισθῇ above) ἡ πολυποίκιλος σοφία τοῦ θεοῦ
and cease toiling.	

---

[28]Because of the reference to the Holy Spirit, which makes the passage look trinitarian, and because of the repetitive nature of the passage, it has been suggested that two interpolations may occur in this passage: "and his bosom is the Holy Spirit" (24:10-11) and "what is hidden of him is his Son" (24:13-14). The former may draw attention away from the locative nature of the reference to "bosom," and the latter may attempt to make a closer connection of this passage to John 1:18, if the interpolator had before him a reading that is found in A and a number of other manuscripts. The reading which is printed in the Nestle-Aland 26th edition is μονογενὴς θεός; it is found in p66 and B, as well as other manuscripts. On the question of the interpolations, see Grobel, pp. 93, 95, nn. 211-213. Of course, trinitarian theology was not fully developed at the time GTr was written, but references to the "spirit" and "Holy Spirit" occur throughout early Christian literature.

[29]Some commentators have proposed Eph 3:9-10 as a parallel to No. 2, GTr 18:11-18 (e.g., van Unnik, p. 116, who draws attention to Eph 3:9), but a better case can be made for its use here.

¹¹ⲉϥⲟⲩ¹²ⲱϩⲉ̅ ⲁⲃⲁⲗ· ⲙ̅ⲡⲓⲛⲉⲉϩⲛ ⲛ̅ⲧⲟ¹³ⲟⲧϥ̅ ⲡⲓⲛⲉⲉϩⲛ ⲛ̅ⲧⲟⲟⲧϥ̅ ⲡⲉ
¹⁴ⲡⲉϥϣⲏⲣⲉ· ϣⲓⲛⲁ ϫⲉ ⲁⲃⲁⲗ ¹⁵₂ⲛ̅ ⲡⲓⲙⲉ₂ⲧ ⲛ̅ⲧⲟⲟⲧϥ̅ ⲙ̅ⲡⲓⲱⲧ ¹⁶ⲛ̅ⲥⲉⲥⲟⲩⲱⲛϥ̅
ⲛ̅ⲥⲉⲗⲟ ⲉⲩ₂ⲁ¹⁷ⲥⲓ ⲛ̅ϭⲓ ⲛⲓⲁⲓⲱⲛ·

A. Context

Eph 3:7-11 (Paul has grace to make God's mystery known). Ps-Paul uses the imagery of the hidden mystery to indicate God's plan to call Gentiles. The church is the medium through which God's wisdom is made known in the heavenly realm.

GTr 24:9-24 (revelation of the Father's secret). Valentinus uses the imagery of uncovering the Father's bosom to indicate the manifestation of the Son, who had been hidden from people as the Father's secret. The manifestation occurred so that all who seek might gain knowledge of the Father and rest in him who is rest itself.

B. Elements of Comparison

(the Father) manifesting	καὶ φωτίσαι . . .
what is hidden of him	τοῦ ἀποκεκρυμμένου

(1) manifesting ≅ φωτίσαι —The syntax differs, but the expressions are similar; Valentinus may have understood φωτίζειν in the sense of "reveal" rather than the more literal "bring to light."

(2) what is hidden ≅ τοῦ ἀποκεκρυμμένου —Both passages use the phrase "what is hidden." It modifies τοῦ μυστηρίου in Eph, whereas it is a substantive in GTr and means "secret." The content of what is hidden is also different in both passages. In Eph, the mystery refers to the admission of the Gentiles to salvation, which was hidden until Christ came (3:11). In GTr, what is hidden is the Father's Son.

in order that	ἵνα
	γνωρισθῇ . . .

through the bowels of the Father,	(cf. διὰ τῆς ἐκκλησίας below)
the aeons	ταῖς ἀρχαῖς καὶ ταῖς ἐξουσίαις ἐν τοῖς ἐπουρανίοις διὰ τῆς ἐκκλησίας
may know	(cf. γνωρισθῇ above)
him	ἡ πολυποίκιλος σοφία τοῦ θεοῦ
and cease toiling.	

(3) in order that = ἵνα —verbatim.

(4) through the bowels of the Father ≅ διὰ τῆς ἐκκλησίας —Ps-Paul understands the church to be the agent which makes known to the heavenly powers and authorities God's wisdom; Valentinus, on the other hand, refers metaphorically to the Father's innermost parts as the agent which makes knowledge of the Father available to the aeons.

(5) the aeons ≅ ταῖς ἀρχαῖς καὶ ταῖς ἐξουσίαις ἐν τοῖς ἐπουρανίοις —The two expressions, "powers" and "authorities," are generalized to "aeons" here. The use of ἀρχή and ἐξουσία to refer to rulers and authorities in the heavenly or spirit world is a feature of Paul's usage (e.g., Rom 8:38; 1 Cor 15:24) and is especially characteristic of the deutero-Pauline school (e.g. Eph 1:21, 6:12; Col 1:16, 2:10, 15) but is not restricted to these authors (e.g. 1 Pet 3:22; T. Levi 3:8; Justin, Dial. 120). Note also that "aeons" occurs in Eph 3:9, which may have suggested it to Valentinus. "Aeons" is an ambiguous term here and could mean "ages," as it often does in Paul (e.g. Rom 12:2; 1 Cor 1:20), but it may already be hypostatized (as in some contemporary philosophical literature, e.g., Epictetus 2,5,13: οὐ γὰρ εἰμι αἰών, ἀλλ' ἄνθρωπος and occasionally in Jewish literature, e.g. 1 Enoch 9:4). Similarly, the meaning is ambiguous in GTr and may be either temporal or hypostatic. If the expression is a generalization of "powers" and "authorities," however, then it is more likely to have a hypostatic sense.

(6) may know ≅ γνωρισθῇ —The mood and tense differ. Moreover, γνωρίζειν has the sense of "make known, reveal" rather than the Coptic "know."

(7) him ≅ πολυποίκιλος σοφία τοῦ θεοῦ —Valentinus may understand "wisdom of God" to refer to the Father himself, or, if the phrase

"what is hidden of him is his son" (24:13-14) is not an interpolation, to the Son.

C. Evaluation of the Parallel

The contexts of the two passages are not especially similar. Only one of the elements of comparison is verbatim (3), but (1), (2), and (6) are quite close. Element (5) may be a generalization of two expressions for heavenly forces. Despite the large number of parallels, it may be preferable to understand the appearance here in GTr of language that occurs in Eph as a reflection of general Pauline terminology (or even use of Col 1:25-27; cf. No. 2), rather than to posit Valentinus' use of a particular text from Eph. This is all the more true since Valentinus uses Eph only rarely, and hence his use of Eph is only possible here.

D. Interpretation

If Valentinus has used Eph here, he has changed ps-Paul's argument to an assertion that what is hidden regarding the Father is the Son, who has been revealed by him so that the aeons (possibly hypostatized) might know the Father. "What is hidden" in both Eph and GTr concerns Christ or the Son; for ps-Paul Christ is the agent of revelation, whereas in GTr the Son himself is what is hidden.[30]

28. GTr 24:21-24 (A²) ∼ 1 Cor 7:31b

Postulated by van Unnik, p. 119. Possible.

He (the Son) expunged the form— the form of it is the world, in which he served.	³¹. . . παράγει γὰρ τὸ σχῆμα τοῦ κόσμου τούτου.

---

[30] The identification of "what is hidden" in GTr with the Son may be part of an interpolation (see No. 26); if so, it may represent a later attempt to bring the passage into line with Eph 3:9 but which uses the usual Valentinian reference "Son" rather than the more typically Pauline "Christ."

²¹ⲁϥⲃⲱⲗ ⲁⲃⲁⲗ ²²ⲙ̄ⲡⲓⲥⲭⲏⲙⲁ· ⲡⲓⲥⲭⲏⲙⲁ ⲛ̄ⲧⲟⲟ²³ⲧϥ ⲡⲉ ⲡⲕⲟⲥⲙⲟⲥ·
ⲡⲉⲉⲓ ⲉⲛ²⁴ⲧⲁϥϣⲱ)ⲡⲉ ⲛ̄ϩⲏⲧϥ̄

A. Context

1 Cor 7:25-31 (advice to the unmarried). After explaining his views on the inadvisability of marriage for those who are not currently married (7:25-28), Paul gives the shortness of time before the end of the world (7:28-31) as a reason.

GTr 24:20-24 (the form is expunged). The passage and its context are grammatically ambiguous. The subject ("he," 24:21) may be either Jesus (cf. 24:8), the Father (cf. 24:18), or the Son (cf. 24:14). "It" may refer either to the defect (i.e., lack), Jesus, or the Son. One logical solution is to understand the passage to say that the Son expunged the form of the defect, which is the world in which the Son served, but the Coptic may also be translated in different ways.[31]

B. Elements of Comparison

he expunged the form—	παράγει γὰρ
the form of it is the world,	τὸ σχῆμα τοῦ κόσμου τούτου.

(1) he expunged ≅ παράγει —The Pauline passage is eschatological: because the end of the world is so near, the form of the world might already be seen as passing away. Valentinus' expression may be one of realized eschatology which takes note of an act of destruction effected through the revelation of the Son. Thus, Paul refers only to the process of the destruction of the world without specifying the cause, whereas Valentinus refers to the actor or cause (the Son).

---

[31] See B. Layton's translation (forthcoming) for an equally plausible rendering of the Coptic ("the realm of appearances, which belongs to it [the lack], is the world").

(2) the form of it is the world ≡ τὸ σχῆμα τοῦ κόσμου —In 1 Cor, the phrase, τὸ σχῆμα τοῦ κόσμου, is an expression which occurs frequently in slightly differing versions through a wide range of Greek literature from Euripides (*Bacchae 832:* τὸ σχῆμα τοῦ κόσμου) to Philostratus (*Vita Apoll.* 8,7, p. 312,9: τὸ σχῆμα τοῦ κόσμου τοῦδε), and in the Greek magical papyri (PGM 4, 1139: σχῆμα κόσμου). Valentinus has apparently divided the two parts of the expression, thereby providing a description of the lack. "It" must refer to the "lack" (24:21), and hence Valentinus explains that the form which the lack takes is the world.

C. Evaluation of the Parallel

The contexts of the two passages are not at all similar. Both of the two elements of comparison are inexact. The first is a much stronger statement in GTr than Paul uses in 1 Cor (see D). The second, though grammatically different, contains the same terminology. Because this terminology is common in Greek literature, one cannot be certain whether Valentinus has used Paul here. He does use 1 Cor in No. 16, however, and his use of it here also is possible.

D. Interpretation

Valentinus' transformation of the Pauline statement is hyperbolic: the form of this world is not passing away but has actually been destroyed or expunged by the Son. This, of course, does not mean that the Son literally destroyed the world but that he filled the world's defect by bringing knowledge of the Father (24:28-32). This may recall to the reader pp. 17-18 as well. There error is said to be without root (17:29-30) and unreal (from the reader's standpoint), whereas true existence comes through knowledge of the Father (18:28). The world, thus, is only a σχῆμα of reality and is, on an epistemological level, destroyed by the knowledge of the Father which the Son brings.[32]

---

[32]The entire passage, 24:22-24, may be an interpolation. See Grobel, p. 97, nn. 218-219 for discussion of the interpolation and the grammatical ambiguities. Thus, the same tentative approach to the possible interpretation of the proposed text should be adopted as in the preceding two instances (Nos. 26, 27). References to other biblical texts have been proposed for these lines, such as van Unnik's suggestion (p. 119) that there may be an allusion to Mark 10:45, but the reference is too short and the text too ambiguous to make a plausible case for any reference besides 1 Cor.

Commentaries

29. GTr 25:1-3 (A²) ~1 Cor 13:10

Postulated by Grobel, p. 99, n. 227. Dubious.

(When he knows, his ignorance dissolves... As darkness dissolves when light appears), so too the defect dissolves in_ perfection.	¹⁰ὅταν δὲ (cf. τὸ ἐκ μέρους καταργηθήσεται, below) ἔλθῃ τὸ τέλειον, τὸ ἐκ μέρους καταργηθήσεται.

¹ⲙ̄ⲡⲓⲣⲏⲧⲉ ⲁⲛ ²ⲡⲓⲱ̣ⲧⲁ ⲱ̣ⲁϥⲃⲱⲗ ⲁⲃⲁⲗ˙ ⲉ̣ⲣⲏ[ⲓ̈] ³ⲉⲛ̄ ⲡⲓϫⲱⲕ

A. Context

1 Cor 13:8-12 (love chapter). Paul compares love, which is eternal, with knowledge and glossolalia, which are temporal. The latter two are imperfect and exist only until the perfect comes, when understanding (or a more complete knowledge) will be available to Christians.

GTr 24:32-25:7 (unity is harmonious). Valentinus contrasts ignorance with knowledge, darkness with light, and lack with perfection. The former term in each group represents what is only apparent and will be replaced by the latter to form unity.

B. Elements of Comparison

the defect ... perfection	τὸ ἐκ μέρους τὸ τέλειον

(1) defect ≅ τὸ ἐκ μέρους —Paul's phrase literally means "what is partial," which is similar to Valentinus' "defect" or "lack." The word

"defect" may be a technical term as in later Valentinian literature (e.g. TriTrac 81:10); in GTr it is the opposite of perfection and the equivalent of ignorance.

(2) perfection = τὸ τέλειον —verbatim. Paul's expression here means "perfection"; use of the substantive with the definite article is a common way to name an abstraction in Greek. The Coptic may be a translation of this Greek model, although two less common words, τελείωσις and τελειότης, which also mean "perfection," could also stand behind the Coptic.

dissolves in | καταργηθήσεται

(3) dissolves in ≅ καταργηθήσεται —Paul's word can mean "abolish," "set aside." Valentinus' phrase is equally vivid (cf. 24:21, where it was translated "expunge"), and some of its meanings overlap with those of καταργεῖν. Both expressions focus on replacing imperfection with perfection. This is especially the case in GTr if "in" is taken instrumentally.

C. Evaluation of the Parallel

The contexts of the two passages are not similar, although they share some terminology. Only one of the three elements of comparison is verbatim (2), the commonplace "perfection." The other two elements of comparison (1, 3) are similar in both passages but are not distinctively Pauline. Paul's view of knowledge as imperfect in 1 Cor 13:8, 12 starkly contrasts with Valentinus' contrast of ignorance and knowledge in this passage. For these reasons, the suggested parallel seems to be more a case of shared terminology, as Grobel originally suggested,[33] than of interpretation of 1 Cor 13:10. Valentinus' use of the Pauline passage is, therefore, dubious.

30. GTr 25:15-19 (A²) ∼ 2 Cor 5:4

Postulated by van Unnik, p. 119. Possible.

(It is from a partial state |

---

[33]Grobel, p. 99, n. 227.

Commentaries 85

into a unity that he will
purify himself,)
 consuming
 matter within himself
as by fire,
and darkness by light,
death by life.

⁴ἵνα καταποθῇ

τὸ θνητὸν ὑπὸ τῆς ζωῆς.

¹⁵ⲉϥⲟⲩⲱⲙ ¹⁶ⲛ̄ϯϩⲩⲗⲏ ⲛ̄ϩⲣⲏⲓ̈ ⲛ̄ϩⲏⲧϥ̄ ⲙ̄¹⁷ⲡⲣⲏⲧⲉ ⲛ̄ⲛⲟⲩⲥⲉⲧⲉ ⲁⲩⲱ
ⲡⲕⲉ ¹⁸ⲕⲉⲓ 2ⲛ̄ ⲟⲩⲁⲉⲓⲛ ⲡⲙⲟⲩ 2ⲛ̄ ⲟⲩ¹⁹ⲱⲛϩ̄

A. *Context*

2 Cor 5:1-5 (death and resurrection). Using terminology drawn from the baptismal liturgy and using building imagery, Paul looks forward to life after death. While on earth we are anxious, not to die, but to obtain eternal life. Then, what is mortal is engulfed by life.

GTr 25:8-19 (the joining into unity). Each person who is, in a metaphorical, cosmological sense, a "way" to the Father will be complete when the harmony of unity occurs. Knowledge is the cause of the harmony (a state of unity, light, and life rather than the former state of multiplicity, darkness, and death). Then, death is engulfed by life.

B. *Elements of Comparison*

consuming | καταποθῇ

(1) [Rhetorical structure] (each Gnostic) consuming matter . . . as by fire, (as) darkness (is consumed) by light, (as) death (is consumed) by life ≅ καταποθῇ, τὸ θνητὸν ἀπὸ τῆς ζωῆς —Valentinus expands Paul's rhetoric but does not retain the same parallelism (see D).

(2) consuming ≅ καταποθῇ —Some of the meanings of these two verbs overlap. Paul's word means, "drink down (liquid), swallow (food), devour," whereas the Coptic of GTr means, more specifically, "eat (food)," a process that includes swallowing but does not refer to liquids. The Greek

verb καταπιεῖν, used here by Paul, is also used in 1 Cor 15:54 (see No. 16) where, as here, one thing (death) is swallowed up in its opposite (victory).

death by life | τὸ θνητὸν ἀπὸ τῆς ζωῆς

(3) death ≅ τὸ θνητόν —Valentinus changes Paul's abstract substantive (formed by using the definite article), "what is mortal" (τὸ θνητόν), which was demanded by the rhetorical structure of the passage, to the more straightforward "death."

(4) by life = ἀπὸ τῆς ζωῆς —verbatim. In both cases, "life" is the focus of the contrast.

C. Evaluation of the Parallel

The contexts are similar insofar as both center on death and its opposite. One of the four elements of comparison (4) is verbatim. The change in rhetorical structure represents an expansion of the rhetoric of 2 Cor, and one of the other two inexact elements (3) is explained by the change in rhetorical structure. The other inexact elements may simply be a variation in word choice in the Coptic translation. Although none of the images is distinctive to 2 Cor, the conjunction of these elements of comparison may make Valentinus' use of the proposed text possible, especially since 2 Cor is known to be used elsewhere in GTr (see No. 55).

D. Interpretation

Paul writes about the death of the earthly body, whereas Valentinus writes of the irrelevance of the concept "death" (much less its actual occurrence) once unity is attained. If Valentinus has used 2 Cor 5:4, he has omitted much of the verse, particularly the garment imagery.[34] This is understandable since its retention might contradict Valentinus' use of such imagery elsewhere (see No. 16). By omitting the garment imagery, he is free to contrast death and life instead of retaining Paul's contrast of "what is mortal" with life. Thus, Paul's contrast is between mortality and immortality (as in 1 Cor 15:54 [No. 16]), but Valentinus' contrast is between death and life (as also in No. 16). Valentinus explicates Paul's

---

[34]Yet, he does retain some of the building imagery within the broader context (GTr 25:23, "house"; cf. 2 Cor 5:1, "house").

notion of the consumption of "what is mortal" as the purification or completion into unity. This is the consumption of matter within the individual human being, as fire consumes what it touches and as darkness is consumed by light.

31. GTr 25:25-35 (A²) ~ 2 Tim 2:20-21

Postulated, with hesitation, by Malinine et al., p. 55. Dubious.

In the manner of some who have moved out from places where they had	²⁰Ἐν μεγάλῃ δὲ οἰκίᾳ οὐκ ἔστιν μόνον σκεύη χρυσᾶ καὶ ἀργυρᾶ καὶ ξύλινα καὶ ὀστράκινα, καὶ ἃ μὲν εἰς τιμὴν
some vessels	(cf. σκεύη above)
which were not good in some places, they broke them,	ἃ δὲ εἰς ἀτιμίαν· ²¹ἐὰν οὖν τις ἐκκαθάρῃ ἑαυτὸν ἀπὸ τούτων, ἔσται σκεῦος εἰς τιμήν, ἡγιασμένον,
and the master of the house did not suffer loss but was glad because in place of those bad vessels, the full ones are made complete.	εὔχρηστον τῷ δεσπότῃ, εἰς πᾶν ἔργον ἀγαθὸν ἡτοιμασμένον. (cf. ἃ μὲν εἰς τιμήν above)

²⁵ⲘⲠⲢⲎⲦⲈ Ⲛ̄ⲀⲀⲈⲒⲚⲈ ²⁶ⲈⲀⲨⲠⲰⲚⲈ ⲀⲂⲀⲖ 2Ⲛ̄ 2Ⲛ̄ⲘⲀ ²⁷ⲈⲨⲚ̄ⲦⲈⲨ ⲘⲘⲈⲨ Ⲛ̄2ⲈⲚ
²⁸ⲤⲔⲈⲨⲞⲤ· Ⲛ̄2ⲢⲎⲒ 2Ⲛ̄ 2Ⲛ̄ ²⁹ⲦⲞⲠⲞⲤ ⲈⲚⲀⲚⲀⲨⲞⲨ· ⲈⲚ ³⁰ⲚⲈⲰⲀⲨⲞⲨⲀⲤⲠⲞⲨ·
ⲀⲨⲰ ⲘⲀϤ³¹ⲀⲤⲒ Ⲛ̄ϬⲒ ⲠⲚⲈⲠ ⲘⲠⲎⲈⲒ ⲀⲖ³²ⲖⲀ ⲰⲀⲤⲢⲈⲰⲈ· ϪⲈ Ⲛ̄2ⲢⲎⲒ ⲄⲀⲢ
³³2Ⲛ̄ ⲠⲘⲀ Ⲛ̄ⲚⲒⲤⲔⲈⲨⲞⲤ Ⲉ³⁴ⲐⲀⲨ· ⲚⲈⲦⲘⲎ2 ⲚⲈⲦⲈⲰⲀⲨ ³⁵ϪⲀⲔⲞⲨ ⲀⲂⲀⲖ

A. Context

2 Tim 2:20-26 (shun passions and controversies). Ps-Paul gives an illustration: a great house uses both high and low quality vessels for different

purposes. He urges his readers to purify themselves in order to become like good vessels, which are used for good purposes.

GTr 25:19-35 (full vessels comprise unity). Valentinus gives an illustration: some people moved and broke bad vessels but did not harm full ones. He urges his readers (who must be [or become] like full vessels) to meditate on all (in the cosmological sense) in order to be ready for unity.

B. Elements of Comparison

some vessels	(cf. σκεύη above)
which were not good ...	ἃ δὲ εἰς ἀτιμίαν·
the full ones	(cf. ἃ μὲν
are made complete	εἰς τιμήν)

(1) vessels = σκεύη —The figurative use of σκεῦος is common in Christian and Jewish literature with which Valentinus may have been acquainted, e.g., Ps 2:9; Jer 18:6; Wis 15:7; 2 Cor 4:7; Rev 2:27; Rom 9:22-23; and Ps Sol 17:23f. It is often a metaphor for people in these examples but also occurs in other literary figures, such as simile, and at other times is used as part of a larger illustration.

(2) some vessels, the full ones ≠ ἃ δὲ (scil. σκεύη), ἃ μέν —2 Tim 2:20 contrasts good and bad vessels. GTr also contrasts good and bad vessels but is more specific about what makes the vessels good or bad: some vessels were broken in moving and others are intact and therefore remain full and perfect. In 2 Tim, the image refers to people who do good and bad deeds, whereas in GTr, the image refers to the elect and non-elect.

| the master of the house | τῷ δεσπότῃ |

(3) the master of the house = τῷ δεσπότῃ —verbatim. Both 2 Tim and GTr use "master of the house" in both its literal sense within the framework of the illustration and also in an (at least implicitly) allegorical sense to refer to God or the Father.

C. Evaluation of the Parallel

Except for the presence of some shared terminology, the contexts of the two passages are not similar. One of the three elements of comparison

Commentaries 89

(2) is inexact; the others (1, 3) are verbatim but are common terms. Valentinus does not use 1 Tim elsewhere, and his use of it here is dubious.

32. GTr 25:35-26:2 (A²) ~ John 3:19

Identified by Grobel, pp. 103, 105, n. 247. Probable.

This (the Word) is the judgment which has come from above having passed judgment on everyone	¹⁹αὕτη δέ ἐστιν ἡ κρίσις (cf. ἐλήλυθεν below) ὅτι τὸ φῶς ἐλήλυθεν εἰς τὸν κόσμον . . .

³⁵Τεει τε ³⁶τεκρισισ ñτα2ει αβαλ· ¹ῆπcα ντπε· εαϲϯ 2επ· αογ²αν νιμ·

A. Context

John 3:16-21 (God's judgment on the world). John explains that judgment has come with the entry of light (Jesus) into the world. Although the Son was not sent (by God) to condemn the world but to effect the world's salvation, those who prefer darkness to light are evil-doers and are condemned. Those who respond to Jesus by believing in him, however, have eternal life.

GTr 25:25-26:6 (the Word's judgment on everyone). Valentinus explains that judgment has come with the appearance of the Word (Jesus). This judgment is like those who break bad vessels in moving but leave full ones intact. The implied allegory must identify the bad vessels with ignorant persons and the full vessels with persons who have knowledge.

B. Elements of Comparison

This is the judgment	αὕτη δέ ἐστιν ἡ κρίσις

(1) this is the judgment = αὕτη δέ ἐστιν ἡ κρίσις —verbatim. The Greek model of GTr may well have had δέ; Coptic translators often omitted the weak connective δέ.

| This (the Word) [cf. 26:5] has come from above | αὕτη (scil. τὸ φῶς, cf. 3:19b) ... ἐλήλυθεν εἰς τὸν κόσμον |

(2) this (the Word) = αὕτη (τὸ φῶς) —John plainly identifies the Word and φῶς at the beginning of his gospel (1:9: ἦν τὸ φῶς τὸ ἀληθινόν ... ἐρχόμενον εἰς τὸν κόσμον); the present passage, then, actually speaks of the Word.

(3) has come = ἐλήλυθεν —verbatim. Both authors see the judgment as already *having come:* they do not speak of a future judgment. Valentinus uses another Johannine motif, "from above," which underlies all of John 3, although John himself does not use the expression in this particular verse.

C. *Evaluation of the Parallel*

The contexts of the two passages are similar, although they use somewhat different imagery in announcing the judgment. All three elements of comparison are verbatim or nearly so. The most telling evidence is the almost identical wording of the phrase, "this is the judgment," in both passages. When one also takes account of Valentinus' frequent use of John, his use of John 3:19 here is all the more probable.

D. *Interpretation*

John implies that persons can determine their own judgment by their choice of light over darkness (i.e., the decision to believe in the name of the Son of God, 3:18), since Jesus has come to earth with the judgment; GTr implies that everyone has already been subject to an absolute judgment (i.e., one is either like a full vessel or like one of the imperfect ones).[35] A later passage (GTr 26:23-26) shows that the judgment brought by the Word would mean the destruction of all those who are not like the

---

[35]As Grobel notes on p. 103, n. 248, it is not clear in GTr how large the role of the individual is in determining one's own judgment.

full vessels. Valentinus retains John's view that the judgment has already come, however, and does not await a climactic judgment scene.[36] In interpreting this passage from John, Valentinus employs motifs that occur in other passages of John, such as "word" and "from above." This use is typical of Valentinus' style in GTr, which often seems to incorporate a melange of allusions, thus making precise identification of the parallel more difficult.[37]

33. GTr 26:2-5 (A[2]) ~ Heb 4:12

Postulated by van Unnik, p. 119. Possible.

it (judgment) being	[12]Ζῶν γὰρ ὁ λόγος τοῦ θεοῦ καὶ ἐνεργὴς καὶ τομώτερος ὑπὲρ πᾶσαν
a drawn, <u>two-edged sword</u> <u>cutting in both directions</u>	μάχαιραν δίστομον καὶ διϊκνούμενος
since <u>the word</u> has come forth.	(cf. ὁ λόγος, above)

²ⲉⲩⲥⲏϥⲉ ⲧⲉ ⲉⲥϫⲁⲗⲙ̄ ³ⲙ̄ⲫⲟ ⲥⲛⲉⲩ ⲉⲥϫⲱⲱⲧ· ⲛ̄⁴ⲥⲁ ⲡⲓⲥⲁ ⲙⲛ̄
ⲡⲉⲉⲓ ⲉⲁϥⲓ ⲁⲧⲙⲏ⁵ⲧⲉ ⲛ̄ϭⲓ ⲡⲓϣⲉϫⲉ·

A. Context

Heb 4:11-13 (the Sabbath rest).[38] The author of Heb exhorts his readers

---

[36]Thus, "destruction" must not be understood literally but in an epistemological sense.

[37]Cf. John 12:31, for example, which is similar to 3:19.

[38]Cf. Giversen, "Evangelium Veritatis and the Epistle to the Hebrews," ST 13 (1959) 92-93, who compares the contexts of these two passages. By looking at a much broader context, he asserts that "rest" is non-eschatological in GTr and that the readers are exhorted to remain in rest rather than to enter into it and that the sword is not a threat but a reminder of what has already passed. This is a fair assessment of this passage, if one bears in mind that the role that each person plays in determining one's own destiny is sometimes ambiguous in GTr (see comments

to strive to enter the Sabbath rest, which is reserved for God's obedient people. No act of disobedience or even an intention can be hidden from God, whose word pierces through each person like a two-edged sword to discern one's inner self.

GTr 25:35-26:8 (judgment of the Word). The coming of the Word has brought judgment, which is described with the image of a two-edged sword. "Word" is not only to be taken literally as a message spoken by those with knowledge, but it has also become embodied, presumably in Jesus.

B. Elements of Comparison

| a drawn, two-edged sword | μάχαιραν δίστομον |
| cutting in both directions | καὶ διϊκνούμενος |

(1) two-edged sword = μάχαιραν δίστομον —verbatim. The expression is not common in literature of the period. It also occurs in Rev 1:16, 2:12, 19:15 (v.l.) but with ῥομφαία rather than μάχαιρα. Since the Greek has not been retained in the Coptic, one cannot be certain which Greek word is the model for "sword" in GTr.

(2) cutting in both directions ≟ καὶ διϊκνούμενος —possibly verbatim. The verb διϊκνεῖσθαι is rare in Greek and means "pierce, penetrate." It is possible that the translator misunderstood the prefix (δι-) to mean "on two sides," like δι- in δίστομον. If this were the case, the two expressions would be identical.

(3) word = λόγος —verbatim. It is not clear whether "word" refers to Jesus in Heb, but Valentinus may have understood it this way, particularly if he also had John 1:14 (see No. 34) in mind.

C. Evaluation of the Parallel

The contexts of the passages are not similar.[39] Two of the elements of comparison are verbatim (1, 3) and a third (2) possibly so. In only one

---

on No. 32), but the passage is not strictly concerned with "rest."

[39]Giversen's analysis of the broader context notwithstanding (cf. preceding note).

other place (No. 11) has Valentinus almost certainly used a passage from Heb. There, as here, the passage was used primarily for the terminology contained therein. Even though the term, "two-edged sword" is striking, it also occurs several times in Rev. If the reason that was suggested for the inexactitude of element (2) were shown to be correct, then Valentinus' use of Heb here would be virtually assured. As it stands now, however, his use of Heb here is only possible.

D. Interpretation

In Heb, God's word is able to discern one's inner self, even more than a two-edged sword is able to pierce whatever it touches. Valentinus has likened the sword to judgment, whereas the sword in Heb is part of an illustration about God's discernment. Valentinus does, however, connect the Word with judgment. Although, as we have seen, judgment is predetermined to a large extent in GTr (No. 32), the appearance of the Word may be understood to bring that judgment into effect. The description of the sword as "drawn" may emphasize the presence of the judgment. Thus, the Word has brought judgment—not in the sense of discernment, as in Heb, but judgment as related in the allegory of the vessels, where some vessels (= people) are full (elect) and others are broken (not elect).

34. GTr 26:4-8 (A^2) ~ John 1:14

Identified by van Unnik, p. 119. Probable.

| ... since the Word which is in the heart of those who speak it came forth. It is not a sound alone, but it became a body (σῶμα). | ^{14}καὶ ὁ λόγος

(cf. vs. 11 εἰς τὰ ἴδια
ἦλθεν)

σὰρξ ἐγένετο
καὶ ἐσκήνωσεν ἐν ἡμῖν. |

---

⁴ⲉⲗϥⲓ ⲁⲧⲙⲏ⁵ⲧⲉ ⲛ̄ϭⲓ ⲡϣⲉϫⲉ· ⲉⲧⲛ̄ⲥⲣⲏⲉⲓ ⁶ⲥⲛ̄ ⲡ₂ⲏⲧ· ⲛ̄ⲛⲉⲧϣⲉϫⲉ ⲛ̄ⲙⲁϥ ⁷ⲟⲩ₂ⲣⲁⲩ ⲟⲩⲁⲉⲉⲧϥ̄ ⲉⲛ ⲡⲉ ⲁⲗ·⁸ⲗⲁ ⲁϥⲣ̄ ⲟⲩⲥⲱⲙⲁ·

94   Biblical Interpretation in the Gospel of Truth

A. Context

John 1:9-14 (prologue). The Word, the agent of creation, was unknown by the world. He came to earth but was rejected by his own people, the Jews, although he enabled those who believed in his name to become children of God. Thus, the Word came in the flesh and lived, as the Father's Son, among humanity.

GTr 25:35-26:8 (judgment of the Word). The coming of the Word has brought judgment, which is described with the image of a two-edged sword. "Word" is not only to be taken literally as a message spoken by those with knowledge, but it has also become embodied, presumably in Jesus.

B. Elements of Comparison

| ... since the Word | καὶ ὁ λόγος |
| ... came forth | (cf. vs. 11 ... ἦλθεν) |

(1) the Word = ὁ λόγος —verbatim. Both John and Valentinus use "Word" to refer to Jesus. John means by λόγος a personified or hypostatized attribute of God, like σοφία in the Wisdom of Solomon or σοφία/λόγος in Philo (as God's agent on earth). The Greek is sometimes retained in GTr (e.g. 37:8), but this is not the case here.

| but it became a body | σάρξ ἐγένετο |

(2) it became = ἐγένετο —verbatim. Both Valentinus and Paul refer to a specific event: the Word's entry into human form.

(3) body ≅ σάρξ —John uses σάρξ in the sense of "a person of flesh and blood," a common use in literature of the period. Valentinus, however, has substituted σῶμα (the living body) for σάρξ. Both terms mean "human being"; evidence for their interchangeability may be found in Paul (Rom 8:11, 13).

C. Evaluation of the Parallel

The contexts of the two passages are not especially similar, although the phrase "it [the Word] became a body" is strikingly similar to John. Two of the elements of comparison are verbatim; one is a common verb and

Commentaries   95

the other a common philosophical term. The inexact element (3) may be explained as a philosophical-sounding replacement for a term that might sound crude and even shocking ("flesh") to Greek ears. Even though all of the vocabulary of the two passages occurs frequently, the idea that the Word became a human being is distinctive enough to make Valentinus' use of this passage probable, especially since John is often used in GTr.

D. Interpretation

By using σῶμα rather than σάρξ in his interpretation of John 1:14, Valentinus focuses on the body as the center of human life and emotion. This facilitates his interpretation of the Word as both a sound[40] which dwells within persons and as a human being. In his interpretation of John, Valentinus retains John's assertion that the Word became a human being, but he also stresses the dual role of the Word as both a body (Jesus) and a sound which is spoken by certain persons. Those who speak the Word are undoubtedly those with knowledge, who are also written in the living book of the living.[41]

35. GTr 26:8-15 (A^2) ∼ Rom 9:21-23

Postulated by Grobel, p. 105, n. 253. Dubious.

A great disturbance happened among the vessels (σκεῦος) because some had been emptied, others filled, because others had been provided, others overturned, some purified, others cleansed.	(cf. σκεῦος below) ^{21} ὃ μὲν εἰς τιμὴν σκεῦος ὃ δὲ εἰς ἀτιμίαν . . . ^{22}σκεύη ὀργῆς κατηρτισμένα εἰς ἀπώλειαν, ^{23}. . . ἐπὶ σκεύη ἐλέους ἃ προητοίμασεν εἰς δόξαν

---

[40]This is surely used metaphorically to refer to the indwelling source of knowledge.
[41]The exposition on letters or passages of text which are like a book (22:38ff.) may suggest this.

⁸ⲟⲩⲛⲁϭ ⲛ̄⁹ⲱ̣ⲁⲣⲧⲡ̄ ⲁϥϣⲱⲡⲉ ⲛ̄ⲟ̣ⲣⲏⲓ̈ ⳉⲛ̄ ¹⁰ⲛ̄̄ⲥⲕⲉⲩⲟⲥ ϫⲉ ⳉⲁⲉⲓⲛⲉ
ⲁ̣ⲟⲩ¹¹ⲁ̣ϭⲟⲩⲱⲟⲩ ⳉⲛ̄ⲕⲁⲩⲉ ⲁ̣ⲟⲩⲙⲉ ¹²ⳉⲟⲩ ϫⲉⲥ ⳉⲛ̄ⲕⲁⲩⲉ ⲁ̣ⲟⲩⲥⳉⲛⲏ¹³ⲧⲟⲩ
ⳉⲛ̄ⲕⲁⲩⲉ ⲁ̣ⲟⲩⲡⲁⲛⲟⲩ ¹⁴ⳉⲁⲉⲓⲛⲉ ⲁ̣ⲟⲩⲧⲟⲩⲃⲁ̣ⲁ ⳉⲛⲕⲉ ¹⁵ⲕⲁⲩⲉ ⲁ̣ⲟⲩⲡⲱⲁϫⲉ

A. Context

Rom 9:19-26 (God's right to choose certain ones for election). Paul gives an illustration of a potter, who can choose which vessels he will make for good and for menial uses. He asserts that God can choose to call not only Jews but also Gentiles to salvation.

GTr 26:8-26 (the disturbance of the ways). Valentinus gives an illustration of vessels (*the* vessels, cf. No. 31) which have come to be in various states of both desirableness and undesirableness. He describes the confrontation between error and knowledge.

B. Elements of Comparison

... vessels (σκεῦος)	(cf. σκεῦος)
... some ...	ὃ μέν ...
others ...	ὃ δέ ...
others had been provided,	σκεύη ὀργῆς
others overturned	... ἐπὶ σκεύη ἐλέους

(1) vessels = σκεύη —verbatim. The use is metaphorical, as in No. 31.

(2) some, others; others, others ≅ ὃ μέν, ὃ δέ; σκεύη, σκεύη —Both passages contrast different kinds of vessels. Paul contrasts vessels made for a good purpose with those made for a menial purpose. Later (9:24) it is clear that "vessel" is meant metaphorically or allegorically; some people will receive mercy and others destruction. Valentinus' contrast has the same import as Paul's, but it is expressed differently. Valentinus employs a binary opposition which contrasts full and empty vessels and then indicates that the full ones have been provided and the empty ones overturned, i.e., destroyed.

C. Evaluation of the Parallel

Both passages form an illustration which uses the word "vessels," but the point is different in the two cases. Of the two elements of comparison, one is verbatim (1) but is a commonplace. The other, a rhetorical construction which indicates the contrast between two kinds of vessels, is inexact. Although Valentinus knows and uses Rom (see, for example, Nos. 71, 73), his use of it here is dubious and no more likely than was his use of 2 Tim in No. 31.

36. GTr 27:7-8 (A²) ~ Col 1:26

Postulated by Grobel, p. 109, n. 270. Possible.

He (the Father) manifested what was hidden of him.	(²⁴ἀνταναπληρῶ τὰ ὑστερήματα τῶν θλίψεων τοῦ Χριστοῦ ἐν τῇ σαρκί μου ὑπὲρ τοῦ σώματος αὐτοῦ, ὅ ἐστιν ἡ ἐκκλησία, ²⁵. . . πληρῶσαι τὸν λόγον τοῦ θεοῦ) (cf. ἐφανερώθη below) ²⁶τὸ μυστήριον τὸ ἀποκεκρυμμένον . . . νῦν δὲ ἐφανερώθη . . . τοῖς ἁγίοις αὐτοῦ . . .

⁷ⲁϥⲟⲩⲱⲛϩ̅ ⲁⲃⲁⲗ ⁸ⲙ̅ⲡⲓⲡⲉⲑⲏⲡ· ⲛ̅ⲧⲟⲟⲧϥ̅

A. Context

Col 1:24-29 (Paul's office and ministry). Ps-Paul reminds his readers of his own mission to preach the account about God to the Gentiles and God's activity through Christ. The content of this account is God's "hidden mystery": it concerns the coming of Christ, who was made known to God's holy people.

GTr 26:36-27:9 (revelation of the Father's secret). Valentinus uses vivid imagery (mouth, tongue) to express the particularly close relationship with the Father that those who are attached to the truth have. They will receive the Holy Spirit, the manifestation of the Father. The Father's medium of revelation is the truth.

B. Elements of Comparison

He (the Father) manifested	(cf. ἐφανερώθη)
	τὸ μυστήριον
what was hidden of him	τὸ ἀποκεκρυμμένον

(1) manifested ≅ ἐφανερώθη —Both ps-Paul and Valentinus contrast something which was formerly hidden with something that is now manifest. By using the passive, ps-Paul focuses the reader's attention not upon the one who made the mystery manifest, but upon those who learned the mystery, namely, God's saints. Valentinus, however, by changing to the active voice, shifts the reader's attention to the Father, who manifested what was hidden. Such a change (from passive to active with specification of the actor) is typical of Valentinus; note also the typical change from God [Col 1:25, 27] to Father.

(2) what was hidden of him = τὸ ἀποκεκρυμμένον —verbatim. Valentinus omits ps-Paul's "mystery," using the participle as a substantive (what was hidden of him = his secret).

C. Evaluation of the Parallel

Although the contexts of the two passages are not especially similar, one of the two elements of comparison (2) is verbatim and the other (1) nearly so (except for a change in voice). Both elements of comparison are indicative of Valentinus' use of Pauline terminology (cf. No. 27 also). A suggested parallel to Col 1:25-27 was shown to be probable in No. 2, but here the evidence is not as strong that Valentinus used the text. Thus, his use of Col is only possible here.

D. Interpretation

In GTr, the mystery is not that Christ has been preached among the Gentiles or that Christ is "in you," as in ps-Paul. Rather, Valentinus closely connects GTr 27:7-8 with 27:8-9: what was hidden but is now

Commentaries   99

manifest is the Father himself (27:5-6).[42] Thus, GTr emphasizes the Father's appearance and manifestation of the mystery. Here the content of the mystery is not the Son (or Jesus Christ; cf. No. 2); rather it is the Father himself, who is of course held by Valentinus to be unknowable except through his Son.

37. GTr 27:8-9 (A²) ~ John 1:18

Postulated by van Unnik, p. 119. Possible.

(Father)	¹⁸... μονογενὴς θεὸς ὁ ὤν
he explained it (his secret).	εἰς τὸν κόλπον τοῦ πατρὸς
	ἐκεῖνος ἐξηγήσατο.

---

⁸ⲁϥⲃⲁⲗϥ̄ ⁹ⲁⲃⲁⲗ

A. Context

John 1:18 (prologue). God is invisible and can only be known through the only begotten Son's explanation of him.

GTr 27:5-9 (the Father's secret). The Father is unknown until he manifests himself in the truth (26:27-28). In this, he has explained his secret, himself.

B. Element of Comparison

he explained it	ἐκεῖνος ἐξηγήσατο

he explained = ἐξηγήσατο —verbatim. In John, the antecedent of

---

[42]Two elements which appear in the context of GTr may be related to Valentinus' interpretation of Col. First, "truth" may be identified with the "word of God" of Col 1:25, and, second, the mention of aeons ("his revelation to the aeons," 27:6-7) may contrast with Col 1:26 ("the mystery hidden for ages" or *from* the aeons"). Both are so tentative that they were not included in the synopsis.

ἐκεῖνος, the grammatical subject, is either "only begotten God" or "only begotten Son"; there is a textual variation, but both surely refer to Jesus. In GTr, the grammatical subject is understood to be the Father. The two phrases in John and GTr are quite similar; the addition of "it" in GTr 27:8 may be a feature of Coptic, which supplies the pronoun object as a matter of course. The Coptic verb, however, could also be translated, "he has unloosed himself," which emphasizes the Father's activity in his self-manifestation as the revelation of his secret.

C. Evaluation of the Parallel

The contexts are similar insofar as both state how God or the Father can be known. The one element of comparison, a frequently used verb in Greek, is verbatim. Because the passage is so short and the Coptic translation ambiguous, Valentinus' use of this passage is only possible, even though he uses John frequently.[43]

D. Interpretation

For Valentinus, the Father is unknowable except through the reception of knowledge about him proclaimed by Jesus in his teaching and crucifixion, as the early pages of GTr make clear. His use of the phrase from John 1:18 is consistent with such a view. What the Father has made manifest in GTr is also what he has explained: himself. This has been done by means of the truth (26:27-28, namely, Jesus; cf. "truth" in John 1:14, 17). Thus, what has been "explained" in both texts is the Father (or God); only the subject differs ("Son" in John and "Father" in GTr).

38. GTr 27:23-24 (A²) ~ Matt 5:48

Identified by van Unnik, p. 119. Probable.

Yet, the Father is perfect	⁴⁸ἔσεσθε οὖν ὑμεῖς τέλειοι ὡς ὁ πατὴρ ὑμῶν ὁ οὐράνιος τέλειός ἐστιν.

---

[43]If No. 26 is not part of an interpolation, he has probably used this text there as well.

²³ⲡⲓⲱⲧ· ⲛ²⁴ⲧⲁϥ· ϥⲭⲏⲕ ⲁⲃⲁⲗ

A. Context

Matt 5:43-48 (Sermon on the Mount). In the last of the antitheses of Matt 5, Jesus commands his disciples to love both their enemies and their neighbors so that they may be children of their heavenly Father. In fact, they are exhorted to perfection in imitation of the heavenly Father's perfection.

GTr 27:11-25 (knowledge and perfection). Children of the Father have come forth from him. They were formerly dormant but have come into existence by their receptiveness to knowledge (at the Father's instigation). Even though some are dormant within the Father, he remains perfect and omniscient.

B. Elements of Comparison

| Yet, the Father is perfect | ὡς ὁ πατὴρ ὑμῶν ὁ οὐράνιος τέλειός ἐστιν |

(1) the Father = ὁ πατήρ —verbatim. Matt's Jesus usually refers to God as "Father" when he speaks to his disciples. Valentinus too uses "Father" more frequently than he does "God." "Father" also occurs frequently in John, as well as in contemporary philosophical literature, especially that which is influenced by Middle Platonism, e.g., Philo, *Spec. Leg.* I, 96 (τῷ τοῦ κόσμου πατρί) and *Corp. Herm.* 1:21 (ὁ πατὴρ ὅλων . . . ὁ θεὸς καὶ πατήρ).

(2) is perfect = τέλειός ἐστιν —verbatim. Matt exhorts his community to perfection,[44] which comes through understanding or knowledge

---

[44]There is a striking parallel to this exhortation in *Did.* 6:2 (τέλειος ἔσῃ), but it is almost certainly dependent upon Matt or Matthean tradition. E. Massaux, "L'influence littéraire de l'Evangile de saint Matthieu sur la Didachè," *EphLov* 25 (1949) 15, argues for a literary dependence of *Did.* upon Matt here. He also draws attention to τέλειος as a particularly Matthean feature.

because the Father himself is understood to be perfect. The command is apparently based on Deut 18:13 (cf. Lev 19:2), with stress upon imitation of God not in his capacity as perfect being but in the perfection of his actions toward and love of humanity.[45] In GTr, the readers are not exhorted to be perfect themselves.

C. Evaluation of the Parallel

Even though the contexts of the two passages are not similar, two verbatim similarities occur. The conjunction of these two in both Matt and GTr is certainly good evidence for Valentinus' use of Matt 5:48, especially since τέλειος, though not unique to Matt, is a particularly Matthean word. Moreover, Matt is used frequently in the latter part of GTr. Thus, the weight of the evidence suggests that Valentinus probably used Matt here.

D. Interpretation

The words of Jesus in Matt which exhort the readers to imitation of the Father's perfection have been transformed in GTr into a theological statement: the Father is perfect. Valentinus does not retain Matt's emphasis on imitation of the Father because this would not be in keeping with his theology, which has at its center a perfect Father who cannot be imitated (but who can be joined by his parts). The perfection of the Father is the perfection of his being; he is removed from the world except as he gives certain persons the impetus to knowledge. Thus, in this passage Valentinus describes the perfection of the Father and the coming into existence (through knowledge) of those who are already latently within the all-encompassing Father. He omits Matt's reference to the "heavenly" Father, as would be expected from his typical disinterest in biblical spatial categories. One is either *within* the all-encompassing Father in a metaphysical sense, or one remains in ignorance and in an existence too sorry even to be considered "real."

---

[45]D. Hill, *The Gospel of Matthew* (Greenwood, SC: Attic, 1972), p. 131, gives a more detailed discussion of this.

Commentaries 103

39. GTr 27:24-25 (A²) ~ 1 John 3:20

Postulated by van Unnik, p. 119. Possible.

and (the Father)	²⁰ὁ θεός . . .
knows every way within him	γινώσκει πάντα.

---

²⁴ⲈϤⲤⲀⲨ²⁵ⲚⲈ ⲀⲘⲀⲈⲒⲦ ⲚⲒⲘ ⲈⲦⲚ̅ϨⲎⲦϤ̅

A. Context

1 John 3:19-24 (God's knowledge). Love enables believers to know that they are of the truth even when they experience doubt. God knows everything and can reassure them.

GTr 27:18-31 (the Father's knowledge). Those who are dormant in the Father must await the Father's impetus before they can have knowledge and attain birth. The perfect Father knows all those who will come into existence (his "ways") when he gives them form and name.

B. Elements of Comparison

and (the Father)	ὁ θεός . . .
knows every way within him.	γινώσκει πάντα

(1) knows = γινώσκει —verbatim. The notion of an omniscient deity is a commonplace in religious and philosophical thought of the first two centuries of the Common Era. Both 1 John and GTr speak of the deity's omniscience. In 1 John, the deity is called God, whereas in GTr, typically, it is called Father.

(2) every $\stackrel{?}{=}$ πάντα —possibly verbatim. Πάντα is a substantive in 1 John, while Valentinus uses it as an adjective, modifying "way." "Way" (ὁδός) is feminine gender in Greek, and hence the Greek model of GTr probably had πάντας τὰς ὁδούς. Whereas 1 John focuses on the moral dimension, the use of "every" to modify "way" in GTr enables Valentinus to introduce the cosmological dimension.

C. Evaluation of the Parallel

The contexts are not similar and can provide no evidence for Valentinus' use of the proposed text. The two elements of comparison are verbatim, though trivial. The brevity of the reference precludes any firm decision on Valentinus' use of 1 John here; in general, however, his use of 1 John is ambiguous.

D. Interpretation

If Valentinus has used 1 John, he has restricted the idea of omniscience to events that occur within the Father because only that which is within the Father is "real." Thus, the focus has been shifted from ethics to the epistemological plane by making clear that the Father is all-encompassing ("within him"). Because of this, the Father knows all his "ways" and is responsible for their existence.

40. GTr 30:14-16 (A²) ~ Gen 3:5

Postulated by Williams.[46] Possible.

And blessed is	⁵ᾔδει γὰρ ὁ θεὸς ὅτι ἐν ᾗ
	ἂν ἡμέρᾳ φάγητε ἀπ' αὐτοῦ.
the one who has opened	διανοιχθήσονται ὑμῶν
the eyes of the blind.	οἱ ὀφθαλμοί,
	καὶ ἔσεσθε ὡς θεοὶ
	γινώσκοντες καλὸν
	καὶ πονηρόν.

¹⁴ⲟⲩⲁ2ⲛ̄ ⲟⲩⲙⲁⲕⲁ¹⁵ⲣⲓⲟⲥ ⲡⲉ ⲡⲉⲉⲓ ⲛ̄ⲧⲁϥⲟⲩⲏⲛ ¹⁶ⲁⲛⲃⲉⲗ ⲛ̄ⲛⲓⲃ̄ⲗ̄ⲗⲉⲉⲩ

---

[46]Standaert, *NTS* p. 270, n. 1, has also tried to understand this section in light of the Gen story of Adam, but he has not attempted to find a specific reference to this verse of Gen.

A. Context

Gen 3:1-7 (the fall). After the serpent convinced the first woman to eat the forbidden fruit, she and the first man ate. The result was that their eyes were opened (metaphorically), and they discerned their nakedness.

GTr 30:12-23 (return from ignorance). Acquisition of knowledge is life awaking from the sleepy state of ignorance. Such a one should be congratulated and is blessed. After one returns from ignorance, the assistance of the quick spirit enables one who is on the ground (as though dazed) to stand up.

B. Elements of Comparison

| the one who has opened | διανοιχθήσονται ὑμῶν |
| the eyes of the blind | οἱ ὀφθαλμοί |

(1) the one who has opened ≅ διανοιχθήσονται —If Valentinus has used Gen, he has phrased the reference to the Gen story as a macarism. "The one who has opened" apparently means the Son (30:25, or, the beloved Son, 30:31-32).[47]

(2) the eyes = οἱ ὀφθαλμοί —verbatim.

(3) of the blind ≅ ὑμῶν —Valentinus uses "the blind" to refer to those whose eyes were opened. If he has used Gen, this is the equivalent of Gen's "your" (ὑμῶν), put into past narrative form.

C. Evaluation of the Parallel

The contexts are similar in that both concern reception of a certain kind of knowledge that comes with the opening of one's eyes. In Gen, reception of knowledge brought unwanted results, whereas in GTr it brought good results. Thus, if Gen is used here it is for purposes of contrast, much as in No. 4. One of the three elements of comparison (2) is

---

[47] One might recall accounts of Jesus healing the blind in the gospels, such as John 9; 10:21; 11:37; Matt 9:27f.; 11:5, as van Unnik, p. 119, suggests, but no direct contact with any of these texts is indicated. Note, however, the figurative use of "blind" in John 9:39-41.

verbatim, and the other two may be understood as changes dictated by a change in form in GTr. This passage seems in line with Valentinus' use of Gen elsewhere, and hence his use of Gen is possible here as well.

D. Interpretation

Elements of a typology seem to be implicit, even though the passage is not as clearly an Adam-Christ typology as is No. 4. "The one who was prone on the ground" (30:20-21) especially recalls Adam, as portrayed in Gen 2:7, although GTr must simultaneously refer to one who comes to knowledge from ignorance.[48] The context of this passage in GTr, though somewhat obscure in its details, presents a highly schematized account of the return from ignorance to knowledge, i.e., the conversion experience. If Valentinus has used Gen 3:5, he contrasts the opening of the eyes of the first man and woman (which brought an unwanted, negative result: they were cast out of Eden) with the Son's action of opening the eyes of those who are figuratively blind with ignorance (which brought a positive result: they "awaken" [to knowledge] from ignorance). The illustration as a whole congratulates one who awakens to sight, i.e., knowledge, and lauds the one (no doubt the Son) by whom the knowledge comes.

41. GTr 30:26-32 (S A²) ∼1 John 1:1-2

Postulated by van Unnik, p. 120. Possible.

For when they had seen him and had heard him,	¹ Ὃ ἦν ἀπ' ἀρχῆς, (cf. ἑωράκαμεν below) ὃ ἀκηκόαμεν, ὃ ἑωράκαμεν τοῖς ὀφθαλμοῖς ἡμῶν,
he let them taste of him and smell him and touch the beloved Son	ὃ ἐθεασάμεθα καὶ αἱ χεῖρες ἡμῶν ἐψηλάφησαν

---

[48]Note that it is the Spirit, not the Son, who helps the one who is prone. This might recall a Gnostic myth in which assistance from the spiritual world comes to the human being who has been created in ignorance by the ruler(s) of the material world (cf. HypArch; ApocryJn).

Commentaries

after he had appeared (to them, add. Sahidic).⁴⁹

περὶ τοῦ λόγου τοῦ ζωῆς—
²καὶ ἡ ζωὴ ἐφανερώθη . . .

Subachmimic text ²⁶ⲚⲀ²⁷ⲦⲀⲢⲞⲨⲚⲈⲨ ⲄⲀⲢ ⲀⲢⲀϤ ⲀⲨⲰ ⲀⲨ²⁸ⲤⲰⲦⲘ ⲀⲢⲀϤ ⲀϤϯ
ⲚⲈⲨ ⲀⲦⲢⲞⲨ²⁹ϪⲒ ϯⲠⲈ ⲀⲂⲀⲖ ⲘⲘⲀϤ ⲞⲨⲀ2Ⲛ ³⁰ⲀⲦⲞⲨϢⲀⲖⲘⲈϤ ⲞⲨⲀ2ⲚⲚ
³¹ⲦⲞⲨⲈⲘⲀ2ⲦⲈ ⲀϪⲚ ⲠϢⲢⲘⲚ³²ⲢⲒⲦ ⲈⲀϤⲞⲨⲰⲚ2 ⲀⲂⲀⲖ
Sahidic fragment ²⁰[ⲀⲨⲰ] ⲚⲈⲦⲤⲰⲦⲘ ⲈⲢⲞ[Ϥ ²¹ [.ⲀϤϯ ⲚⲀⲨ ⲚϯϯⲠⲈ [ⲘⲚ
ⲠⲒⲤⲦⲞⲒ Ⲛ̣] ²²[ⲞⲨⲤ] ⲘⲞⲦ ⲚⲦⲀϤ ⲠϢ[ⲎⲢⲈ ⲘⲘⲈⲢⲒⲦ] ²³[ⲀϤⲞ]ⲨⲰⲚ2 ⲚⲀⲨ ⲈⲂⲞⲖ

A. Context

1 John 1:1-4 (introduction). Using Johannine motifs that have been altered (cf. John 20:24-29) to suit a new format and situation, the author of 1 John attests the reality of the Word of life by using verbs which refer to the senses. He affirms that the human Jesus had historical continuity with the Word and that the readers have historical continuity with Jesus.[50]

GTr 30:23-32 (appearance of the beloved Son). Valentinus stresses the reality of the Son's appearance by using concrete language which refers to the five senses. The readers have been given a dual sense of understanding, namely, knowledge from the Father and the revelation of his Son.

B. Elements of Comparison

when they had seen . . .	(cf. ἑωράκαμεν)
had heard . . .	ἀκηκόαμεν . . .
(he let them) taste . . .	
smell . . .	
touch . . .	ἐψηλάφησαν . . .

---

[49] The Sahidic version seems to have been phrased differently but probably attests an identical or similar Greek text of the passage. The Sahidic manuscript is fragmentary.

[50] See J. M. Lieu, "'Authority to Become Children of God': A Study in 1 John," *NovT* 23 (1981) 213-215, 220-221 on the reworking of Johannine ideas in 1 John, and 213 on eyewitness language.

(1) when they had seen ≅ ἑωράκαμεν —Two words for "see" occur in the Johannine passage (θεᾶσθαι, ὁρᾶν). Of the two, ὁρᾶν has a broader range of meanings which center around sense perception but which include visions and catching sight of those who have become visible by supernatural means. The syntax of the two passages differs with the literary form: 1 John reads almost like an affirmation of faith, whereas GTr is a past narrative.

(2) (when they) had heard ≅ ἀκηκόαμεν —Both passages mention the sense of hearing but with the same syntactical difference as in (1).

(3) (he let them) touch ≅ ἐψηλάφησαν —Both passages mention the sense of touch but with the same syntactical difference as in (1).

| the beloved Son after he had appeared | τοῦ λογοῦ τῆς ζωῆς— καὶ ἡ ζωή ἐφανερώθη |

(4) he (beloved Son) had appeared ≅ ἡ ζωή ἐφανερώθη —"Life" in 1 John and "beloved Son" in GTr must both refer to Jesus. There is metonymy in 1 John (result for cause, "life" appeared) which is resolved by Valentinus (he, the Son appeared). "Son" or "beloved Son"[51] is the name for Jesus that Valentinus prefers from this point in GTr until the end. The same syntactical difference occurs in these phrases as in (1).

C. Evaluation of the Parallels

The contexts are similar insofar as both stress the reality of experience with Jesus (or the Son). Not one of the elements of comparison is verbatim, however, because the difference in syntax is so vast. The shared vocabulary centers around references to the senses; three senses are mentioned in 1 John and all five in GTr. How to weigh this evidence is a problem. The differences between the two passages are too great to be certain that Valentinus has used 1 John, but the shared references to the senses which stress the reality of experience are striking. As usual, Valentinus' use of 1 John is ambiguous.

---

[51]There is apparently an early Christian tradition referring to Jesus as God's beloved Son (Matt 3:17; 17:5; 2 Pet 1:17; *Mart. Pol.* 14:13; *Diog.* 8:11), which may have been associated especially with Jesus' baptism and transfiguration.

D. Interpretation

Both 1 John and GTr refer to the senses figuratively in order to affirm the reality of later experience with Jesus. Mention of the sense of smell and taste, which 1 John does not include in his list, may make clear to the readers that a figurative sense is intended, that is, that Valentinus no longer is referring to the earthly Jesus. Thus, if Valentinus has used this passage, he has separated seeing and hearing the beloved Son from tasting, smelling, and touching him. He may wish to separate Jesus' earthly life from his resurrected life (cf. No. 42). In this case, sight and hearing would refer to Jesus' earthly life and taste, smell, and touch would refer to Jesus' post-resurrection state.[52]

42. GTr 30:34-35 (S A²) ~ Gen 2:7

Postulated by Williams. Possible. Cf. No. 43.

(the beloved Son)	⁷καὶ ἔπλασεν ὁ θεὸς τὸν ἄνθρωπον χοῦν ἀπὸ τῆς γῆς καὶ
after he had breathed into them what was in the thought,	ἐνεφύσησεν εἰς τὸ πρόσωπον αὐτοῦ πνοὴν ζωῆς, καὶ ἐγένετο ὁ ἄθρωπος εἰς ψυχὴν ζῶσαν.

Subachmimic text ³⁴ⲉⲁϥⲛⲓϥⲉ ⲛ̄ϩⲏⲧⲟⲩ ³⁵ⲙ̄ⲡⲉⲧϩⲛ̄ ⲡⲓⲙⲉⲉⲩⲉ
Sahidic fragment ²⁵[ⲁϥⲛⲓϥ]ⲉ ⲙ̄ⲡⲉϥⲙⲉⲉⲩ [ ]

---

[52] An intriguing idea is that Valentinus might refer to different stages of one's relationship with the beloved Son. Sight and hearing would then refer to an early stage in that relationship and taste, smell, and touch to a later stage. There is no support for this in the text of GTr itself, however.

110 Biblical Interpretation in the Gospel of Truth

A. Context

Gen 2:4b-7 (creation of the first human being). God has made the heavens and the earth and also the first human being. That one has been formed from dust, and God has made him alive by breathing into him.

GTr 30:26-36 (action taken by the beloved Son). The Son has appeared in order to tell the ignorant about the Father. Intimate acquaintance with the Son has led them to receive what was in the Father's thought, which has been transmitted by the Son's breathing.

B. *Elements of Comparison*

(the beloved Son)	. . . ὁ θεός . . .
after he had breathed	ἐνεφύσησεν
into them	εἰς τὸ πρόσωπον αὐτοῦ
what was in the thought	πνοὴν ζωῆς

(1) the beloved Son ≅ ὁ θεός —Rather than "God," Valentinus refers to "the beloved Son," a typical change in aspect of the deity.

(2) after he had breathed ≅ ἐνεφύσησεν —verbatim, except for a slight difference in syntax.

(3) into them ≅ εἰς τὸ πρόσωπον αὐτοῦ —nearly verbatim. Τὸ πρόσωπον is untranslatable in this prepositional idiom, which simply means "into him." The Coptic may presuppose the plural of this Greek model.[53] Valentinus has pluralized the object of the preposition, extending the reference in Gen to the first human being so that it applies to all who have heard the Son.

(4) what was in the thought ≠ πνοὴν ζωῆς —These two expressions are not similar, although "what is in the thought" may be Valentinus' interpretation of "the breath of life" (see D).

---

[53] ⲚϨⲎⲦⲞⲨ after ⲚⲒϤⲈ is almost certainly a writing of ⲈϨⲎⲦⲞⲨ which etymologically means "toward face (ϨⲎⲦ ⸗) of them."

C. Evaluation of the Parallel

The contexts of the two passages are not similar, but this is not significant since Valentinus often uses Gen typologically. The similarity in phrasing between the two passages is striking, but no one of the four elements of comparison is verbatim. They occur in the same order, however, and all can be understood as typical changes made by Valentinus or as changes dictated by the syntax or interpretation. The similarity to No. 43, which almost certainly uses John, makes the use of Gen only possible.[54]

D. Interpretation

Hints of an Adam-Christ typology may continue to arise in this passage.[55] Valentinus contrasts the breath of life that God has breathed into the first human being in the Gen story with what the beloved Son has breathed into those who have listened to him, namely, what was in the Father's thought. He does not say that God's breath was somehow deficient; rather, it initiated life. The breath that the Son breathes into persons bestows light, however (30:36-37); this light is conversion (30:37-31:1).

43. GTr 30:34-35 (S A²) ∼ John 20:22

Identified by van Unnik, p. 120. Probable. Cf. No. 42.

(the beloved Son)	(ὁ 'Ιησοῦς)
after he had breathed into them what was in the thought (scil. of the Father)	²³καὶ τοῦτο εἰπὼν ἐνεφύσησεν καὶ λέγει αὐτοῖς· λάβετε πνεῦμα ἅγιον·

---

[54]This might be a double allusion, to both Gen and John. GTr 30:19 may refer to Jewish haggadah about the Golem; this also occurs in some forms of Gnostic myth (e.g., HypArch). If that is so, the reader would already have Adam in mind.

[55]As in the case of No. 40; see Standaert, p. 270, n. 1 on this.

Subachmimic text ³⁴ⲉⲁϥⲛⲓϥⲉ ⲛ̄ⲍⲏⲧⲟⲩ ³⁵ⲙ̄ⲡⲉⲧⲍⲛ̄ ⲡⲓⲙⲉⲉⲩⲉ
Sahidic fragment ²⁵[ⲁϥⲛⲓϥⲉ ⲙ̄ⲡⲉϥⲙⲉⲉⲩ [   ]

A. Context

John 20:19-23 (reception of the Holy Spirit). After his resurrection, Jesus has appeared to his disciples to commission them to carry on his mission. In so doing, he has breathed into them and has commanded them to receive the Holy Spirit.

GTr 30:26-36 (action taken by the beloved Son). The Son has appeared in order to tell the ignorant about the Father. Intimate acquaintance with the Son has led them to receive what was in the Father's thought, which has been transmitted by the Son's breathing.

B. Elements of Comparison

(the beloved Son)	(ὁ 'Ιησοῦς)
after he had breathed	. . . ἐνεφύσησεν
into them	. . . αὐτοῖς
what was in the thought	. . . πνεῦμα ἅγιον

(1) the beloved Son ≡ ὁ 'Ιησοῦς —Jesus and the beloved Son are surely one and the same, but Valentinus prefers "Son" or "beloved Son" in the latter half of GTr.⁵⁶

(2) after he had breathed ≡ ἐνεφύσησεν —verbatim, except for a slight difference in syntax.

(3) into them = αὐτοῖς —possibly verbatim. Strictly speaking, "breathe on" is conveyed by ἐμφυσᾶν (and "disciples" is the understood object). 'Αυτοῖς, however, can mean "into them," but for Valentinus to have read it this way, he would have to have omitted καὶ λέγει and λάβετε (see D).

---

⁵⁶See Standaert, *NTS*, pp. 269-274 on this.

Commentaries   113

(4) what is in the thought ≠ πνεῦμα ἅγιον —In John, Jesus is not said to have actually breathed the Holy Spirit into his disciples. Rather, he is said to breathe onto them and then to have commanded them to receive the Holy Spirit. "What is in the thought" may be Valentinus' interpretation of "Holy Spirit" (see D).

C. Evaluation of the Parallel

The contexts of both passages are similar (post-resurrection in John and possibly also in GTr), as are the subjects (Jesus in John, beloved Son in GTr). If taken at face value, the proposed elements of comparison do not look as convincing as those suggested in No. 42 because the grammatical structure of John 20:22 is not as close to GTr as is that of Gen. John himself, however, was probably alluding to Gen. Since Valentinus frequently uses John, his use of it here as well is more probable than is his use of Gen in No. 42, although a simultaneous allusion to both is also possible.

D. Interpretation

Valentinus has recalled to his readers Jesus' resurrection appearance in which Jesus commands his disciples to receive the Holy Spirit. Although John does not actually say that Jesus breathed the Holy Spirit into his disciples, Valentinus apparently understood this to be the case (strictly speaking, he had to ignore καὶ λέγει and λάβετε to make such a reading possible). Thus he interprets the Johannine passage with an eye to his own conception of the work of Jesus, the beloved Son. Those who listened to the Son (both while he was on earth and afterwards through proclamation of his message) learned about the Father, and the Son transmitted to them what was in the Father's thought. The mediation of what was in the Father's thought has occurred through the Son's breathing into certain persons so that they received the light which comes through conversion (30:36-31:1). "Light" should thus be understood as the equivalent of "what was in the Father's thought."

44. GTr 30:35-36 (S A²) ~ John 6:38

Identified by Schenke, p. 46, n. 8. Probable.

(When the beloved Son | 38ὅτι καταβέβηκα

114   Biblical Interpretation in the Gospel of Truth

had appeared ...)   ἀπὸ τοῦ οὐρανοῦ
doing   οὐχ ἵνα ποιῶ [' Ιησοῦς]
                                   τὸ θέλημα τὸ ἐμὸν ἀλλὰ
his (the Father's) will   τὸ θέλημα τοῦ πέμψαντός με.

Subachmimic text ³⁵ⲉϥⲉⲓ³⁶ⲣⲉ ⲙ̄ⲡⲉϥⲟⲩⲱϣⲉ
Sahidic fragment ²⁵ⲉϥ ²⁶ⲛⲉϥⲉⲓⲣⲉ]ⲉ ⲙ̄ⲡⲉϥⲟⲩⲱ[ϣ)

A. Context

John 6:35-40 (bread of life discourse). The Son (Jesus) has come from heaven to earth in order to do his Father's will, which is to bestow eternal life upon those who believe in him (the Son).

GTr 30:32-31:1 (appearance of the Son). The beloved Son has appeared on earth in order to do his Father's will, which is to enlighten those who will convert.

B. Elements of Comparison

(the beloved Son) doing   [' Ιησοῦς] ... ποιῶ
his (the Father's) will   τὸ θέλημα τοῦ πέμψαντός με

(1) doing ≅ ποιῶ —Although the syntax differs, both texts express the notion that Jesus does his Father's will. In John, Jesus ("the Son," 6:30) is the speaker; in GTr, the beloved Son (Jesus) is described.

(2) his will ≅ τὸ θέλημα τοῦ πέμψαντός με —Both passages refer to the Father's will, although Valentinus has used the simpler "his" for John's phrase, τοῦ πέμψαντός με. The omission of the Johannine motif of the sending of the Son is not surprising since Valentinus shows no interest in it elsewhere.[57]

---

[57] See C. K. Barrett, p. 211 on the lack of interest in this motif in GTr. In 41:23ff., the "parts" send their thought to the Father.

C. Evaluation of the Parallel

The contexts of the two passages are similar. The two passages share the same motif, i.e., that the Son does the Father's will. Of the two elements of comparison, one (1) is nearly verbatim and the other (2) inexact because it has been simplified. The appearance of the motif of Jesus' doing the Father's will outweighs the fact that only two verbal parallels exist because it is a motif peculiarly associated with John (see also 4:34).[58] In fact, it is nearly peculiar to John, although in Heb 10:7, 9, the prophetic-christological exegesis of Ps 39:9 has Christ say that he has come to do God's will. The weight of the evidence suggests that Valentinus used John here.

D. Interpretation

Valentinus does not mention who sent Jesus; the beloved Son is said merely to appear. This shifts the emphasis from the Father's activity in sending Jesus to the beloved Son's activity in converting people. Otherwise, in both passages, the Son is said to do his Father's will. What is his Father's will? It is for him to impart what is essential to salvation: in John, eternal life; in GTr, what is in the Father's thought, which is light (30:36-37). Yet, "light" is possibly a Valentinian equivalent of "life," as we have seen in No. 3, where "light" is substituted for "life."

45. GTr 31:4-6 (A²) ~ Rom 8:3

Identified by Schenke, p. 46, n. 9. Probable.

(the beloved Son)	³ὁ θεὸς τὸν ἑαυτοῦ υἱὸν
he came forth	πέμψας
by means of a likeness	ἐν ὁμοιώματι
of flesh (σάρξ)	σαρκὸς ἁμαρτίας

---

⁴ⲚⲦⲀϤⲈⲒ Ⲁ⁵ⲂⲀⲖ ϨⲒⲦⲞⲞⲦⲤ ⲚⲞⲨⲤⲀⲢⲜ Ⲛ⁶ⲤⲘⲀⲦ·

---

[58] Van Unnik, p. 120, suggested this as a parallel.

A. Context

Rom 8:1-4 (salvific nature of the incarnation). The incarnation of the Son leads to the condemnation of sin and the setting free of believers from the power of the law of sin and death to the power of the law of the Spirit of life.

GTr 30:32-31:14 (salvific nature of the incarnation). The incarnation of the beloved Son is necessary in order for persons to gain acquaintance with the Father through Jesus and to understand the incorruptibility of the Word.

B. Elements of Comparison

(the beloved Son)	ὁ θεὸς τὸν ἑαυτοῦ υἱὸν
he came forth	πέμψας

(1) beloved Son = υἱόν —"Beloved Son," last mentioned in 30:31-32, is still the topic of discussion.

(2) came forth ≅ πέμψας —Paul's emphasis is on God's initiative in sending his Son, whereas Valentinus does not mention God's action of sending but rather focuses on the appearance and activity of the beloved Son among humanity.

by means of a likeness	ἐν ὁμοιώματι
of flesh (σάρξ)	σαρκὸς ἁμαρτίας

(3) by means of a likeness of flesh = ἐν ὁμοιώματι σαρκός —verbatim. The presence of the word "likeness" in both passages may recall Gen 1:26, which is quoted by early Christian writers (e.g., 1 Clem 33:5). Philo gives the verse a Middle Platonist interpretation. In *De Opif. Mundi* 69-70, he explains that κατ' εἰκόνα θεοῦ in Gen 1:26 refers to the mind (νοῦς) of the first human rather than to his bodily form. He maintains that the author of Gen further brought out his meaning by adding the phrase καὶ καθ' ὁμοίωσιν to indicate that the image did indeed correspond to its archetype. Thus, in both Rom and GTr, an implicit comparison of Adam and Christ may be at work.

C. Evaluation of the Parallel

The two passages occur in similar contexts, and two of the three elements of comparison are verbatim or nearly so. The inexactness of (2) results from a theological change typical of GTr. The occurrence of the striking phrase, "by means of a likeness of flesh," in both Rom and GTr is particularly telling. Coupled with Valentinus' clear use of Rom elsewhere (e.g., 71, 73), it increases the likelihood of his use of Rom here.

D. Interpretation

Two changes made by Valentinus hint at his interpretation. The first is his use of the intransitive verb, "come forth," rather than Paul's transitive, "send" (or "be sent"). This shifts the emphasis away from God's initiative in the incarnation and may suggest a less agential process, such as emanation. The second is his omission of Paul's reference to the sinful nature of Jesus' flesh; this shifts the interest away from the ethical plane, which is central here for Paul, to the intellectual plane. Conversion results from reception of the light, which we have seen[59] is a symbol for "knowledge." Knowledge of the Father is seen in his likeness borne by the beloved Son, who became human for this purpose. In GTr, the Son's incarnation was not salvific because his flesh was sinful, like that of all people (as Paul believes), but because he proclaimed the incorruptible and unseizable Word (31:11-13).[60]

46. GTr 31:28-29 (S A²) ~ John 14:6

Identified by Grobel, p. 129, n. 346. Probable.

He (bel. Son) became a way	⁶λέγει αὐτῷ [ὁ] 'Ιησοῦς· ἐγώ εἰμι ἡ ὁδός

---

[59]E.g., in the discussion of No. 3.

[60]A textual corruption, probably due to scribal omission, makes it difficult to say more about Valentinus' interpretation of Rom 8:3. "Matter" (ὕλη) is mentioned in GTr 31:4 and clearly marked in Coptic as the subject, but there is no verb which agrees with this subject. The original text may have stated that the Son was made out of matter in the likeness of flesh.

for those who were lost | καὶ ἡ ἀλήθεια καὶ ἡ ζωή.

Subachmimic text ²⁸ⲁϥϣⲱⲡⲉ ⲉϥⲟⲉⲓ ⲛ̄ⲟⲩ²⁹ⲙⲁⲉⲓⲧ· ⲛ̄ⲛⲉⲉⲓ ⲉⲛⲉⲩⲥⲁⲣⲙ̄
Sahidic fragment[61] ²¹ⲟ[ⲩⲙⲟ]²²[ⲉⲓⲧ ⲁϥϣⲱⲡ]ⲉ ⲛ̄ⲛⲁⲉⲓ ⲉⲧⲥⲟⲣ[ⲙ·

A. Context

John 14:1-7 (opening of Jesus' farewell discourse). For those who want knowledge of the Father, Jesus ambiguously "is" a true way of life that is or imparts salvation.

GTr 31:26-31 (the beloved Son's work among humanity). For those whom the beloved Son has released from the captivity of error (ignorance) by knowledge, he may be seen as having "become" a way or path.

B. Elements of Comparison

He (bel. Son) became a way | ἐγώ εἰμι ἡ ὁδός

(1) he became ≅ ἐγώ εἰμι —The self-proclamation of Jesus in John has been changed to past narrative form in GTr.

(2) a way ≅ ἡ ὁδός —In John, Jesus proclaims that he is *the* way par excellence. In GTr, however, the definite article is not used.

C. Evaluation of the Parallel

The contexts of the two passages are not similar, but the image of Jesus (or the Son) as a "way" is strong and distinctly recalls John 14:6. One of the two elements of comparison (2) is nearly verbatim, and the other can be explained as a change dictated by the form of incorporation into GTr. Moreover, John 14:6 was probably used earlier (No. 3). Although

---

[61]S: "a [way came into existence (?)] for those who were lost". This restoration, however, is very uncertain.

Commentaries 119

this reference is briefer than No. 3, the one phrase used in No. 46 is closer to the Johannine text.[62]

D. Interpretation

Valentinus explains that the beloved Son (= Jesus) is a way or path to the Father; as such he is the medium of salvation. Moreover, he has bestowed attributes of the Father on those whom he has converted (31:16-20). The beloved Son is not called *the* way but rather is said to have become *a* way. He is closely identified with knowledge (31:30), however, and probably is to be regarded as a model for others to follow in their search for the Father (31:31-32). Thus, all those whom the Son has converted (i.e., the children of the Father) are also called "ways" in GTr (see 27:24-25).

47. GTr 31:35-32:4 (S A²) ~ Matt 18:12-13

Identified by van Unnik, pp. 112-113. Probable.

He (the beloved Son) being the shepherd	¹²... ἐὰν γένηταί τινι ἀνθρώπῳ ἑκατὸν πρόβατα καὶ πλανηθῇ ἓν ἐξ αὐτῶν,
who left behind the ninety-nine sheep which had not gone astray, came, (and) he searched for the one which had gone astray.	οὐχὶ ἀφήσει τὰ ἐνενήκοντα ἐννέα (cf. πρόβατα above) ἐπὶ τὰ ὄρη καὶ πορευθεὶς ζητεῖ τὸ πλανώμενον; ¹³καὶ ἐὰν
He rejoiced when he found it because the ninety-nine...	γένηται εὑρεῖν αὐτό... χαίρει ἐπ' αὐτῷ (cf. ἐὰν γένηται εὑρεῖν αὐτό above) μᾶλλον ἢ ἐπὶ τοῖς ἐνενήκοντα ἐννέα τοῖς μὴ πεπλανημένοις.

---

[62]Comparison of the Sahidic text with John 14:6 does not change the interpretation substantially.

120   Biblical Interpretation in the Gospel of Truth

Subachmimic text ³⁵ENTAq πe παχωc ³⁶ENTA2KωE NCωq· MΠΙΠCTE· ψιc
NECAY ETE MNOYCωPM ²Aqei Aq(ω)ine NCA Πeei NTAq ³CωpM Aqpea)e
NTApeq⁴6INE MMAq ϫe πιπcτeψειc

Sahidic fragment ²⁵πλει π[e παχωc] ²⁶[eqκω e2p]λ[η̄] MΠΙΨ̄TAEIO[Y
MN̄ ψιc] ²⁷[NECOOY] NAEI ETE MΠOYCω[PM Aq] ²⁸[(ω)INE NC]A
πλι NTAqCωPM [   ]

A. Context

Matt 18:10, 12-14 (the lost sheep). Matt's Jesus tells a parable about a
shepherd who leaves behind ninety-nine sheep in his flock in order to
search for one that had gone astray. Finding it is a cause for great rejoicing. Matt's application of the parable (put into the mouth of Jesus) is that
the Father does not want a single believer not to be saved.

GTr 31:28-32:17 (the lost sheep). Valentinus presents a parable about a
shepherd who leaves behind ninety-nine sheep in his flock in order to
search for one that had gone astray. Finding it is a cause for great rejoicing. Valentinus' interpretation (which he says is symbolic) is that the addition of one to ninety-nine is the occasion for the finger-reckoning to move
from the left hand (where it is positioned through ninety-nine) to the right
hand. When one was added and a total of one hundred attained, the
number could be expressed with the right hand.

B. Elements of Comparison

(1) [Rhetorical structure] the shepherd who left behind, he came (and)
he searched for, he rejoiced when he found it ≅ ἀφήσει, καὶ πορευθεὶς
ζητεῖ, ἐὰν γένηται εὑρεῖν αὐτό . . . χαίρει —Valentinus has
changed Matt's generalization into a specific description of someone's
activity, while keeping the parable form. This change accounts for differences of tense.

| He (the beloved Son) being | . . . ἐὰν γένηταί |
| the shepherd | τινι ἀνθρώπῳ |

(2) he (the beloved Son), the shepherd ≅ τινι ανθρώπῳ —Valentinus

Commentaries

has identified the subject of Matt's generalization as being the Father's beloved Son. He may recall the identification of Jesus as a good shepherd in John 10:11, 14.[63]

(3) the ≅ τινι . . . —Valentinus speaks of "the" well-known shepherd, familiar to his readers from Matt 18:12-13.[64]

who left behind the ninety-nine sheep	οὐχὶ ἀφήσει τὰ ἐνενήκοντα ἐννέα (cf. πρόβατα)

(4) the ninety-nine sheep = τὰ ἐνενήκοντα ἐννέα πρόβατα —verbatim.

he came (and) he searched for the one which had gone astray	καὶ πορευθεὶς ζητεῖ τὸ πλανώμενον

(5) he came (and) he searched for the one which had gone astray ≅ καὶ πορευθεὶς ζητεῖ τὸ πλανώμενον —nearly verbatim.

He rejoiced when he found it because the ninety-nine . . .	ἐὰν γένηται εὑρεῖν αὐτό . . . χαίρει ἐπ' αὐτῷ (cf. ἐὰν γένηται εὑρεῖν αὐτό) μᾶλλον ἢ ἐπὶ τοῖς ἐνενήκοντα ἐννέα τοῖς μὴ πεπλανημένοις.

(6) he rejoiced ≅ χαίρει —see (1).

(7) when he found it ≅ ἐὰν γένηται εὑρεῖν αὐτό —see (1).

(8) because the ninety-nine = μᾶλλον ἢ ἐνενήκοντα ἐννέα —The explanation for the shepherd's joy differs in each passage. Matt explains that the shepherd rejoices more over the one found than the ninety-nine which did not stray; Valentinus substitutes "because" for Matt's "more than," enabling him to give as a reason a deficiency inherent in the number ninety-nine itself (32:4-6).

---

[63] Schenke, p. 47, n. 1 and then Grobel, p. 129, n. 351 also observed this.
[64] As Grobel, p. 129, n. 351 suggests.

C. Evaluation of the Parallel

The contexts are similar insofar as both speak of sheep (clearly to be identified with persons) who have gone astray. Those who have gone astray in GTr are the ignorant, whereas Matt refers to believers who yield to temptation. All but two (2, 8) of the elements of comparison are verbatim,[65] if one allows for minor variations in word order. Because Valentinus knows and uses Matt elsewhere, his use of it here is all the more probable.

D. Interpretation

Valentinus' reference to the finger-reckoning system is discussed throughout the secondary literature,[66] but the interpretation which he gives to Matt has been less frequently understood. First, Valentinus identifies the beloved Son with the shepherd of Matt's parable. He then gives the outline of the parable. With the word "because" in 32:4, he introduces the interpretation of the parable.[67] Thus, the reason for the shepherd's rejoicing is said to be the change from left to right hand in the counting system when one is added to ninety-nine to make one hundred. As an interpretation of the parable, however, this surely is not apparent to the reader, and so Valentinus says outright that it is a symbol (32:16-17).

What clues to the interpretation lie in this mass of confusion? The shepherd has been identified as Jesus, and so the reader can begin to work out the allegory from there. The ninety-nine are counted on the left hand, which is deficient. This detail is only important insofar as it leads to understanding that the addition of one causes the number to be counted on

---

[65] Story, p. 21, also noticed this. Moreover, he also examined the Lukan parallel and concluded that it is not used in GTr because it has details (which may be particularly Lukan touches) that are not present in either Matt or GTr.

[66] See, e.g., van Unnik, pp. 96-97, 113; Grobel, pp. 129, 131, 133, nn. 353-358; and Marrou, pp. 99-103.

[67] GTr 32:4-17 reads: "because ninety-nine is a number which is on the left hand (and) is grasped there, but on the occasion when the one will be found, the whole number turns to the right hand. Thus, the one which lacks a unit, that is, the entire right hand, which draws what has become deficient, takes it from its left part and moves it over to the right hand. Thus, the number equals one hundred; it is the sign of the one who is in their voice."

the propitious right hand. A similar interpretation of the number ninety-nine (and also one) is attributed to the Marcosians in Irenaeus, Adv. Haer. I 16, 2. Here in GTr, the left hand, where the ninety-nine (sheep = people) are situated, may be the lack (the realm that is not within the Father). The addition of one lost (= ignorant) person makes the entire number go to the right hand (the realm of the Father, namely, "all"). Thus, the total is on the propitious side, which may indicate unity. Valentinus has allegorized sheep as people and then has referred to them collectively as numbers symbolizing the lack and unity. Finally, he says that one hundred is a symbol of the *spoken* form of the numbers (now taken individually as people = sheep). By this, he probably means that the numbers are persons who are called, i.e., whose names are spoken, and who comprise the Father. When those who were defiled (31:34-36) convert, they complete what is lacking for the perfection of all (18:36-38) and represent the finding of the lost sheep.

48. GTr 32:17-22 (A²) ~ Matt 12:11

Identified by van Unnik, pp. 113-114. Probable.

The Father is he who	¹¹τίς ἔσται ἐξ ὑμῶν ἄνθρωπος ὃς ἕξει πρόβατον ἓν
when	καὶ ἐὰν
the sheep which he found	(cf. πρόβατον above)
fell	ἐμπέσῃ τοῦτο
into the pit	(cf. εἰς βόθυνον below)
even on the Sabbath (σάββασιν)	τοῖς σάββασιν εἰς βόθυνον,
labored over it. He gave life to the sheep,	οὐχὶ κρατήσει αὐτὸ,
having brought it up from the pit	καὶ ἐγερεῖ;

---

[17]ΠⲰⲦ ⲚⲈⲠⲈⲈⲒ· [18]ⲔⲀⲚ 2Ⲛ̄ ⲮⲀⲂⲂⲀⲦⲞⲚ ⲈⲠⲈⲤⲀϤ [19]Ⲛ̄ⲦⲀϤϬⲒⲚⲦϤ ⲈⲀϤ2ⲀⲈⲒⲈ· ⲀⲠⲒ[20]2ⲒⲈⲒⲦ· ⲀϤⲢ̄ 2ⲰⲂ ⲀⲢⲀϤ ⲀϤⲦⲚ̄2Ⲟ [21]Ⲙ̄ⲠⲒⲈⲤⲀⲨ ⲈⲀϤⲚ̄ⲦϤ Ⲁ2ⲢⲎ̄Ⲓ [22]2Ⲛ̄ ⲠⲒϢⲒⲈⲒⲦ

A. Context

Matt 12:9-14 (the sheep that fell into a pit). Matt tells a story of Jesus' healing on the Sabbath, when labor is forbidden. To justify his action to the Pharisees, Jesus uses an *a fortiori* argument about a man rescuing a sheep that fell into a pit on the Sabbath.

GTr 32:17-34 (the sheep that fell into a pit). Immediately after the interpretation of an earlier story about sheep, Valentinus continues with this one. Herein, a man rescues a sheep that fell into a pit on the Sabbath. The man, Valentinus explains, means the Father; the Sabbath means (a) the intervention of the Father into the affairs of the world and (b) the Gnostics.

B. Elements of Comparison

(1) [Rhetorical structure] he who, when the sheep which he found fell, labored, having brought it up ≅ τίς ἔσται, ὃς ἕξει πρόβατον, καὶ ἐὰν ἐμπέσῃ, οὐχὶ κρατήσει, ἐγερεῖ —Valentinus has changed Matt's generalization into a specific description of someone's activity. This change accounts for differences of tense, mood, and clause subordination.

The Father is	τίς ἔσται ἐξ ὑμῶν
he who	ἄνθρωπος ὃς
	ἕξει πρόβατον ἓν
when	καὶ ἐάν
the sheep which he found	(cf. πρόβατον)

(2) the Father, he ≅ ἄνθρωπος —Valentinus has identified the subject of Matt's generalization as the Father.

(3) the sheep which he found ≅ πρόβατον —The added phrase, "the ... which he found," cross refers to the finding of a lost sheep mentioned in the preceding passage (No. 47). Thus, Valentinus identifies the sheep as the one known to his readers from that passage.

fell	ἐμπέσῃ τοῦτο
into the pit	(cf. εἰς βόθυνον)
even on the Sabbath	τοῖς σάββασιν
	εἰς βόθυνον
labored over it.	οὐχὶ κρατήσει αὐτὸ

Commentaries

He gave life to the sheep,
having brought it up
from the pit.

καὶ ἐγερεῖ

(4) fell ≅ ἐμπέσῃ —see (1).

(5) into the pit ≅ εἰς βόθυνον —The definite article in GTr refers to "the (well-known)" pit mentioned in Matt 12:11, the source of this passage. Valentinus by now assumes that his reader has recognized this source.

(6) on the Sabbath = τοῖς σάββασιν —verbatim. Use of the plural (by Matt) is idiomatic in Greek. Since Coptic idiom requires a singular, nothing prevents us from assuming that the Greek model of GTr here had the plural.

(7) labored over it ≅ κρατήσει —Valentinus uses a vaguer expression for the Father's personal care for the sheep than does Matt, perhaps to prepare for his allegorization of the text (see D).

(8) having brought it up ≅ ἐγερεῖ —verbatim, except for the difference dictated by rhetorical structure. The verb ἐγείρειν can refer to resurrection and enters into the allegorization of the parable (see D).

C. *Evaluation of the Parallel*

The contexts of the two passages are utterly different. Matt is a healing and legal controversy, and GTr is allegory *per se*. Yet, five of the elements of comparison are verbatim or nearly so, and the order of presentation is almost identical. The inexact elements of comparison (2, 7), introduce interpretive material (Father, labored). The use of Matt here is all the more probable because Valentinus knows and uses Matt elsewhere (e.g., No. 47).

D. *Interpretation*

By introducing the Father as the one who brings the sheep up from the pit, Valentinus sets in motion an allegory of the passage in Matt. He even explicitly refers to his allegorical intent in 32:22-23 ("understand the interior meaning"). Perhaps because of the plural form of "Sabbath" in Greek, Valentinus provides two resolutions of Sabbath, i.e., alternative or superimposed hyponoias. "Sabbath" is interpreted as the day on which salvation must not be idle, that is, the day on which the normally inactive Father intervened in the affairs of the world by means of the incarnation of the Son, who brought knowledge of the Father to humanity. Moreover, the readers (those who have knowledge of the Father = the Gnostics) *are* that day ("Sabbath" taken as a plural, σάββασιν).

Other details of the implied allegory are unstated and have to be surmised by the reader. The sheep must represent the Gnostics, collectively. Jesus must be identified with the Father as the one who brought the sheep up from the pit; here, as often in GTr, the roles of Jesus and the Father cannot be entirely separated. The pit must represent this world or, on the epistemological plane of which this text mainly speaks, the ignorance in which most people live. Valentinus adds that the Father "gave life" (perhaps ζῳοποιεῖν) to the sheep, which may refer to the imparting of knowledge, since in GTr (No. 3) life is interpreted as "light," which further signifies knowledge. "Having brought it up" may refer to the resurrection, which may be interpreted as a realized event or present reality for the Gnostic.

These details of the allegory are not stated in the text, but in any event, this interpretation of Matt 12:11 sets forth Valentinus' understanding of the magnitude of an event which would induce the Father to intervene in human affairs. Just as Jesus says in Matt that healing a person is more important than observing the Sabbath, so too Valentinus interprets the incarnation as the impassive Father's statement that saving humanity is more important than remaining unknowable.

49. GTr 32:26-28 (A²) ∼ Rev 21:25

Postulated by Grobel, p. 137, nn. 370-371. Possible.

You should speak from the higher day, this one which does not have night.	(ἡ πόλις ἡ ἁγία ᾽Ιερουσαλήμ) ²⁵καὶ οἱ πυλῶνες αὐτῆς οὐ μὴ κλεισθῶσιν ἡμέρας, νὺξ γὰρ οὐκ ἔσται ἐκεῖ

²⁶ⲉⲣⲉⲧⲛ̅ϣⲉϫⲉ ⲁⲃⲁⲗ ²⁷ϩⲛ̅ ⲡⲓϩⲟⲟⲩ ⲉⲧⲛ̅ϩⲣⲏⲉⲓ ⲡⲉⲉⲓ ²⁸ⲉⲧⲉ ⲙⲛ̅ⲧⲉϥ ⲟⲩϣⲏ ⲙ̅ⲙⲉⲩ

Commentaries   127

A. Context

Rev 21:23-27 (new Jerusalem). John's vision of the new Jerusalem is a symbolic interpretation of the renewal of creation. When this occurs (at the end of days), there will be an eternal day; there will no longer be night. The eternal day will need no sun or other luminary.

GTr 32:22-39 (the higher Sabbath). "Sabbath" is understood allegorically. The higher day is an eternal day. The readers are then identified as the perfect day and as the dwelling place of the eternal luminary.

B. Element of Comparison

| the higher day, this one which does not have night | μὴ κλεισθῶσιν ἡμέρας, νὺξ γὰρ οὐκ ἔσται ἐκεῖ |

does not have night ≅ νὺξ γὰρ οὐκ ἔσται ἐκεῖ —The word "night" occurs in both passages; the wording of the rest of the phrase is nearly exact, once one accounts for John the Seer's future tense as required by the literary conventions of a vision. The notion of an eternal day occurs also in IV Ezra 2:35 and may be implied in Isa 60:19.[68]

C. Evaluation of the Parallel

Both passages use similar imagery in contexts that obviously lend themselves to symbolic or allegorical interpretation, but the contexts themselves are not obviously similar. Furthermore, there is only one nearly verbatim element of comparison; it is a single phrase about the eternal day, and this idea occurs elsewhere in literature of the period. These limitations of evidence might cast doubt upon use of Rev here. Nevertheless, Valentinus knows and uses Rev in other parts of GTr (see Nos. 9, 10), and thus his use of it is possible here as well.

D. Interpretation

If Valentinus has used Rev 21:25, by "the higher day" he may understand the new Jerusalem of Rev, a symbolic representation of the situation after the end of days. Valentinus may have understood this situation as

---
[68] See Malinine et al., p. 57 for other references (most later than GTr).

already present for those who possess interior understanding. Thus, some of the vivid imagery used in Rev to describe the new Jerusalem or renewal of creation would be used here to describe one who can understand scripture allegorically. The readers themselves are said to be the "higher" or perfect day, in which an everlasting light dwells. The eternal light that they possess is undoubtedly the knowledge of the Father which was brought by Jesus; this is suggested by the preceding passage (No. 48), an interpretation of the illustration of the sheep that fell into a pit.

50. GTr 33:4-5 (A²) ~ Matt 11:28

Identified by Grobel, p. 141, n. 380. Probable.

And as for those who labor, give them rest.	²⁸Δεῦτε πρός με (scil. 'Ιησοῦς) πάντες οἱ κοπιῶντες καὶ πεφορτισμένοι, κἀγὼ ἀναπαύσω ὑμᾶς.

⁴ⲁⲩⲱ ⲛⲉⲧⲁⲗ⁵ⲥⲓ ⲛ̄ⲧⲉⲧⲛ̄ϯ ⲙ̄ⲧⲁⲛ ⲛ̄ⲛⲉⲩ

A. Context

Matt 11:28-30 (invitation to rest). In these verses, which are peculiar to Matt, Jesus alludes to the "yoke" of the Jewish Law and contrasts that yoke, which is burdensome, with his own yoke (discipleship), which is not burdensome. He beckons all those who are burdened thus to come to him, i.e., to follow him, in order to receive rest (salvation).

GTr 33:1-9 (allegorical paraenesis). In these lines, which are meant allegorically as Valentinus has indicated in GTr 32:26-27, the readers are exhorted to perform certain actions which will benefit others.[69] Among

---

[69] The hypothesis is given as the first item in the paraenesis (32:35-37): "Speak of the truth with those who seek after it and about knowledge to those who have sinned in their error."

Commentaries 129

these are giving rest to persons who labor, that is (presumably), providing knowledge to those who seek it so that they might be a part of the Father.

B. *Elements of Comparison*

(1) [Rhetorical structure] and as for, give ≅ Δεῦτε πρός με, κἀγὼ ἀναπαύσω —Valentinus' alteration of the form of the passage from an invitation of Jesus to an exhortation to the readers of GTr occasions changes in tense and mood.

And	Δεῦτε
as for	πρός με (scil. ' Ιησοῦς)
those who labor	πάντες οἱ κοπιῶντες
	καὶ πεφορτισμένοι
give them rest.	κἀγὼ ἀναπαύσω ὑμᾶς

(2) those who labor ≅ πάντες οἱ κοπιῶντες —GTr omits Matt's "all."

(3) give them rest ≅ κἀγὼ ἀναπαύσω ὑμᾶς —The change in rhetorical structure provides a shift in focus: the reader is exhorted to give rest to those who labor. The notion of "rest" (ἀναπαύω, καταπαύω, and their cognate nouns) is a commonplace metaphor in early Christian literature (e.g., Matt 12:43; Heb 3:11, 18; 4:1, 3, 5; Rev 6:11; 14:13; GTh 90; 2 Clem 5:5) and can refer to the Sabbath rest, especially as interpreted to mean an eschatological rest (Heb 4).[70]

C. *Evaluation of the Parallel*

The contexts are quite different, but, once the changes in rhetorical structure are taken into account, the passage in GTr is quite similar to that in Matt. Two elements of comparison (2, 3) are nearly verbatim, and they appear in the same order in both passages. Although there is nothing particularly distinctive about the elements of comparison taken individually, their occurrence together in both GTr and Matt increases the likelihood that Valentinus used Matt here, just as he often uses it in this central section of GTr (e.g. Nos. 47, 48).

---

[70] In GTr 37:7-8, "rest" is equated with knowledge of the Father.

D. Interpretation

The readers of GTr have just been exhorted to "speak from the perspective of the higher day" (32:26-27; see No. 49), which means that they are to understand allegorically the exhortations which follow. Valentinus instructs his readers to perform actions which Jesus also performed while on earth, such as helping the sick and feeding the hungry. In so doing, Valentinus employs a saying of Jesus that would apparently have been recognized as such, namely, the invitation to rest. The readers would then understand that, just as Jesus beckoned those who labored to come to him and rest, so too they are to beckon those who labor and give them rest. The readers are instructed to imitate Jesus, but not Jesus as Matt portrays him—rather, Jesus as understood by the readers of GTr, as the one who has brought knowledge of the Father. Thus, the interior understanding of the passage is that the readers must themselves impart knowledge of the Father unto others. This will give others rest, or metaphorically, true Sabbath rest (see No. 48).

51. GTr 33:5-8 (A²) ~ Eph 5:14

Postulated, with hesitation, by Malinine et al., p. 11 supp. Dubious.

And awaken those who wish to arise and wake up those who sleep	¹⁴. . . διὸ λέγει· ἔγειρε, ὁ καθεύδων, καὶ ἀνάστα ἐκ τῶν νεκρῶν, καὶ ἐπιφαύσει σοι ὁ Χριστός.

---

⁵ⲚⲦⲈ⁶ⲦⲚⲦⲞⲨⲚⲈⲤ ⲚⲈⲈⲒ ⲈⲦⲞⲨⲰϢⲈ Ⲁ⁷ⲦⲰⲰⲚ ⲚⲦⲈⲦⲚⲚⲈϨⲤⲈ ⲚⲚⲈⲦⲚ⁸ⲔⲀⲦⲔⲈ·

A. Context

Eph 5:11-14 (paraenesis). Ps-Paul exhorts his readers not to act like those who are unconverted but instead to expose the evil deeds of the unconverted so that they will be apparent to all. Christ imparts a spiritual reawakening to those who are evil.

GTr 33:1-9 (paraenesis). Valentinus exhorts his readers to convert others, that is, to bring them from ignorance to knowledge. This is a spiritual reawakening, which is likened to awaking from sleep.

B. Elements of Comparison

(1) [Rhetorical structure] awaken, to arise ≅ ἔγειρε, καὶ ἀνάστα —Even though Eph 5:14 occurs within a paraenetic context, the verse is apparently an excerpt from a hymn or poem. The strophic arrangement of Eph 5:14 is absent in GTr: there is no indication that these lines are from a hymn; they simply continue the exhortations begun in 32:26.

| and awaken those | ἔγειρε, ὁ καθεύδων |

(2) awaken ≅ ἔγειρε —The Greek verb (and its Coptic representation) here could refer to resurrection. Eph almost certainly alludes to the resurrection from the dead as a figure of moral improvement by those who are evil. GTr here uses "awaken" as a figure of intellectual activation in those who "slumber" in ignorance.

| those who wish to arise | καὶ ἀνάστα |

(3) to arise ≅ ἀνάστα —Again, the Greek verb (and its Coptic representation) could refer to resurrection. Each is to be taken figuratively as in (2).

C. Evaluation of the Parallel

Although both references occur in paraenetic contexts, the strophic form of Eph is quite different from the paraenetic form of GTr. The two elements of comparison (2, 3) that are nearly exact are single items of vocabulary and, even in their figurative sense, are utter commonplaces.[71] The two passages share nothing more than a common terminology for spiritual renewal, which Valentinus need not have taken from Eph 5:14. The postulation of this source is therefore dubious.

---

[71] See BAG, s.v. for numerous references.

52. GTr 33:16-18 (A²) ~ Matt 6:19

Identified by Malinine et al., p. 12 (supp.). Probable.

Do not	¹⁹Μὴ θησαυρίζετε ὑμῖν
be moth-eaten,	θησαυροὺς ἐπὶ τῆς γῆς,
do not be worm-eaten	ὅπου σὴς
	καὶ βρῶσις ἀφανίζει καὶ
	ὅπου κλέπται διορύσσουσιν
because you (pl.) have already	καὶ κλέπτουσιν·
cast it (earthly treasure?) off.	

¹⁶ⲘⲠⲢ̄Ⲣ̄ ⲬⲀⲀⲈⲤ ¹⁷ⲘⲠⲢ̄Ⲣ̄ ϤⲚⲦ ⲬⲈ ⲀⲦⲈⲦⲚ̄ⲞⲨⲰ ¹⁸ⲈⲢⲈⲦⲚ̄ⲚⲞⲨⲌⲈ ⲘⲘⲀϤ ⲀⲂⲀⲖ

A. Context

Matt 6:19-21 (Sermon on the Mount). Jesus exhorts his disciples not to hoard their wealth because it is vulnerable to theft or even corruption by natural means, such as insects. One's true wealth is shown by what the heart contains, e.g., either spiritual thoughts or thoughts of material wealth.

GTr 33:11-12 (paraenesis). In a series of exhortations directed toward the spiritual state of his readers (perhaps as part of a community), Valentinus urges his readers themselves not to become the object of earthly influence. Earthly concerns are to be of no regard to them.

B. Elements of Comparison

(1) [Rhetorical structure] do not be moth-eaten, worm-eaten ≅ Μὴ θησαυρίζετε ὑμῖν, ὅπου σὴς καὶ βρῶσις ἀφανίζει —Both passages take the form of a command or exhortation, but Valentinus has changed the rhetorical structure slightly so that the readers become the objects of potential corruption.

... moth-eaten,	ὅπου σὴς
do not be worm-eaten	καὶ βρῶσις ἀφανίζει

Commentaries   133

(2) moth = σής —verbatim.

(3) worm = βρῶσις —verbatim. The meaning of βρῶσις is uncertain. It seems originally to have meant "meat," but in this period it may be a general term for "decay" (e.g., Galen 6, 422; 12, 879). Other possible meanings are "rust" and "worm" (as the LXX [cod. A] renders the verb אָכַל in Mal 3:11), but the Coptic translator of the passage, in making the connection with Matt 6:19, clearly thought the meaning was "worm" since that is the usual translation of the Coptic [ϥⲚⲦ] (so also GTh 76).[72]

(4) (moth-)eaten, (worm-)eaten ≅ ἀφανίζει —Both expressions have to do with corruption.

C. Evaluation of the Parallel

The two passages occur in similar contexts (hortatory or paraenetic) and have similar rhetorical structures (negative commands). The lexical elements of comparison are verbatim or nearly so. Moreover, the imagery is relatively rare, and it occurs in a strong and probably well-known passage in Matt. Valentinus uses Matt elsewhere (e.g., Nos. 47, 48), probably including the Sermon on the Mount (e.g., No. 38), and his use of Matt here is thus all the more likely.

D. Interpretation

Valentinus' alteration of the rhetorical structure alters the reader's relationship to the biblical pericope: it focuses the danger of corruption upon the readers rather than upon their material wealth and thus converts the images of "moth" and "rust" to allegory. Here the readers are commanded not to become moth-eaten or worm-eaten, that is, not to become prey to earthly influence. Valentinus gives an intriguing justification to this command: "because you (pl.) have already cast it off." The antecedent of "it" (or "him")[73] is obscure. It is possible that, as in No. 48, the reader is expected to have recognized the biblical source (Matt 6:19) and perhaps also is expected to supply an antecedent from there. In this case, "it"

---

[72]See Grobel, pp. 143, 145, nn. 391, 392 for a more complete discussion; he thinks the passage alludes to Luke 12:33, even though "worm" is not used there.
[73]If indeed the manuscript should not be emended to "them."

could refer to the moth, worm, or even earthly treasure of the biblical pericope. In any case, "it" must refer to the origin of the corruption (possibly even a real person ["him"] who is now outside of Valentinus' community).

53. GTr 33:19-21 (A²) ～ Eph 4:27

Identified by Grobel, p. 145, n. 396. Probable.

| Do not become a place (τόπος) of the devil (διάβολος) because you have already brought him to naught. | ²⁷μηδὲ δίδοτε τόπον τῷ διαβόλῳ |

---

¹⁹ⲘⲠⲢⲰⲰⲚⲈ ⲈⲢⲈⲦⲚⲞⲈⲒ ⲚⲦⲞ²⁰ⲠⲞⲤ ⲘⲠⲆⲒⲀⲂⲞⲖⲞⲤ ϪⲈ ⲀⲦⲈ²¹ⲦⲚⲞⲨⲰ ⲈⲢⲈⲦⲚⲞⲨⲰⲤϤ ⲘⲘⲀϤ

A. Context

Eph 4:25-27 (paraenesis). Because the Christian community is to be close-knit, ps-Paul urges his readers to tell the truth, not to remain angry for long periods of time, and not to give evil (literally, the devil) a chance to work among them.

GTr 33:11-32 (paraenesis). Moving the paraenesis now away from the readers' treatment of others and turning to their own condition, Valentinus urges them not to concentrate on those whom they have rejected lest they become a place where evil (ignorance; literally, the devil) can be active, for it has already been vanquished.

B. Elements of Comparison

(1) [Rhetorical structure] do not become ≅ μηδὲ δίδοτε —As in No. 52, both passages take the form of an admonition.

Do not become | μηδὲ δίδοτε
a place (τόπος) | τόπον
of the devil (διάβολος) | τῷ διαβόλῳ

(2) become ≅ δίδοτε —δίδωμι is often used in Greek with τόπος to mean, "give opportunity" (+ dat., "to"). With the verb "become," τόπος in GTr probably means "place" (although it is just possible that the Greek idiom translated here meant "become an opportunity for").

(3) place = τόπον —verbatim. Cf. (2).

(4) of the devil ≅ τῷ διαβόλῳ —GTr may possibly be translated "for the devil" (cf. [2]). If not, these expressions are identical except for a difference of grammatical case dictated by the choice of verb.

C. Evaluation of the Parallel

The contexts of both passages are similar, as are their rhetorical structures. At least two elements of comparison are verbatim or nearly so, and a third (2) may be so. Now, an admonition similar to that of Eph and GTr occurs in 1 Tim 5:14 and (attributed to Jesus) in Ps-Clementine *Hom.* XIX. 2.[74] Research on the background of the admonition has suggested that it originated in a Jewish context and may have become traditional in early Christianity.[75] Only in Eph and GTr, however, are both τόπος and διάβολος used. Thus, Valentinus is likely to have gotten the admonition from Eph 4:27, and not from another known source.

D. Interpretation

The meaning of the admonition is much the same in both passages. The readers are instructed not to allow evil (the devil) to work among them as members of a Christian community. Valentinus adds an explanatory phrase, however: "because you (pl.) have already brought him to naught." This indicates that evil has already been vanquished and precludes any notion of an eschatological triumph of good over evil. It is therefore

---

[74] 1 Tim 5:14: μηδεμίαν ἀφορμὴν διδόναι τῷ ἀντικειμένῳ λοιδορίας χάριν; ps-Clementine *Hom.* XIX.2: μὴ δότε πρόφασιν τῷ πονηρῷ.
[75] See W. D. Stroker, *The Formation of Secondary Sayings of Jesus* (Ph.D. dissertation, Yale, 1970), pp. 61-63.

136   Biblical Interpretation in the Gospel of Truth

questionable whether "devil" is to be taken literally (as Satan), especially since the word is not used elsewhere in GTr and since the problem of evil is usually discussed within the context of error and ignorance of the Father in GTr. More likely, the appearance of the word "devil" in GTr is due to its presence in the passage of Eph which here underlies GTr.[76]

54. GTr 33:37-39 (A²) ~ Matt 7:16 = Matt 7:20

Identified by Grobel, p. 149, n. 416. Probable.

For (γάρ) by the fruits	¹⁶ἀπὸ τῶν καρπῶν
	αὐτῶν
those who are yours (pl.) are known.	ἐπιγνώσεσθε αὐτούς.

³⁷ⲀⲂⲀⲖ ⲄⲀⲢ ⲌⲚ ⲚⲒ³⁸ⲞⲨⲦⲰⲰⲈ· ϢⲀⲨϪⲒ ⲤⲀⲨⲚⲈ ⲀⲚⲈ³⁹ⲦⲈ ⲚⲞⲨⲦⲚ̄ ⲚⲈ

A. Context

Matt 7:15-20 (Sermon on Mount). Matt attempts to strengthen his community's self-identity by giving as words of Jesus an admonition about false prophets. These are recognized by the results their prophecy brings and not by their outward appearance.

GTr 33:33-34:3 (the Father). Valentinus explains to his readers that the Father is able to recognize those whom he has called by their deeds or condition. Those who are called exude the Father's goodness and sweetness.

B. Elements of Comparison

for by the fruits	ἀπὸ τῶν καρπῶν
	αὐτῶν

---

[76]It might also allude to someone who had been ostracized by Valentinus' community.

Commentaries 137

those who are yours (pl.)
are known. | ἐπιγινώσεσθε αὐτούς

(1) by the fruits ≅ ἀπὸ τῶν καρπῶν αὐτῶν —nearly verbatim. Valentinus apparently deletes Matt's αὐτῶν (if indeed this difference is not entirely a feature of the Coptic translation). In both passages, "fruits" figuratively refers to one's actions and their results (Matt's elaboration of the points with various kinds of trees and the fruits produced by them may have been the original setting of the saying[77] but is not retained by Valentinus). This use was extremely common in literature of the period, even proverbial (Proverbia Aesopi 51 P., Δῆλος ἔλεγχος ὁ καρπὸς γενήσεται Παντὸς δένδρου ἣν ἔχει φύσιν).

(2) those who are yours ≠ αὐτούς —Matt is concerned with how one distinguishes members of the community, insiders, from outsiders. Valentinus focuses on the interior life of his own community of *electi* and is not concerned here with outsiders at all.

(3) are known ≅ ἐπιγνώσεσθε —The shift to the passive may result in ambiguity regarding the agent of "know," which could be the Father or the fellow *electi*. Apparently the latter are those whom the Father knows, although the *electi* may also recognize that they are among those called.

C. *Evaluation of the Parallel*

The contexts of the two passages are different, but the passage in GTr looks much like it has been reshaped from Matt. Of the three elements of comparison, one (1) is nearly verbatim, and the other two involve possible alterations in the grammar. Despite the proverbial ring of the passage in both Matt and GTr, it seems that Matt himself was the first to omit the reference to "trees" (found in Aesop's version) in constructing the saying. Since Valentinus knows and uses Matt, it is more likely that he has taken the saying from Matt in the form which does not refer to trees and then

---

[77]This is apparently the consensus of scholarship. See, for example, D. Hill, *The Gospel of Matthew*, p. 151. To be more precise, the form in 12:33, which is similar to Luke 6:44, is considered to be closer to the original saying; Matt is then considered to have constructed the admonition about "fruits" in 7:16, 20 by omitting the reference to "tree."

interpreted it than that he took a proverb, omitted the reference to trees, and then changed the grammatical structure.

D. Interpretation

Valentinus clearly uses "fruits" in a figurative sense to refer to the results of one's actions. If the readers are still to understand that this has "interior" meaning, as stated in 32:22-23, then the actions of those who are within the community or who are "children of the Father" have certain results which enable them to be recognized by the Father. These results are characteristics which are integrally related to the Father himself, such as sweetness and goodness. In this way, the children of the Father can be seen as his "fragrance" (see No. 55).

55. GTr 34:3-5 (S A²) ~ 2 Cor 2:14

Identified by Grobel, p. 149, n. 418. Probable.

Therefore the Father loves his fragrance and manifests it everywhere	¹⁴Τῷ δὲ θεῷ χάρις τῷ πάντοτε θριαμβεύοντι ἡμᾶς ἐν τῷ Χριστῷ (cf. τῷ θεῷ above) καὶ τὴν ὀσμὴν τῆς γνώσεως αὐτοῦ (cf. τὴν ὀσμὴν above) φανεροῦντι [sc. τῷ Χριστῷ] δι' ἡμῶν ἐν παντὶ τόπῳ

Subachmimic text ³ⲉⲧⲃⲉ ⲡⲉⲉⲓ ⲡⲓⲱⲧ ⲙⲁⲓⲉ ⁴ⲙ̄ⲡⲉϥⲥⲧⲁⲉⲓ ⲁⲩⲱ ϥⲟⲩⲱⲛϩ̄
ⲙ̄ⲙⲁϥ ⁵ⲁⲃⲁⲗ 2ⲙ̄ ⲙⲁ ⲛⲓⲙ
Sahidic fragment ¹[   ] 2ⲙ̄ ⲙⲁ ⲛ[ⲓⲙ

A. Context

2 Cor 2:14-16 (the fragrance of God). Knowledge of God is like a

Commentaries   139

fragrance which spreads everywhere by means of Christ through Paul (and his fellow workers), both to those who are being saved and to those who are not.

GTr 33:37-34:5 (the fragrance of the Father). The children of the Father are like his fragrance because they originate in him by whom it is also spread everywhere.

B. Elements of Comparison

Therefore the Father loves	Τῷ δὲ θεῷ χάρις . . . (cf. τῷ θεῷ above)
his	καὶ τὴν ὀσμὴν τῆς γνώσεως αὐτοῦ
fragrance	(cf. τὴν ὀσμήν above)

(1) the Father ≅ τῷ . . . θεῷ —Valentinus has made a typical change from "God" to "Father."

(2) his fragrance ≅ τὴν ὀσμὴν τῆς γνώσεως αὐτοῦ —Paul speaks of the fragrance of God's knowledge (not clear whether "God's" is a subjective or objective genitive), whereas Valentinus speaks of the Father's fragrance outright. He may have resolved the ambiguity of the genitive by omitting the explicit reference to "knowledge," although "knowledge" is surely implicit in what Valentinus means by fragrance (see D). "Fragrance" is a common motif in religious literature of the time. For example, Ode of Solomon 11:15 speaks of the "pleasant fragrance of the Lord."[78] ThCont 144:19-21 (which may be later than GTr) speaks of the fragrance imparted by the sun and moon, and in the later Manichean *Psalm-Book*, Thomas is identified with a fragrance. "Fragrance" occurs in a parallel construction with "light," and the two should probably be identified (194:3; 214:28-215:4).[79]

---

[78] J. H. Charlesworth, *The Odes of Solomon* (Missoula: Scholars, 1977) notes this on pp. 52, 56 n. 27 and also draws attention to 1 Enoch 24:1-6.

[79] J. D. Turner, *The Book of Thomas the Contender* (Missoula: Scholars Press, 1975) pp. 183-184, discusses the term "fragrance" as a metaphor of salvation. He draws attention to the passages in 2 Cor and GTr as well as to those in the Manichean *Psalm-Book* and ThCont.

and manifests it	φανεροῦντι
everywhere	δι' ὑμῶν
	ἐν παντὶ τόπῳ

(3) manifests = φανεροῦντι —verbatim. In both passages, the deity manifests the fragrance.

(4) everywhere = ἐν παντὶ τόπῳ —verbatim.

C. *Evaluation of the Parallel*

The contexts are not altogether different, and the similarity of the elements of comparison is quite close. Of the four elements of comparison, two are verbatim (3, 4) and the other two nearly so, especially if one takes account of typical changes made by Valentinus. The imagery of "fragrance," however, is relatively common. Reference to the fragrance of God or the Father is more distinctive but is still not unique. In view of the widespread use of the image as a metaphor of salvation, one cannot be certain that 2 Cor is the source, especially since Valentinus' use of 2 Cor is infrequent.

D. *Interpretation*

Valentinus has apparently identified Paul's reference to the fragrance of God's knowledge with the Father's fragrance itself. The latter, however, is surely knowledge of the Father. The children of the Father are considered to be the Father's fragrance because they have knowledge of the Father. The children of the Father are not the Father's fragrance because of their response to the gospel, as in Paul, but because they originate in him (34:2-3). After this passage, the motif of the Father's fragrance is developed in a long section, which apparently bears no further relationship to 2 Cor.

56. GTr 34:19-19 (S A^2) ∼ Gen 2:7

Postulated by Williams. Possible. An alternative to No. 57.

^{7}καὶ ἔπλασεν ὁ θεὸς
τὸν ἄνθρωπον χοῦν
ἀπὸ τῆς γῆς . . . καὶ

Commentaries 141

And it (the fragrance) is
a soul-endowed (ψυχικόν)
modeled form (πλάσμα)

ἐγένετο ὁ ἄνθρωπος
εἰς ψυχὴν ζῶσαν
(cf. ἔπλασεν above)

Subachmimic text ¹⁸ⲟⲩⲉⲉⲓ2ⲛⲛ ⲟⲩⲡⲗⲁⲥⲙⲁ ¹⁹ⲙ̄ⲯⲩⲭⲓⲕⲟⲛ ⲡⲉ
Sahidic fragment ¹³[ ] ⲯⲩⲭⲓⲕⲟⲛ ⲙ̄[ⲡⲗⲁⲥⲙⲁ

A. *Context*

Gen 2:4b-7 (creation and condition of the first human being). When God made heaven and earth, he also formed a human being out of dust and breathed into him the life-principle.

GTr 34:5-26 (the divine constituent of human beings). The Father's "fragrance" (i.e., the life-principle) mixes with matter, and the spirit is the intermediary by which the life-principle once again returns to its origin in the Father. The combination of life-principle with matter is a human being, although the life-principle is not apparent, just as one cannot see the water in mud.

B. *Elements of Comparison*

it (the fragrance) is
a soul-endowed (ψυχικόν)
modeled form (πλάσμα)

καὶ ἔπλασεν ὁ θεὸς
τὸν ἄνθρωπον χοῦν
ἀπὸ τῆς γῆς . . . καὶ
ἐγένετο ὁ ἄνθρωπος
εἰς ψυχὴν ζῶσαν
(cf. ἔπλασεν above)

(1) it is ≅ ἐγένετο ὁ ἄνθρωπος —The two expressions are similar, but the use of "became" (following ἔπλασεν earlier) in Gen underlines God's direct role in the formation of the human being. The Father's role in the formation of the human being in GTr is more indirect. He is said to manifest his aroma everywhere, but Valentinus does not say that the Father directly mixes the aroma with the matter.

(2) a soul-endowed (ψυχικόν) modeled form ≅ εἰς ψυχὴν ζῶσαν

—Ψυχή in Gen means that which possesses life (or a soul), whereas ψυχικόν in GTr means something pertaining to life (or the soul).[80]

(3) modeled form (πλάσμα) ≅ ἔπλασεν, εἰς ψυχὴν ζῶσαν —Ἔπλασεν in Gen refers to the action of forming the human being, whereas πλάσμα in GTr refers to the result of that act, which is expressed by ψυχὴν ζῶσαν in Gen. Πλάσμα and the verb πλάσσειν distinctly refer to Gen 2. In Philo, for example, this is nearly always the case. In *De Opif. Mundi* 134, he quotes Gen 2:7 and says that the human being formed by God here refers to an object of sense perception with body and soul, i.e., a real person, whereas the human being mentioned in Gen 1:26 referred to an idea or type, an object of thought, which is incorporeal.

C. Evaluation of the Parallel

The contexts are similar in that both refer to the constitution of the first human being, but this is expressed in a very different fashion in each passage. None of the three elements of comparison is exact (although in two [2, 3] of them the Coptic preserves Greek words that are related to the Greek of Gen). Valentinus' use of Gen is possible but perhaps no more possible than his use of 1 Cor in No. 57 since Paul himself quotes Gen. The use of πλάσμα in particular increases the likelihood that Valentinus refers to Gen in some form.

D. Interpretation

If Valentinus has interpreted Gen 2:7, he has understood the ψυχή of the first human being to be the fragrance of the Father. Without the Father's fragrance, presumably the first human being would be nothing more than a lump of clay that has been shaped into a form with arms, legs, and so forth. In 34:26 he mentions "fragrances" in the plural, and so Valentinus may take the first human being, who was endowed with the life-principle, as a type of those later persons who would be endowed with the Father's fragrance and hence have knowledge of the Father (or as a type of the one who brought knowledge of the Father, i.e., Christ).[81]

---

[80] For references see BAG, s.v.
[81] For this, cf. No. 57.

Commentaries 143

57. GTr 34:18-19 (S A²) ~ 1 Cor 15:45

Postulated by Grobel, p. 153, n. 437. Possible. An alternative to No. 56.

And it (the fragrance) is a soul-endowed (ψυχικόν) modeled form (πλάσμα)	⁴⁵οὕτως καὶ γέγραπται· ἐγένετο ὁ πρῶτος ἄνθρωπος ᾽Αδαμ εἰς ψυχὴν ζῶσαν ὁ ἔσχατος ᾽Αδαμ εἰς πνεῦμα ζῳοποιοῦν.

Subachmimic text ¹⁸ⲞⲨⲈⲈⲒ2ⲚⲚ ⲞⲨⲠⲖⲀⲤⲘⲀ ¹⁹ⲘⲮⲨⲬⲒⲔⲞⲚ ⲠⲈ
Sahidic fragment ¹³[   ] ⲮⲨⲬⲒⲔⲞⲚ Ⲙ̄[ⲠⲖⲀⲤⲘⲀ

A. Context

1 Cor 15:42-50 (resurrection of the dead). In his contrast of the earthly and the resurrection states, Paul contrasts the present physical body with a future spiritual body. He quotes a version of Gen 2:7 in order to make an exegetical type of Christ. Just as the first Adam initiated the physical life, so the "last Adam" (Christ) has initiated the spiritual life. The first Adam was earthly; the last Adam is heavenly. Christians as mortal are like the first Adam but in the resurrection will be like the last Adam.

GTr 34:5-26 (the divine constituent of human beings). The Father's "fragrance" (i.e., the life-principle) mixes with matter, and the spirit is the intermediary by which the life-principle once again returns to its origin in the Father. The combination of life-principle with matter is a human being, although the life-principle is not apparent, just as one cannot see the water in mud.

B. Elements of Comparison

it (the fragrance) is a soul-endowed (ψυχικόν) modeled form (πλάσμα)	ἐγένετο ὁ πρῶτος ἄνθρωπος ᾽Αδαμ εἰς ψυχὴν ζῶσαν

(1) it is ≅ ἐγένετο ὁ πρῶτος ἄνθρωπος —The two expressions are similar, but, even though the word "became" occurs in 1 Cor, there is no reference to πλάσσειν (as Gen 2:7; cf. No. 56). Consequently, there is no explicit reference to the craftsman in either passage. "Became" implies that a process of formation did occur, whereas GTr is merely descriptive.

(2) a soul-endowed (ψυχικόν) modeled form (πλάσμα) ≅ εἰς ψυχὴν ζῶσαν —Ψυχή in Gen means that which possesses life (or a soul), whereas ψυχικόν in GTr means something pertaining to life (or the soul). There is no reference to πλάσσειν or πλάσμα in 1 Cor.

C. Evaluation of the Parallel

The contexts are similar in that both refer to the constitution of the first human being, but the similarities in context end there. Neither of the two elements of comparison is exact (although in one of them [2] the Coptic preserves two Greek words, one of which is related to the Greek of 1 Cor). Because Valentinus uses this section of 1 Cor elsewhere (No. 16), his use of 1 Cor is possible here (even though Paul does not refer to πλάσμα).

D. Interpretation

If Valentinus has used 1 Cor, he may also have retained an allusion to Paul's comparison of the first Adam with the last Adam, especially since Valentinus may establish an Adam-Christ typology in No. 4. The passage seems more likely to refer to one person as a prototype for all people (34:26), but the crucial step, that of comparing the first Adam with Christ, is only implicit at best. Paul's reference to ψυχή would in any event be interpreted as the divine constituent of human beings, the "true" life-principle.

58. GTr 35:5-6 (S A²) ∼ 1 John 1:5

Identified by Grobel, p. 157, n. 457. Probable.

(their likeness)	⁵(ὁ θεός)
the l̲i̲g̲h̲t̲	φῶς ἐστιν
i̲n̲ w̲h̲i̲c̲h̲	καὶ (cf. ἐ̲ν̲ α̲ὐ̲τ̲ῷ̲)
	σκοτία ἐν αὐτῷ

Commentaries 145

there is no | οὐκ ἔστιν οὐδεμία
shadow | (cf. σκοτία)

Subachmimic text ⁵ποyοein ετε μν̄ 2λειβες ⁶ν̄2ητϥ
Sahidic fragment ¹ποyϳοein πλϊετε

A. *Context*

1 John 1:5-7 (God is light). The author of 1 John strives to reinforce his community's strength and identity by urging them to be like God, who is pure. In so doing, he uses the imagery of light and darkness and stresses that cleansing from sin comes through Jesus' death.

GTr 34:34-35:8 (discovery of the fullness). Valentinus expounds to his readers what the fullness (of deity) means. In so doing, he uses the imagery of light and further identifies it with salvation, hope, and their (his readers') likeness.

B. *Elements of Comparison*

the light	φῶς ἐστιν
in which	καὶ (cf. ἐν αὐτῷ)
	σκοτία ἐν αὐτῷ
there is no	οὐκ ἔστιν οὐδεμία
shadow	(cf. σκοτία)

(1) light = φῶς —verbatim; a commonplace as associated with the divine and a characteristic image of the Johannine school.

(2) in which ≅ καὶ . . . ἐν αὐτῷ —The parataxis of 1 John is made syntaxis in GTr.

(3) there is no shadow ≅ σκοτία ἐν αὐτῷ οὐκ ἔστιν οὐδεμία — Valentinus has used a slightly different image, "shadow," for ps-John's image, "darkness," but has retained the point that the light is pure or complete.

C. *Evaluation of the Parallel*

The context of both passages speaks of the image of light in connection with the deity. Of the three elements of comparison, one is verbatim (but a commonplace) and another nearly so (and more distinctive). The third (2) simply represents a grammatical modification which was necessary to incorporate the reference into GTr. Although there are no other cases in which Valentinus has almost certainly used 1 John (cf., No. 39, 41, 61), this particular reference is virtually a paraphrase. Thus, his use of 1 John is likely here.

D. *Interpretation*

"Fullness" is the practical equivalent of God in GTr; it is "in the Father's thought and intellect" (16:35-36). In this passage, the fullness is said to be the image of those who are saved (the Gnostics), and it is light. Thus, Valentinus is able to assert implicitly that those who are the saved are incorporated into the fullness and into the light. "Light," however, is no longer an ethical image (cf. part A) which is contrasted with darkness. Rather, it is a metaphysical image which is contrasted, not with its logical or diametrical opposite ("darkness") but with "shadow," imagery which suggests a deficiency of (or in) light. There can be no deficiency in the fullness, and thus the light is complete in GTr, much as it is pure in 1 John.

59. GTr 35:30-31 (S A^2) ∼ Agraphon
(apud Ephraem, Syr. Evang. Concord. Expos., Chap. 17)[82]

Identified by Malinine et al., p. 17 (supp.). Probable.

Sed ubi dolores sunt, ait, illic

---

[82]See L. Leloir, ed., *Ephrem de Nisibe: Commentaire de L'Evangile Concordant ou Diatessaron*, SC 121 (Paris: le Cerf, 1966) 302-303 for text and translation. This passage in Ephraem is commonly identified as Agraphon 176 [A76], according to the classification of Resch. See the discussion in A. Resch, *Agrapha: Aussercanonische Schriftfragmente* (Leipzig: Hinrichs, 1906), p. 202.

Commentaries

For (γάρ) the physician hastens to the place where there is sickness.	festinat medicus. (Cf. above)

Subachmimic text ³⁰ⲡⲥⲁⲉⲓⲛ ⲅⲁⲣ ϣⲁϥⲡⲱⲧ· ⲁⲡⲙⲁ ⲉ³¹ⲧⲉ ⲟⲩⲛ̄ ϣⲱⲛⲉ ⲛ̄ϩⲏⲧϥ̄
Sahidic fragment ²⁵ⲅ]ⲁⲣ ⲉϣⲁϥ[ⲡ]ⲱⲧ ⲉⲡ[ⲙⲁ ⲉⲧ]

A. Context

Agraphon apud Ephraem, Skyr. Evang. Concord. Expos., Chap. 17 (original context unknown).[83]

GTr 35:24-35 (forgiveness). Valentinus describes the occasion of salvation as the reception of incorruptibility. Forgiveness is interpreted as the fact that the Word came to this world (the lack), just as a doctor goes to the sick and supplies their needs. In this way, the world's defect was rectified.

B. Element of Comparison

For (γάρ) the physician hastens to the place where there is sickness.	Sed ubi dolores sunt, ait, illic festinat medicus. (cf. above)

The two passages are nearly verbatim, except for the order of the clauses, which could be a function of style of the Coptic or Latin translations.

---

[83] In Ephraem, the context is a commentary on the resurrection of Lazarus: When Jesus wants to return to the ailing Lazarus in Judea, where he is hated by the Jews, the disciples protest, but Jesus replies with this aphorism about the physician's duty.

C. Evaluation of the Parallel

In the absence of any information on the agraphon, it is not possible to compare the contexts of the two passages. Obviously, the use that Ephraem (date c. 306-373) makes of it is not relevant. I am unable to find the saying in any text from Valentinus' own time. It is present in Ephraem's *Diatessaron*, whose Greek original may have been written toward the end of Valentinus' lifetime.[84] Thus, Valentinus might have known it from a written source, but the aphorism might also have been current in oral tradition, either Christian or common.

D. Interpretation

Valentinus uses this saying to show the role played by the Word in salvation as well as the role played by those who are to be saved. The Word acts like a doctor, who is eager to help those who are sick. The latter may be identified with those who are to be saved; these do not hide the fact that they are seeking salvation. The result is that the fullness, mediated by the Word, undoubtedly Jesus, supplies the lack which those who are not saved have and thus bestows grace upon them (35:35-36:3).

60. GTr 36:15-16 (S A^2) ~ Matt 7:7

Postulated by Grobel, p. 167, n. 502. Possible.

Seek and those who are (lit., have become) disturbed will receive a sending back	^{7}ζητεῖτε καὶ εὑρήσετε

---

[84] The *Diatessaron*, as is well-known, was written by Tatian, a former pupil of Justin Martyr, around the middle of the second century. The question of its original language (Greek or Syriac) is still disputed, and very little is known about its early history. Tatian is known to have lived and worked in Rome (with Justin Martyr and possibly at the same time Valentinus was in Rome) before he returned to his native Assyria. M. Elze gives a concise critical assessment of the evidence for Tatian's activity in his classic monograph, *Tatian und seine Theologie* (Göttingen: Vandenhoeck & Ruprecht, 1960), pp. 106-124. Leloir also includes sections on the origin, contents, importance, and order of the *Diatessaron* on pp. 15-24.

Commentaries   149

(and he will anoint them
   with anointing)

Subachmimic text ¹⁵ϣⲓⲛⲉ ⲛ̄ⲥⲉⲭⲓ ⲛ̄ⲛⲟⲩⲥⲧⲟ ¹⁶ⲛ̄ϭⲓ ⲛⲉⲉⲓ ⲛ̄ⲧⲁ2ⲱⲧⲁⲣⲧⲣ̄
Sahidic fragment ¹⁹ⲅ]ⲩ [ⲛ]ⲁⲭⲓ ⲛ̄ⲟ[ⲩⲥⲧⲟ] ²⁰[ⲛ̄ϭⲓ ⲛⲁϥⲓ̀ⲉⲧⲱⲧⲣ̄ⲧⲱⲣ

A. Context

Matt 7:7-11 (Sermon on the Mount). Jesus says that the Father will supply the needs of those who pray, just as an earthly father supplies the needs of his children.

GTr 36:13-20 (restoration into the fullness). Christ was proclaimed so that those who are in need of salvation may receive forgiveness, which is restoration to the fullness. Christ brings that which will supply their need (called the Father's mercy), and thus those who are saved are called perfect.

B. Elements of Comparison

| Seek and | ζητεῖτε καὶ |

(1) seek and = ζητεῖτε καί —verbatim.

| those who are (lit., have become) disturbed will receive a sending back | εὑρήσετε |

(2) will receive ≅ εὑρήσετε —Valentinus may have modified Matt's "you will find" to "those . . . will receive."

C. Evaluation of the Parallel

The contexts of the two passages are not closely related. Of the two elements of comparison, one (1) is verbatim and the other (2) inexact. The verbatim element may be distinctive in that it is an imperative, but the verb used ("seek") is extremely common. Thus, there is simply not enough evidence to demonstrate Valentinus' use of Matt here, although, given his frequent use of Matt, the possibility that he used it here as well cannot be ruled out.

D. Interpretation

Valentinus may call Matt 7:7 to the reader's mind by using the imperative, "Seek." The inexact element of comparison would then provide a clue to the interpretation. If "receive" is understood as an interpretation of the Matthean "find," then "a sending back" may be the object of Matt's objectless verb, "find."[85] What those who seek will find (i.e., get) is their restoration to the fullness. This may be understood as an interpretation of "repentance" (35:22-23).[86] The one who repents is restored to the fullness, which has no defect or lack (35:35-36) and which is, as we have seen, identified with the Father in GTr. Thus, the passage uses earlier motifs to explain that the goal of salvation through knowledge is to return to one's origin within the Father.

61. GTr 36:15-19 (S A²) ∼ 1 John 2:27

Postulated by Grobel, p. 169, n. 504. Possible.

... And those who were disturbed (will) receive a sending back and he (will) anoint them with the anointing.[87] The anointing is the mercy of the Father who will have mercy on them.	²⁷καὶ ὑμεῖς τὸ χρῖσμα ὃ ἐλάβετε ἀπ' αὐτοῦ μένει ἐν ὑμιν . . . (cf. τὸ χρῖσμα above) . . . τὸ αὐτοῦ χρῖσμα διδάσκει ὑμᾶς περί πάντων καὶ ἀληθές ἐστιν . . .

---

[85]This seems to be the logic behind Grobel's reasoning (p. 167, n. 502).
[86]"For, as for this conversion, it is called repentance."
[87]Sah. frg. apparently adds, "[and] they will receive the anointing," an even closer parallel to the Johannine text.

Subachmimic text ¹⁵ⲚⲤⲈⲬⲒ ⲚⲚⲞⲨⲤⲦⲞ· ¹⁶ⲚϬⲒ ⲚⲈⲈⲒ ⲚⲦⲀ2ⲰⲦⲢⲠⲦⲠ· ⲚϤⲦⲀ2 ¹⁷ⲤⲞⲨ ⲘⲠⲒⲦⲰ2Ⲥ· ⲠⲒⲦⲰ2Ⲥ ⲚⲈ ¹⁸ⲠⲚⲀⲈ· ⲘⲠⲒⲰⲦ· ⲈⲦⲀϤⲚⲀⲚⲀⲈ ¹⁹ⲚⲈⲨ·
Sahidic fragment ¹⁹ⲈⲒⲨ [Ⲛ]ⲀⲬⲒ ⲚⲞ[ⲨⲤⲦⲞ] ²⁰[ⲚϬⲒ ⲚⲀⲒ᪻ⲈⲦⲰⲦⲢⲦⲰⲠ ⲀⲨⲰ Ⲛ[ϤⲦⲀ2] ²¹[ⲤⲞⲨ ⲚⲤ]ⲈⲬⲒ ⲘⲠⲒⲦⲰ2Ⲥ· Ⲛ[ϤⲦⲰ]

A. Context

1 John 2:18-27 (anointing by the Holy Spirit). The ointment which the Holy One has bestowed upon members of the Johannine community gives the ability to discern the truth, which brings eternal life. This ointment is the Holy Spirit (John 14:26) and remains within those who have received it.

GTr 36:13-26 (anointing of the Father's mercy). The ointment which Christ has bestowed upon the Gnostics brings a renewal and perfection. The ointment is the Father's mercy which is shown to those who have received it.

B. Elements of Comparison

and he (will) anoint them
with the anointing   (cf. τὸ χρῖσμα above)

(1) the anointing = τὸ χρῖσμα — verbatim. The word χρῖσμα occurs only in 1 John in the New Testament and only infrequently (e.g., PGM 7, 874) in other literature of the period.[88] "Anointing" figures prominently in some later Christian Gnostic texts (e.g., GPh 74:12ff.; there it is no longer a metaphor for the reception of the Spirit or the mercy of the Father but has become a sacrament, i.e., the chrism). There is, however, no indication that a sacrament underlies this passage in GTr.[89]

---

[88] See Grobel, p. 169, n. 508 and F. Schmidtke, "Zum Evangelium Veritatis 36, 17 ff.," *TLZ* 85 (1960), col. 713-714 for the background of the image of anointing on a jar.
[89] E. Segelberg, "Evangelium Veritatis—A Confirmation Homily and its Relation to the Odes of Solomon," *Orientalia Suecana* 8 (1959) 1-42, attempts to find sacramental references throughout GTr, but his arguments are not convincing.

... (will) receive a sending back | ὃ ἐλάβετε ἀπ' αὐτοῦ

(2) (will) receive ≅ ἐλάβετε —The person, number, and tense differ.

C. Evaluation of the Parallel

The contexts are superficially similar, but 1 John addresses problems within the community, whereas Valentinus refers to a state in which those who have responded to Christ are found. One of the elements of comparison (1) is verbatim. The other is lexically verbatim but grammatically different. Valentinus' use of 1 John here is only possible because the reference is quite brief and does not escape the general ambiguity surrounding possible parallels to 1 John in GTr.

D. Interpretation

A word-play in Greek (χριστός, χρῖσμα; "anointed one," i.e., Christ, anointing) plays an important role in the interpretation. Christ is said to be proclaimed publicly and is said to anoint with ointment (36:13-17) those who are disturbed. Valentinus clearly states that ointment ("anointing") is to be interpreted allegorically to mean "mercy of the Father" (36:17-18). If 1 John is used here, Valentinus may have understood 1 John's "Holy Spirit" as "mercy of the Father" which is like an ointment and is brought by Christ. What Christ has bestowed upon the Gnostics, then, is not the Holy Spirit as in 1 John but the anointing of perfection brought about by the mercy of the Father. Those who receive the anointing are those who have already been predestined for salvation, as 36:21-22 suggests, although predestination may not provide irrevocable assurance (36:22-24). The interpretation of 1 John 2:27 may illustrate especially well the way Valentinus can use references to entirely different texts in close succession in the composition of GTr because, if he has used both 1 John and Matt 7:7 (No. 60), this passage completes the imperative "seek," which he drew from Matt 7:7.[90]

---

[90] As Grobel, p. 167, n. 502 suggests.

Commentaries 153

62. GTr 36:35-38 (A²) ~ Gen 2:15

Postulated by Grobel, p. 171, n. 517. Possible.

He (the Father) knows	¹⁵καὶ ἔλαβεν κύριος ὁ θεὸς
his plantings	τὸν ἄνθρωπον, ὃν ἔπλασεν,
for it is he who planted them	καὶ ἔθετο αὐτὸν
in his paradise.	ἐν τῷ παραδείσῳ
	ἐργάζεσθαι αὐτὸν
	καὶ φυλάσσειν . . .

³⁵ϥⲥⲁⲩ³⁶ⲛⲉ ⲛ̄ⲛⲓϫⲟ ⲛ̄ⲧⲟⲟⲧϥ̄ ϫⲉ ⲛ̄ⲧⲁϥ ⲡⲉ ³⁷ⲛ̄ⲧⲁϥϫⲟ ⲙ̄ⲙⲁⲩ ϩⲛ̄
ⲡⲓⲡⲁⲣⲁⲇⲓⲥ³⁸ ⲥⲟⲥ ⲛ̄ⲧⲟⲟⲧϥ̄

A. Context

Gen 2:8-17 (description of Eden). God made a garden in which the man whom he had formed would live. God also made a great number of trees for the garden which would provide him with food and aesthetic pleasure.

GTr 36:35-39 (description of paradise). God put certain plants into a garden where God knows each one. This is an allegory: the garden (paradise) means God's place of rest.

B. Element of Comparison

in his paradise	ἐν τῷ παραδείσῳ

in his paradise ≅ ἐν τῷ παραδείσῳ —In Gen 2:15, "paradise" has its original (literal) sense of a garden or enclosed park. In later references to "paradise," however, the word often figuratively refers to a "place of blessedness above the earth" (e.g. Test. Levi 18:10; 2 Cor 12:4); in GTr it is specifically allegorized: paradise = the Father's place of rest (36:38-39). Because Valentinus uses the verb "plant" or "sow" (36:37), he evidently was aware of the original meaning.[91]

---

[91]Grobel, p. 171, n. 517 gives a more complete discussion.

C. Evaluation of the Parallel

The contexts are similar insofar as both refer to plants in a garden, but Valentinus clearly intends GTr to be taken allegorically. There is only one element of comparison; it is nearly verbatim, though brief. Because Valentinus does seem to know and use Gen (e.g., No. 4) at least the creation story, his use of Gen here is possible.

D. Interpretation

Valentinus may have generalized the account in Gen of God's placing the first human being in paradise (Eden) so that it now extends to all those who possess the first human being's status before the fall, i.e., the Gnostics. He makes his allegorical intention clear by equating paradise and the Father's place of rest. He further seems to equate (by parallelism) the Father's sowings with the words of the Father's ponderings (37:2-3).[92] Thus, an implicit identification of "sowings" with "Gnostics" or "those who are within the Father, who have knowledge of the Father" is almost certainly intended. The Father's place of rest is itself probably used figuratively to refer to the all-encompassing Father within whom all those with knowledge dwell, in a metaphysical sense (cf. 18:31-35).

63. GTr 37:22-24 (A²) ∼ Matt 10:29

Postulated by van Unnik, pp. 120-121. Possible.

(And it is the will in which the Father rests himself . . .)	²⁹οὐχὶ δύο στρουθία ἀσσαρίου πωλεῖται; καὶ ἓν ἐξ αὐτῶν
nor does anything happen without the will of the Father.	οὐ πεσεῖται ἐπὶ τὴν γῆν ἄνευ τοῦ πατρὸς ὑμῶν.

---

[92] This is a striking parallel to Philo's explanation of this in Q. Ans. Gen. I.6: "And his ideas the Creator planted like trees in the most sovereign thing, the rational soul" [Loeb translation].

²²ⲟⲩⲇⲉ ⲙⲁⲣⲉⲗⲗⲁⲩ²³ⲉ ϣⲱⲡⲉ ⲁϫⲛ̄ ⲡⲟⲩⲱϣⲉ· ⲛ̄ⲧⲉ²⁴ⲡⲓⲱⲧ·

A. *Context*

Matt 10:26-31 (on discipleship). Jesus exhorts his disciples not to fear those who are hostile to them because the Father cares for all of them. He cares so much that without the Father not even a sparrow dies.

GTr 37:15-24 (on the Father's will). The Word was the first manifestation of the Father's will. The Father reposes in his will, without which nothing happens.

B. *Element of Comparison*

| nor does anything happen | οὐ πεσεῖται ἐπὶ τὴν γῆν |
| without the will of the Father | ἄνευ τοῦ πατρὸς ὑμῶν |

without the will of the Father ≅ ἄνευ τοῦ πατρὸς ὑμῶν —Whereas Matt does not mention "will," Valentinus does. Valentinus may have read "without the will of your Father" in his text of Matt (as a variant against our received text). Such a reading, as van Unnik[93] noted, is found in Irenaeus *Adv. Haer.* II 26.2, *sine patris vestri voluntate*, and quotations in Tertullian, Cyprian, and some old Latin manuscripts also attest that the phrase, "without the will of your Father" was known in some versions of Matt. Valentinus does not retain "your" from Matt, which is also contained in the passage from Irenaeus just cited and which may have been in his Greek text of Matt.

C. *Evaluation of the Parallel*

The contexts of the two passages are not similar, but both passages make the point that nothing happens unless the Father wants it to happen. The element of comparison is inexact, however, and the suggested parallel is brief. These two considerations weigh against the similar phrasing of

---

[93]Pp. 120-121.

the two passages and hence preclude certainty of Valentinus' use of Matt here, despite his frequent use of it elsewhere.

D. Interpretation

If Valentinus has used Matt here, he has taken the phrase out of context and has used it in a very different way. First, he has removed any personal reference ("*your* Father") because the Father is consistently portrayed as removed from humanity in GTr. Second, he has made the Father's will the agent of his action toward humanity, but he has equated the Father's will with his place of rest, stating that it is incomprehensible, like the Father himself. There is, therefore, a deliberate tension in the passage. The Father remains incomprehensible, even in his will, but yet the Father's will is his agent.

64. GTr 38:10-11 (A²) ~ Heb 1:5

Postulated by van Unnik, p. 121. Possible.

And	^{5}Τίνι γὰρ εἶπέν [sc. θεός] ποτε τῶν ἀγγέλων·
he (the Father) begot him as a son.	(cf. ἐγὼ . . . γεγέννηκά σε) υἱός μου εἶ σύ, ἐγὼ σήμερον γεγέννηκά σε;

¹⁰ⲁⲩⲱ ⲁϥⲙⲉⲥⲧϥ̄ ⲛ̄ⲛⲟⲩϣⲏ¹¹ⲣⲉ·

A. Context

Heb 1:1-14 (Christ's superiority to angels). The author demonstrates that a series of quotations is about Christ's person, role, and importance. Christ is shown to be God's son, begotten by God his Father.

GTr 38:6-15 (the Son has God's name). The Father named the one whom he begot as a son. The Father named him "Son," but paradoxically the Father's name is "Son."

Commentaries 157

B. *Elements of Comparison*

| he (the Father) begot him as a son. | (cf. ἐγὼ . . . γεγέννηκά σε) υἱός μου εἶ σύ, ἐγὼ σήμερον γεγέννηκά σε; |

(1) he begot him ≅ ἐγὼ . . . γεγέννεκά σε —In Heb 1:5, the author quotes from Ps 2:7; this is a good example of the prophetic-christological exegesis of scripture, which was common in the first two centuries of Christianity. The exegesis of Ps 2 occurs in other New Testament texts, e.g. Acts 13:33, Heb 5:5, and reflects an early Christian tradition that Jesus was begotten as God's son (e.g. 1 Clem. 36:4). Valentinus makes his typical change in referring to the deity as Father rather than God. The person is also changed because the passage is put into past narrative form.

(2) a son ≅ υἱός μου —nearly verbatim.

C. *Evaluation of the Parallel*

In both passages, the point is that the deity begot a son, but the contexts are very different. The two elements of comparison are nearly verbatim if one accounts for a change in form in GTr. If these were the only considerations, the certainty of Valentinus' use of Heb here would be virtually assured. Ps 2 was frequently interpreted in early Christianity, and hence these lines in GTr may not reflect an independent exegesis of Heb since it is probably part of a common Christian tradition by this time. Valentinus does use Heb elsewhere in GTr (e.g., No. 11), however, and his use of it here cannot be ruled out.

D. *Interpretation*

Valentinus apparently knows the traditional exegesis of Ps 2:7 in early Christian circles, but he has disguised the motif of fulfillment of prophecy by putting the statement into past narrative form. The contexts of the two passages share references to "name" (GTr 11; Heb 1:4) and "Father" (GTr 38:14; Heb 1:5b). Valentinus, however, brings the Father and Son into an even closer relationship than does the exegesis of Ps 2:7 in Heb. According to GTr, the Son has the Father's name. That name is "Son." Who is the Father? He is the Son! This is, of course, in keeping with the view that the Father is incomprehensible except as he can be known through the Son (Jesus, Word, etc.).

65. GTr 38:11-12 (A²) ~ John 17:11

Postulated by Malinine et al., p. 58.[94] Possible.

He (Father) gave him (Son) his name which was his.	¹¹... πάτερ ἅγιε, τήρησον αὐτοὺς (cf. ᾧ δέδωκάς μοι below) ἐν τῷ ὀνόματί σου ᾧ δέδωκάς μοι, ἵνα ὦσιν ἓν καθὼς ἡμεῖς.

¹¹ⲁϥϯ ⲡⲉϥⲣⲉⲛ ⲁⲣⲁϥ ⲉⲧⲉ ⲛⲉ ¹²ⲟⲩⲛ̄ⲧⲉϥⲥ̄

A. Context

John 17:6-11 (high priestly prayer). Jesus has manifested the Father's name to those who believe that the Father has sent him. He prays that these may be kept in God's name, which has been given to Jesus, so that they may experience the unity which Jesus and the Father have.

GTr 38:6-15 (the Son has God's name). The Father names the one whom he begot as a Son. The Father named him "Son," but paradoxically the Father's name is "Son."

B. Elements of Comparison

He (Father) gave him (Son) his name which was his	(cf. ᾧ δέδωκάς μοι below) ἐν τῷ ὀνόματί σου ᾧ δέδωκάς μοι

(1) he gave him ≅ ᾧ δέδωκάς μοι —Valentinus rephrases words of Jesus into past narrative; otherwise the phrases are identical.

---

[94] But van Unnik, p. 121, noted John 17:12.

(2) his name ≅ τῷ ὀνόματί σου —Valentinus rephrases words of Jesus into past narrative; otherwise the phrases are identical.

C. Evaluation of the Parallel

Both passages maintain that the Father has given Jesus or the Son his own (the Father's) name, but the contexts are not very similar. The two elements of comparison are nearly verbatim if one takes account of the change to past narrative form. Both John and GTr, however, probably reflect the background of speculation on the "Name" in contemporary Jewish literature and in Christian literature influenced by Judaism.[95] Thus, even though Valentinus knows and uses John frequently, his use of it here is no more than possible.

D. Interpretation

The Johannine Jesus describes both the unity of Father and Son and also the Son as the manifestation of the Father's name. If Valentinus has used John 17:11, he has extracted the lines from their context, put them into the third person, past narrative form, and has referred to Jesus as "Son." Beyond this, he has done little to interpret the passage; he underscores John's statement of Jesus' unity with the Father by giving a description of Jesus' unity with the Father that is more explicit than John's.

66. GTr 38:33-39:1 (A²) ∼ Phil 2:9, 11

Postulated by Malinine et al., p. 59. Possible.

It is he (the Father) who alone begot him for himself as a name . . .	⁹διὸ καὶ ὁ θεός . . . ἐχαρίσατο αὐτῷ τὸ ὄνομα
in order that the name of the Father might be upon their head	τὸ ὑπὲρ πᾶν ὄνομα . . .

---

[95]The secondary literature on this is abundant. Two good, representative studies are those of J. Daniélou, pp. 147-157 and J. D. Dubois, pp. 198-216.

as Lord— | ¹¹ κύριος Ἰησοῦς Χριστός . . .
this name which is the true name.

³³ⲚⲦⲀϤ ⲞⲨⲀⲈⲈⲦϤ ⲠⲈⲚ³⁴ⲦⲀϤⲘⲒⲤⲈ ⲘⲘⲀϤ ⲚⲈϤ ⲚⲞⲨⲢⲈⲚ ³⁵...
³⁶ϢⲒⲚⲀ ⲚϤϢⲰⲠⲈ ⲀⲬⲚ ⲦⲞⲨⲀ³⁷ⲠⲈ ⲚϬⲒ ⲠⲢⲈⲚ
ⲘⲠⲒⲰⲦ· ⲈϤⲞⲈⲒ ³⁹ⲚⲬⲀⲈⲒⲤ· ⲈⲦⲈ ⲠⲈⲈⲒ ⲠⲈ ⲠⲢⲈⲚ ¹ⲘⲀⲘⲎⲈ

A. Context

Phil 2:6-11 (early christological hymn). The hymn speaks of Christ Jesus' pre-existence, incarnation, service, obedience, voluntary death, exaltation, and the bestowal of the Name on him.

GTr 38:32-39:3 (the Name). The passage speaks of the Name's pre-existence so that the Father's name might be Lord over the aeons.

B. Elements of Comparison

It is he (the Father) who alone | διὸ καὶ ὁ θεός . . .
begot him for himself | ἐχαρίσατο αὐτῷ
as a name | τὸ ὄνομα

(1) he (the Father) ≅ θεός —Valentinus makes his typical change in referring to the deity as Father rather than God.

(2) begot ≅ ἐχαρίσατο —Valentinus may have understood the bestowal of the Name to have occurred on the occasion of the Son's begetting.

(3) for himself ≅ αὐτῷ —nearly verbatim.

(4) a name ≅ τὸ ὄνομα —Both passages show contact with the Jewish and early Christian tradition of reference to the divine name.[96] This tradition builds on the Jewish refusal to pronounce the Tetragrammaton (YHWH); reverence for the divine name was carried over from Hebrew

---

[96] This tradition is often abbreviated as, simply, "the Name."

Commentaries   161

into Greek usage, where it was regularly translated "Lord" (κύριος). Thus, "Lord" might be recognized as a reference to the divine name.

| ... upon their head | τὸ ὑπὲρ πᾶν ὄνομα ... |
| as Lord | κύριος 'Ιησοῦς Χριστός |

(5) upon their head ≅ ὑπὲρ πᾶν ὄνομα —Paul speaks of a name which surpasses all other names, whereas Valentinus indicates that the Father's name is (metaphorically) "upon" each Gnostic's head.

(6) Lord = κύριος —verbatim. In both passages, "Lord" probably recalls the Tetragrammaton, at least indirectly. In Phil, it is Jesus Christ who is Lord, who has the Name. In GTr, it is the Son who has the Father's name; this name is Lord.

C. Evaluation of the Parallel

The contexts of the two passages are utterly different. Both passages, however, refer to "Lord" and "Name," common designations for God. Both epithets also were applied to Jesus in some circles of early Christianity. One of the elements of comparison is verbatim, and two others are nearly so. A third (1) reflects Valentinus' preferred reference to the deity as "Father" rather than "God." Because Valentinus' use of Phil elsewhere in GTr is uncertain (see No. 15), his use of Phil here is only possible.

D. Interpretation

Both passages assert that the exalted name is κύριος, "Lord." Moreover, in both cases Christ Jesus, or the Son, has this name. The two passages differ as to when this name is bestowed. In the hymn that Paul uses in Phil, the Name seems to be understood as bestowed on Christ Jesus as a consequence of his earthly life and obedience unto death. Valentinus, however, seems to have understood bestowal of the name to have occurred at the Father's begetting of the Son, presumably in his pre-existent state. Thus, Valentinus may attempt to clarify the ambiguous status given to the pre-existent Christ Jesus in the hymn of Phil.

67. GTr 38:36-37 (A²) ~ Rev 22:4

Postulated by van Unnik, p. 121. Dubious.

(He begot for him a name . . . in order that) the name of the Father might be upon their head.	⁴καὶ ὄψονται τὸ πρόσωπον αὐτοῦ (sc. θεοῦ), καὶ τὸ ὄνομα αὐτοῦ ἐπὶ τῶν μετώπων αὐτῶν.

³⁶ⲚϤϢⲰⲠⲈ ⲆⲬⲚ ⲦⲞⲨⲀ³⁷ⲠⲈ Ⲛ̄ϬⲒ ⲠⲢⲈⲚ ⲘⲠⲒⲰⲦ·

A. Context

Rev 22:1-5 (the new Jerusalem). In John's vision, the city's street has a river flowing down its middle; on its banks is the tree of life. The city has no evil, and all the inhabitants worship God. They will even be allowed to see his face because his name is on their foreheads. The city will have eternal day and will be lighted by the Lord God.

GTr 38:32-39:3 (the Name). The Name was pre-existent so that the Father might be Lord over the aeons or so that the Father's name might be upon the heads of the sons of the Name.

B. Elements of Comparison

the name of the Father might be upon their head	καὶ τὸ ὄνομα αὐτοῦ ἐπὶ τῶν μετώπων αὐτῶν

(1) the name of the Father ≅ τὸ ὄνομα αὐτοῦ —Both passages refer to the name. In Rev 22:4, "name" must be the name of God (cf. Rev 22:3, 5), the Tetragrammaton or κύριος, as "Lord God" in Rev 22:5 suggests. In GTr 38:36-37, "name" specifically refers to the name of the Father, Valentinus' typical expression for the deity in GTr; this name must be κύριος, or, indirectly, the Tetragrammaton.

(2) upon their head ≅ ἐπὶ τῶν μετώπων αὐτῶν —"Forehead" (μέτωπος) is more specific than "head." "Upon their forehead(s)" is also found in Rev 7:3, 9:4 (with a reference to sealing rather than to name); 13:16; 14:1

Commentaries   163

(with name). All of these may derive directly or indirectly from an interpretation of Ezek 9:4.

C. Evaluation of the Parallel

The contexts of the two passages are different. Both elements of comparison are inexact. Each of the passages refers to "Name," which is common in early Christian literature. The other element (2) contains different terms ("foreheads" in Rev and "head" in GTr). Even though Valentinus does use certain strong passages of Rev (e.g., No. 10), his use of Rev here is dubious.

68. GTr 39:15-19 (A²) ~ Rev 19:12

Postulated by Malinine et al., p. 59. Possible.

But this one who exists	(ὁ καθήμενος ἐπὶ τὸν ἵππον λευκόν)
exists with his name also	¹²ἔχων ὄνομα γεγραμμένον
and he alone knows it	ὃ οὐδεὶς οἶδεν εἰ μὴ αὐτός
(the next clause is corrupt)[97]	

---

¹⁵ⲡⲉⲉⲓ ⲛ̄ⲧⲁϥ ⲉⲧϣⲟⲟⲡ· ϥϣⲟ¹⁶ⲟⲡ ⲙⲛ̄ ⲡⲉϥⲕⲉⲣⲉⲛ ⲁⲩⲱ ¹⁷ϥⲥⲁⲩⲛⲉ ⲙ̄ⲙⲁϥ ⲟⲩⲁⲉⲉⲧϥ̄
¹⁸ⲁⲩⲱ ⲁⲧⲣⲉϥϯ ⲣⲉⲛ ⲁⲣⲁϥ ⲟⲩ¹⁹ⲁⲉⲉⲧϥ̄ (18-19 are corrupt)

A. Context

Rev 19:11-16 (the rider on the white horse). John describes a vision of someone on a white horse, who has eyes like flames, crowns on his head, and a name inscribed which only he knows. He also has a name inscribed on his robe and on his thigh: King of Kings and Lord of Lords.

GTr 39:7-20 (the name). The antecedents of the pronouns in this passage are not clear, but the import of the passage is that the Father alone gave

---

[97]"And to cause him to name it (or him) alone."

the Son a name. The Son exists with his name. Only the Father knew him and could give him a name. Because the Father's name is "Son," the passage speaks of the Father's self-manifestation as Son.

B. Elements of Comparison

| exists with his name also, | ἔχων ὄνομα γεγραμμένον |
| and he alone knows it | ὃ οὐδεὶς οἶδεν εἰ μὴ αὐτός |

(1) exists with his name ≅ ἔχων ὄνομα —nearly verbatim, if one understands the Coptic existential construction to translate ἔχειν. The Coptic translation does suggest, however, that Valentinus may have understood the passage in a metaphysical sense.

(2) and he alone knows it ≅ ὃ οὐδεὶς οἶδεν εἰ μὴ αὐτός —nearly verbatim, when one takes account of the Greek idiomatic use of the double negative.

C. Evaluation of the Parallel

The contexts of the two passages are not similar except that both use the tradition of the Name. When syntactical differences arising from the incorporation of the phrases into GTr and grammatical differences due to Coptic idiom are taken into account, the two elements of comparison are nearly verbatim. Together with Valentinus' use of Rev elsewhere in GTr (e.g., No. 9, 10), these similarities make his use of Rev possible here as well.

D. Interpretation

Both passages affirm that someone has a name which only he knows. In Rev, this person is the one on a white horse (i.e., Jesus; Rev 19:11), and in GTr, this one is Lord (GTr 38:39). If Valentinus has used Rev, he has replaced the imagery of the rider on the white horse, which is specific to Rev, with a stream of ambiguous pronouns. The ambiguity may serve to underscore the unity between Father and Son as exemplified in the Name. A poor Coptic translation of the Greek might be responsible for the ambiguity, but the ambiguity is more likely a deliberate theological expression. Valentinus' point seems to be that only the Father could name the Son but that the Son is named only because he exists.

69. GTr 39:19-20 (A²) ~ John 10:30

Postulated by Standaert, *NTS*, p. 272.[98] Dubious.

He is the Father.	³⁰ἐγὼ [ὁ 'Ιησοῦς] καὶ
The Son is his name.	ὁ πατὴρ ἕν ἐσμεν.

¹⁹ πιωτ πε πϣηρε˙ ²⁰ πε πεϥρεν

A. Context

GTr 10:22-30 (Jesus the shepherd). In response to the Jews' question about Jesus' Messiahship, Jesus states that his works bear witness to him, but the questioners cannot see them since they are not his followers. Jesus asserts his unity with the Father and his ability to give life to his followers.

GTr 39:19-26 (the name). The Father's name is "Son," but the Father did not hide himself and his name in activity. He remained as he was and allowed his self-manifestation, Son, to distribute names.

B. Element of Comparison

	ἐγὼ [ὁ 'Ιησοῦς] καὶ
He is the Father.	ὁ πατὴρ ἕν ἐσμεν.
The Son is his name.	

the Father = ὁ πατήρ —verbatim. The self-proclamation of Jesus in John is not retained in GTr; GTr is expository and uses the third person.

---

[98] Standaert does not refer to these lines specifically but rather rightly notes the similarity of thought underlying John 10:30 and much of the long exposition on the Name in GTr 38-40.

C. Evaluation of the Parallel

The contexts are quite different, but both passages assert the unity of Father and Son. The element of comparison is verbatim but can hardly be seen as peculiar to John, although the Johannine Jesus does refer to God as "Father" when he speaks. John 10:30 may have influenced this passage as a whole in a way that can no longer be reconstructed, but Valentinus' use of John 10:30 in a specific way is dubious, despite Valentinus' frequent use of John in GTr.

70. GTr 41:16-17 (A^2) ~ Rev 22:16

Postulated by Williams.[99] Dubious.

and he (the Father) is the root of all his parts (?).	^{16}ἐγώ εἰμι [ʾΙησοῦς] ἡ ῥίζα καὶ τὸ γένος Δαυίδ . . .

---

^{16}ⲁⲩⲱ2ⲛ̄ ⲛⲉϥϯⲏ ^{17}ⲧⲏⲣⲟⲩ ⲧⲟⲩⲛⲟⲩⲛⲉ ⲡⲉ

A. Context

Rev 22:12-16 (epilogue). After the conclusion of John's revelation, Jesus promises to come soon to distribute recompense for each one's deeds. Christians will be able to enter the new Jerusalem, but others must remain outside. Jesus is the true Davidic Messiah, as his titles, such as "root," show.

GTr 41:7-20 (the fullness). Each Gnostic must speak about the Father, from whom he or she came and to whom each one must return in order to be within the realm of repose. There each one is also his or her own realm

---

[99]As with No. 69, this example is included not because GTr is actually dependent on the suggested parallel but in order to highlight an important element present in both texts.

Commentaries 167

of repose and is a fullness within the Father, who is the root of all his parts.[100]

B. Elements of Comparison

and he (the Father) is | ἐγώ εἰμι [' Ἰησοῦς]
the root | ἡ ῥίζα

(1) he is ≅ ἐγώ εἰμι —The self-predication of Jesus' Messiahship ("I am the root and offspring of David") is not retained in GTr; GTr is expository and uses the third person.

(2) the root = ἡ ῥίζα —verbatim. "Root" is used in Rev together with "offspring of David" in a prophetic-christological exegesis of Isa 11:1, 10 (cf. Rev 5:5 for "root" also). The word was frequently used in a figurative sense in literature of the time (e.g. *Corp. Herm.* 4:10, ἡ γὰρ μόνας, οὖσα πάντων ἀρχὴ καὶ ῥίζα; Plutarch, *De Lib. Educ.* 4C, πηγὴ γὰρ καὶ ῥίζα καλοκἀγαθίας; Heb 12:15, ῥίζα πικρίας). "Root" may also have become a technical term in some Gnostic circles. For example, ApocryJn II, 30:30 refers to a "root of life," and TriTrac 68:8-9 says that the Father created the aeons as "roots."

C. Evaluation of the Parallel

Only one point of comparison might seem to be noteworthy, namely, the metaphor of the deity (Father, Jesus) as "the root." Rev 22:16, however, clearly alludes to Isa 11:10 ("root of Jesse"), whereas GTr exhibits none of the distinctive, Messianic features of Isaiah's imagery. Without such features, the metaphor of "root" is only a commonplace. Thus, even though Valentinus clearly uses Rev elsewhere (e.g., Nos. 9, 10), there is no compelling reason to conclude that he did so here.

---

[100]The word translated "parts" here is unknown outside of GTr; it is often translated "emanations but may be a feminine collective of ⲧⲁⲓⲉⲓⲉ (GTr 32:14; 41:5) which means "art, share, portion." Grobel discusses this on p. 81, 83, n. 171.

71. GTr 42:3-4 (A²) ~ Rom 3:23

Identified by van Unnik, p. 121. Probable.

| ... nor have they (the parts) fallen short of the glory of the Father | ²³πάντες γὰρ ἥμαρτον καὶ ὑστεροῦνται τῆς δόξης τοῦ θεοῦ |

³ⲞⲨⲦⲈ ⲘⲠⲞⲨⲰϪⲰⲰⲦ· ⲘⲠⲈⲀⲨ ⁴ⲘⲠⲒⲰⲦ·

A. Context

Rom 3:21-26 (righteousness through faith). God makes no distinction between Jew and Gentile. All are sinners and lack God's glory; believers are justified by God's free grace through Christ Jesus' redemption.

GTr 41:23-42:9 (the Father's parts). The Father's parts think of their root, which lifts them up to him (the Father). They have not exceeded themselves, however, nor do they lack the Father's glory or think of him as partaking of human emotion because he is without evil, is imperturbable, sweet, and omniscient.

B. Elements of Comparison

| ... nor have they (the parts) fallen short of the glory of the Father | πάντες γὰρ ἥμαρτον καὶ ὑστεροῦνται τῆς δόξης τοῦ θεοῦ |

(1) they (the parts) ≠ πάντες —Valentinus has restricted "all" (people) to those who are "parts" of the Father, i.e., the Gnostics.

(2) have (not) fallen short ≅ ὑστεροῦνται —These expressions are effectively identical in tense. Valentinus negates the Pauline statement.

(3) of the glory of the Father ≅ τῆς δόξης τοῦ θεοῦ —These expressions are identical, except for the typical change in GTr from "God" to "Father."

C. Evaluation of the Parallel

The contexts are very different because Paul speaks of the lack of distinction between Jew and Gentile, whereas Valentinus speaks of the state of rest that Gnostics may attain. Two of the three elements of comparison (2, 3) are virtually identical and the third is determined by the context in GTr. Valentinus knows and uses Rom elsewhere (e.g., No. 45), and his use of it here as well is almost certain.

D. Interpretation

GTr practically paraphrases Rom 3:23, but Valentinus has made four important changes. First is the change of subject from "all" to "parts." Second is the typical change from "God" to "Father." Third is the addition of "nor," which completely transforms Paul's passage from an assertion of a lack shared by all humanity to an assertion that the Father's parts did *not* lack his glory. Fourth, there is no mention of sin in this passage in GTr. This, of course, is understandable because "sin" is not a category which Valentinus finds applicable to Gnostics. Those who know that they are from the Father effectively become parts of the Father, and, therefore, there can be no sin in them (cf. 42:6-7). Because he does not mention sin, Valentinus alters the shape of the Pauline passage (omitting reference to the lack of distinction between Jew and Gentile as regards sin, justification, and grace). Since he speaks only to those who are "parts" of the Father, Valentinus can say that they have not fallen short of the Father's glory. In so doing, Valentinus stands the passage from Rom on its head.

72. GTr 42:18-21 (A²) ~ Rev 21:4

Postulated by Malinine et al., p. 60. Possible.

(And they do not go down to Hades) nor do they have envy (φθόνος) or sighing nor is there death in them.	⁴(Καὶ ἐξαλείψει πᾶν δάκρυον ἐκ τῶν ὀφθαλμῶν αὐτῶν) (cf. κραυγή below) καὶ ὁ θάνατος οὐκ ἔσται ἔτι οὔτε πένθος οὔτε κραυγὴ οὔτε πόνος οὐκ ἔσται ἔτι . . .

¹⁸ΟΥΤΕ ΜΝΤΕΥ ¹⁹ΦΘΟΝΟС ΜΜΕΥ ΟΥΤΕ ²⁰ΛϢΕ2ΛΜ ΟΥΤΕ ΜΝ ΜΟΥ Ν²¹2ΡΗΪ
Ν2ΗΤΟΥ

A. Context

Rev 21:1-4 (the new Jerusalem). In John's vision, the new city comes from heaven to be with humanity. God himself will dwell with humanity, who will be his people. He will make sorrow, death, and other painful emotions disappear.

GTr 42:11-26 (the Father's parts). Those who have possessions from above, that is, those who are the Father's parts, strain toward him. Thus, they do not go down to Hades, nor can they suffer painful emotions or death. They rest in the Father. They never tire of truth because they are the truth.

B. Elements of Comparison

nor do they have envy or sighing	(cf. κραυγή below)
nor is there death in them	καὶ ὁ θάνατος οὐκ ἔσται
	. . . κραυγή . . .

(1) sighing ≅ κραυγή —Both passages list components of human pathos, but the details vary. There are no common elements in the lists, but "sighing" and "crying" are similar.

(2) nor is there death in them ≅ καὶ ὁ θάνατος οὐκ ἔσται —The chief difference between those two is the change in tense from future to present in GTr. In Rev, the future tense is appropriately used for a vision, whereas in GTr the present is used to describe what now obtains.

C. Evaluation of the Parallel

The contexts are not similar nor is either of the elements of comparison verbatim. One is only very inexact ("sighing"/"crying"). The other (2) could, however, almost be a paraphrase of the corresponding phrase in Rev, and for this reason Valentinus' use of the suggested parallel is

Commentaries

possible, although not as certain as in some other cases where the use of Rev has been proposed (e.g., Nos. 9, 10).

D. Interpretation

Valentinus may interpret this passage as if the new Jerusalem has already arrived for his readers. For those who belong to the Father, death may not be considered a relevant category or event. Yet, in this passage, Valentinus retains some contact with traditional spatial notions of "above" and "below," as seen in the mention of going up to the Father and (not) going down to Hades. This is rare, for Valentinus generally ignores traditional, biblical spatial categories due to his philosophical conception of an all-encompassing Father. Although Valentinus does not deny that there is a Hades, the place is not important for his readers because they are beyond death, groaning, and presumably all other factors which comprise human pathos. John's vision is thus in GTr no longer a vision of future reality which employs vivid imagery but rather has been appropriated and transformed to fit the situation of those who are the Father's "parts." One of the elements in Valentinus' list of envy, sighing, and death is not typical of the kind of list we have in Rev, namely, envy (or jealousy, φθόνος). Ἄφθονος is a common attribute of God in Middle Platonism,[101] and thus Valentinus may be saying that the "parts" have the same attributes as the Father.

73. GTr 43:6-7 (A²) ~ Rom 5:5

Identified by van Unnik, p. 121. Probable.

these (brothers/sisters) on whom the love (ἀγάπη) of the Father is poured forth	(cf. καρδίαις ἡμῶν below) ⁵ἡ ἀγάπη τοῦ θεοῦ ἐκκέχυται

---

[101] Negative characteristics such as this are frequently used in Middle Platonism to describe the transcendent deity who is removed from humanity (cf. No. 48, in which an exception made by the Father is described). J. Dillon, *The Middle Platonists* (London: Duckworth, 1977), pp. 45-49 gives a concise summary of the dominant themes of Middle Platonism. GTr 18:38-40 says that the Father is not jealous and that there can be no jealousy between him and his members (μέλος, found also in Rom 12:4-5; 1 Cor 12:12).

ἐν ταῖς καρδίαις ἡμῶν
διὰ πνεύματος ἁγίου
τοῦ δοθέντος ἡμῖν.

⁶ⲚⲈⲈⲓ ⲈⲢⲈϯⲀⲄⲀⲠⲎ Ⲙ̄⁷ⲠⲒⲰⲦ· ϢⲞⲨⲞ ⲀϪⲰⲞⲨ

A. Context

Rom 5:1-5 (results of justification). Those who have been justified through faith have peace with God and have access to his grace. They rejoice in the hope of sharing God's glory as well as in their sufferings because through the latter they will be strengthened to hope and not be disappointed. God's love has been poured into their heart.

GTr 43:1-8 (the place of rest). Valentinus says that he has come into existence in the place of rest. Moreover, he will be there again and hence is always concerned with the Father of all and with those who are truly brothers and sisters (presumably the Father's "parts") on whom the Father's love is poured so that they are not deficient.

B. Elements of Comparison

these (brothers/sisters) on whom the love (ἀγάπη) of the Father is poured forth	(cf. καρδίαις ἡμῶν below) ἡ ἀγάπη τοῦ θεοῦ ἐκκέχυται ἐν ταῖς καρδίαις ἡμῶν

(1) these ≅ καρδίαις ἡμῶν —Both Paul and Valentinus refer to insiders. Paul refers, by synecdoche, to his readers, the Roman Christians, as "hearts." Valentinus resolves this trope, speaking of his fellow-Gnostics by the ingroup jargon of "brothers"/"sisters," which had become the common way of addressing insiders in Christian communities from the earliest years of Christianity.

(2) the love of the Father ≅ ἡ ἀγάπη τοῦ θεοῦ —nearly verbatim, except for the typical change from "God" to "Father."

(3) is poured forth ≅ ἐκκέχυται —Only the tense differs.

C. Evaluation of the Parallel

Both Paul and Valentinus refer to insiders, believers or Gnostics, respectively; to this extent the contexts are similar. Valentinus, however, is not concerned with the theological concepts, such as justification and grace, that concern Paul in the passage in Rom. Nevertheless, the passage in GTr is virtually a paraphrase of that in Rom, and despite the difference in context, there can be little doubt that Rom is used here as elsewhere in GTr (e.g., No. 45).

D. Interpretation

This passage is fascinating because of the insight it gives us into Valentinus' eschatological perspective. He says that he has been in the place of rest and that he will be there. He speaks as one who has experienced a vision, and GTr must be seen, in large part, as the interpretation of that vision. In the conclusion of GTr, he gives his motivation for writing: he is always occupied with the Father of all (owing to his vision). In so doing, he incorporates a strong phrase from Paul which speaks of the Father's love as poured forth and which conjures up images of things which overflow, such as a bubbling spring. He does not include Paul's theological concepts; they do not apply for those who have come into true existence and who are, in a sense, already a "part" of the Father. Valentinus may intentionally recall to his readers Paul's vision in which he was caught up to the third heaven (2 Cor 12:2-4) and so present himself as standing in the tradition of Paul.

3
Evaluation of Valentinus' Use of Texts

After the detailed analyses presented in the preceding chapter, a more general evaluation of Valentinus' use of texts may help to clarify underlying issues. Valentinus' use of texts is intriguing because he never quotes them verbatim. This is in keeping with a general practice in antiquity; ancient literary authors typically did not cite their sources word for word but brought them into agreement with their own style.[1] In light of this practice, what is particularly striking about GTr is not the absence of references to a source but rather the type of sources that are used, namely, texts that were to become part of the New Testament. Such texts had not been incorporated into a literary work in an interpretive manner in early Christianity before the time of GTr. The earliest Christians used the Jewish Scriptures as their own, and modern study of early Christian interpretation has largely focused on citations of Jewish Scriptures. In recent years, scholars have done important research on the use of quotation formulae (used to cite words of Jesus) in early Christian literature,[2] but quotation formulae are not used in GTr. Valentinus' use of texts in GTr, then, appears to be in keeping more with general literary practice than with typical early Christian methods of citing sources.

---

[1] See the discussion of this in E. Norden, *Die antike Kunstprosa vom VI. Jahrhundert v. Chr. bis in die Zeit der Renaissance*, I (Leipzig: Teubner, 1898) 89-90.

[2] The pioneering work was done by H. Koester, *Synoptische Überlieferung*, who showed that sayings collections (rather than one or more of the synoptic gospels) may underlie many of the citations of words of Jesus in the Apostolic Fathers. In addition, J. M. Robinson has made a fruitful attempt to delineate a genre or gattung for such sayings collections in "*Logoi Sophon:* On the Gattung of Q," *Trajectories through Early Christianity*, pp. 71-113, especially pp. 85-103.

The complete absence of explicit citations in GTr raises the question of whether the texts used by Valentinus were considered scriptural by either him or his readers. The question is particularly acute because only a few of the texts discussed in chapter 2 are from Jewish Scriptures. Valentinus and his followers did not abandon Jewish Scriptures,[3] but they generally preferred to use words of Jesus,[4] and the present study confirms such an assessment.[5] How to interpret Jewish Scriptures in light of Christian convictions remained a problem for some Christians who were contemporaneous with Valentinus. Justin Martyr, for example, successfully developed the typological form of exegesis so that Jewish Scriptures could be retained as Christian: figures and events from the Jewish Scriptures were only a type of Christ and events surrounding him. Marcion rejected these Scriptures outright in favor of his "Gospel" and "Apostle" (Luke and letters of Paul respectively, edited by Marcion to remove what he considered to be interpolations by Judaizers). Valentinus also showed a marked preference for using passages from Christian books rather than Jewish Scriptures, but what distinguished him from either Justin or Marcion is the particular way in which he incorporated these texts into a larger literary work. He evidently considered the texts that he used to be significant, but there is no overt indication of their importance. Evidently, he would expect his readers to recognize particular texts that he used and thereby to understand that he was interpreting these passages.

Because the Christian material incorporated in GTr is never a verbatim citation, is it possible that Valentinus simply had a bad memory? If this were the case, the imprecise nature of the allusions to certain texts could be easily understood. It is the case, however, that ancient writers frequently relied on a good memory. Seneca claimed to have been able to recite correctly a list of two thousand names after hearing it read one

---

[3]As Ptolemy's "Letter to Flora" (Epiphanius, *Panar.* 33.3-7) clearly demonstrates.

[4]Von Campenhausen, pp. 80-81. For a detailed study of the problems faced by Christians as they continued to use Jewish Scriptures as their own, see especially Campenhausen, chap. 3, "The Crisis of the Old Testament in the Second Century," pp. 62-102.

[5]If one looks only at the gospel material used in GTr, one quickly observes that most of it comes from passages which relate words of Jesus. The lack of formula citations is thus all the more striking.

Valentinus' Use of Texts 177

time.[6] GTr is a literary work with a complex rhetorical structure,[7] which does not appear to be hastily constructed; this fact also would tend to indicate that the allusions in GTr are not merely haphazard citations from memory. Rather, Valentinus interprets the sources that he incorporates into his work. He alters each text, even those that appear to be paraphrased, in accordance with his style; all have undergone a subtle interpretive process. In fact, any incorporation of one text into another requires interpretation, and this is especially true when both texts are theological or philosophical. Thus, Valentinus' interpretive skill in interweaving texts (that may have a theology different from his own) into a new theological composition shows both his literary and his theological acumen.

While it is clear that Valentinus used written works, whether he depended also upon oral tradition must remain an open question. For the first hundred and fifty years of Christian history both oral and written traditions often stood side by side, intersected, and interacted with each other.[8] From the analyses given in the preceding chapter, it is clear that Valentinus worked from texts, although the possibility that he was also in contact with oral traditions cannot be excluded, as an examination of Nos. 14 and 59 may suggest.[9] Despite the fact that the text of his sources may not have been fixed in Valentinus' lifetime and despite the fact that many traditions about Jesus remained fluid, there is no indication that Valentinus did not work from texts. Even minor alterations which he made yield clues to his theological perspective, as the analyses in Chapter 2 show. Of course, Valentinus may also have been dependent upon written traditions other than those known to us, but, if so, this is difficult to determine now. In the same manner, it is impossible to ascertain with any precision just when Valentinus has used an oral tradition. If, however, he may have used a text known to us, we can evaluate the probability of his use of it. The

---

[6]*Controversiae* 1, Preface 2-4. This is noted in G. Kennedy's discussion in W. Walker, ed., *The Relationships Among the Gospels* (San Antonio: Trinity University, 1978), pp. 142-143. Although Kennedy has used this example to explain how some major agreements and minor disagreements could have arisen among the synoptic gospels, the question of citation from memory invariably arises in study of GTr.

[7]See Standaert's analysis in *NTS*, for example.

[8]Campenhausen, ch. 4, especially p. 121.

[9]No. 14 may reflect knowledge of a tradition of a document, identified with Jesus, that is nailed to a cross. No. 59 is presumed to be an agraphon, previously known to us only in Ephraem's commentary on the *Diatessaron*.

sources studied in Chapter 2 all come from either Genesis or works that would eventually become part of the New Testament. In constructing GTr, Valentinus may have used other sources as well, but these sources have not yet been identified.

Because Valentinus was so successful in incorporating texts into GTr, identification of the texts used is not simple, nor is it possible in many cases to be certain whether a particular text has been used. Rather, only a relative degree of certainty can be established—hampered, of course, by the lamentable fact that GTr has survived only in Coptic translation. Nevertheless, the analyses of Chap. 2 show that Valentinus used numerous texts in composing GTr; these analyses, however, by their nature cannot prove that Valentinus used a given text. A catalogue showing the relative certainty of use of each particular text in the corpus not only may indicate which writings he used but also may give some clues as to their importance for him. In Chap. 2, each suggested parallel was assigned an evaluation of probable, possible, or dubious based primarily on the results of Part B, Elements of Comparison. Evaluation of the likelihood that Valentinus used a particular text is a difficult procedure that cannot yield results of absolute certainty. The results can be compiled into these three categories of relative certainty. These categories are here collected and arranged in different configurations which enable the reader to have easy access to the results. The corpus numbers along with the textual references are listed, first, in the order of their use in GTr (Table 1) and, second, in biblical order (Table 2).

Table 1

SOURCES LISTED BY DEGREE OF CERTAINTY

1. Probable

Corpus No.	Source	Corpus No.	Source
2	Col 1:25-27	32	John 3:19
3	John 14:6	34	John 1:14
4	Gen 2:17, 3:7	38	Matt 5:48
5	Col 1:16-17	43	John 20:22
6	Col 1:16-17	44	John 6:38
9	Rev 13:8	45	Rom 8:3
10	Rev 5:3, 6-7	46	John 14:6
11	Heb 2:17-18	47	Matt 18:12-13
12	Matt 20:28	48	Matt 12:11
14	Col 2:14	50	Matt 11:28
16	1 Cor 15:53-54	52	Matt 6:19
17	John 10:17-18	53	Eph 4:27
18	John 12:32	54	Matt 7:16 = 7:20
19	Rom 8:29-30	55	2 Cor 2:14
23	John 3:8	58	1 John 1:5
26	John 1:18	71	Rom 3:23
		73	Rom 5:5

Table 1 (Continued)

2. Possible

Corpus No.	Source	Corpus No.	Source
1	Rom 1:21, 23, 25, 27	41	1 John 1:1-2
13	Heb 9:17	42	Gen 2:7
15	Phil 2:8	49	Rev 21:25
20	John 10:3	56	Gen 2:7
22	John 3:31	57	1 Cor 15:45
25	John 10:4	60	Matt 7:7
27	Eph 3:9-10	61	1 John 2:27
28	1 Cor 7:31b	62	Gen 2:15
30	2 Cor 5:4	63	Matt 10:29
33	Heb 4:12	64	Heb 1:5
36	Col 1:26	65	John 17:11
37	John 1:18	66	Phil 2:9, 11
39	1 John 3:20	68	Rev 19:12
40	Gen 3:5	72	Rev 21:4

3. Dubious

Corpus No.	Source	Corpus No.	Source
7	Luke 2:46-47	31	2 Tim 2:20-21
8	1 Cor 13:12	35	Rom 9:21-23
21	Rom 10:14	51	Eph 5:14
24	Luke 15:17	67	Rev 22:4
29	1 Cor 13:10	69	John 10:30
		70	Rev 22:16

Table 2

SOURCES LISTED IN BIBLICAL ORDER

Source	Probable	Possible	Dubious
Gen		2:7 (42, 56)	
		2:15 (62)	
	2:17, 3:7 (4)		
		3:5 (40)	
Matt	5:48 (38)		
	6:19 (52)		
		7:7 (60)	
	7:16 = 7:20 (54)		
		10:29 (63)	
	11:28 (50)		
	12:11 (48)		
	18:12-13 (47)		
	20:28 (12)		
Luke			2:46-47 (7)
			15:17 (24)
John	1:14 (34)		
	1:18 (26)	1:18 (37)	
	3:8 (23)		
	3:19 (32)		
		3:31 (22)	
	6:38 (44)		
		10:3 (20)	
		10:4 (25)	
	10:17-18 (17)		
			10:30 (69)
	12:32 (18)		
	14:6 (3, 46)		
		17:11 (65)	
	20:22 (43)		

Table 2 (Continued)

Source	Degree of Certainty		
	Probable	Possible	Dubious
Rom		1:21,23,25,27 (1)	
	3:23 (71)		
	5:5 (73)		
	8:3 (45)		
	8:29-30 (19)		
			9:21-23 (35)
			10:14 (21)
1 Cor		7:31b (28)	
			13:10 (29)
			13:12 (8)
		15:45 (57)	
	15:53-54 (16)		
2 Cor	2:14 (55)		
		5:4 (30)	
Eph		3:9-10 (27)	
	4:27 (53)		
			5:14 (51)
Phil		2:8 (15)	
		2:9, 11 (66)	
Col	1:16-17 (5,6)		
	1:25-27 (2)	1:26 (36)	
	2:14 (14)		
2 Tim			2:20-21 (31)
Heb		1:5 (64)	
	2:17-18 (11)		
		4:12 (33)	
		9:17 (13)	

Table 2 (Continued)

	Degree of Certainty		
Source	Probable	Possible	Dubious
1 John	1:5 (58)	1:1-2 (41)	
		2:27 (61)	
		3:20 (39)	
Rev	5:3,6-7 (10)	19:12 (68)	22:4 (67)
	13:8 (9)	21:4 (72)	22:16 (70)
		21:25 (49)	

Aside from Gen, which is usually interpreted typologically,[10] the texts that are used fall into three distinct groups: Matthew, Johannine literature (considering Rev to be Johannine, as did most Christians in the second century),[11] and Pauline literature (including deutero-Pauline works, whose authority was not questioned in the second century).[12]

---

[10] Typological exegesis in GTr is discussed in Chapter 4.

[11] At least until the time of Gaius, who lived in Rome c. 180-185, when Gaius challenged the Johannine authorship of Rev. The most extensive study of Gaius' challenge has been done by J. D. Smith, *Gaius and the Controversy over the Johannine Literature* (Ph.D. Dissertation, Yale, 1979).

[12] There is no certain attestation for the pastorals in the tradition of early Christianity before the third quarter of the second century. W. Meeks evaluates the evidence in *The Writings of St. Paul* (New York: Norton, 1972), pp. 132-133. At any rate, there is little evidence for their use in GTr for whatever reason. Heb may have been considered Pauline in the second century, although the only evidence is Clement's statement (preserved in Eusebius, *H. E.* VI 14,4) that Pantaenus considered it

Matt is used frequently in GTr, particularly in the second half. From fragments that have survived in other Christian literature, Valentinus is known to have used Matt elsewhere,[13] as did his student Ptolemy in his "Letter to Flora."[14] Matt was in wide use in many circles of Christianity in the second century,[15] and its use by Valentinus may be due to its general popularity rather than any particular theological reason. The Matthean passages used in GTr are in every case words of Jesus, either sayings or parables. Several of the sayings are taken from the Matthean Sermon on the Mount (Matt 5-7).[16] One is taken from a section on discipleship in Matt 10,[17] although this particular passage is not on discipleship. One passage[18] comes from material that is peculiar to Matt (the so-called "M" material),[19] at least among the synoptic gospels.

Valentinus' use of Matt rather than Mark or Luke[20] is sometimes

---

Pauline. Clement and Pantaenus worked in Alexandria; no good evidence survives regarding attribution of its authorship in Rome in the second century.

[13] See frg. 2, where several allusions to Matt occur.

[14] Preserved in Epiphanius, *Panar.* 33.3-7. Campenhausen, pp. 82-86, gives a detailed discussion of the letter.

[15] E. Massaux, *Influence de l'Evangile de saint Matthieu sur la littérature chrétienne avec saint Irénée*, gives a careful analysis of the similarities and differences between Matt and specific passages in early Christian literature that may show knowledge of it. He concludes that literary use of Matt was frequent in second-century Christian literature. Although subsequent work may indicate that his corpus should be narrowed, in general his results are convincing. See also G. N. Stanton, "5 Ezra and Matthean Christianity in the Second Century," *JThS* n.s. 28 (1977) 67-83. Ignatius and the Didache also seem to know Matt (or perhaps the Matthean tradition). On the latter, see E. Massaux, *EphLov*, p. 15.

[16] Nos. 38, 52, 54, 60.

[17] No. 63.

[18] No. 50. Logion 90 of the GTh has a similar saying but omits the word "labor" which is common to Matt and GTr.

[19] This term is common parlance among New Testament scholars, although whether it refers to written or oral tradition is debated. See, for example, W. D. Davies, *The Setting of the Sermon on the Mount* (Cambridge: University Press, 1966), p. 9.

[20] It is not possible to exclude Valentinus' use of Mark, but each time he may allude to Mark, there is a Matthean parallel; simplicity of hypotheses suggests that he used Matt rather than Mark. Similarly the evidence for Valentinus' use of Luke is slim. Some of the Matthean examples have parallels in Luke, but in each case, the passage in GTr either retains

indicated because GTr includes either the Matthean story-line or shares details with the Matthean text in question. For example, the use of "sheep" in a story of an animal that fell into a pit[21] indicates that Matt was used rather than the Lukan parallel (which has "ox or ass" [or, variant reading, a man]), even though there are no particularly Matthean theological motifs in the passage. Shared details as well as a shared story-line make it probable that another passage on sheep, the parable of the lost sheep,[22] was taken from Matt rather than Luke. Finally, it is more probable that Valentinus has used Matt 10:28[23] rather than Mark 10:45, which is almost identical, simply because there is no other evidence that he has used Mark.

Identification of Johannine passages used in GTr is more difficult. John is certainly important theologically for Valentinus, but it is sometimes difficult to be certain which texts are used. In other words, Valentinus often uses motifs that occur more than once in John. The problem is partially a result of John's own ambiguity, that is, his reworking of themes throughout his gospel. Valentinus apparently reworks these themes again. Thus, GTr shares a number of theological motifs with John. In many cases the analyses have shown that these were derived from John, but in others (i.e., those considered possible), while Johannine motifs are present, it is difficult to show direct contact with the text. Outside of Valentinus' use of the prologue to John, in every case but one[24] the texts are either words of Jesus or are taken from summary accounts that Valentinus may have understood as words of Jesus. The role of 1 John is even more ambiguous than that of John since 1 John has reworked many themes from the gospel of John. An element of control is lacking when one discusses any proposed source in which an earlier theme is reworked, and hence if both the author of 1 John and Valentinus have reworked Johannine motifs, identification of a specific passage is extremely difficult. Similar problems of control exist in certain of the proposed references to Rev, although in this case the problem is that similar themes recur in many works of apocalyptic literature. In a few passages it is possible to be relatively certain that Valentinus used Rev and not other apocalyptic literature or traditions that we can no longer identify, but many of the

---

Matthean characteristics (or story-line) or is devoid of peculiarly Lukan features.
[21]No. 48.
[22]No. 47.
[23]No. 12.
[24]No. 43, which reports an action of Jesus.

proposed references[25] to Rev may simply reflect a general knowledge of apocalyptic literature or traditions. Valentinus' use of Paul differs from his use of Matt or the Johannine literature because the form and content of the Pauline material differs from the other two groups. Clearly Paul is not "the" apostle for Valentinus, if by that one means that Pauline conceptions have dominated his writing. Formerly scholars had maintained that Paul was virtually the exclusive property of Gnostics in the second century and that Gnostics claimed him as "the" apostle and traced the authority of their tradition back to Paul.[26] Recent scholarship on the use of Paul in the second century has shown that Gnostics laid no special claim on Paul and that Paul's writings were increasingly used by Christians in general throughout the second century, depending on the genre and purpose of the writing.[27] Sometimes Valentinus seems only to have drawn terminology from the Pauline texts,[28] but other times he appears to have alluded to a "strong" passage which his readers immediately would have recognized, either paraphrasing it or altering it in some way.[29] Although the authority of Paul himself is not obviously central to Valentinus, Paul's thought is of considerable importance to him. This is most clear in passages where Valentinus has provided further development of Pauline passages.[30] Especially if the analysis of No. 73 in Chap. 2 is at all convincing, Valentinus may have seen himself as continuing the apostolic tradition, even though he lays no specific claim on Paul's authority.

In summary, the interpretation of texts and traditions in GTr represents a transition point from Christian interpretation of Jewish Scripture

---

[25]E.g. Nos. 49, 72.

[26]The secondary literature on this problem is vast. For a cogent review of it, see D. Rensberger, *As the Apostle Teaches* (Ph.D. Dissertation, Yale, 1981), pp. 1-45. He includes works from the Tübingen school through W. Bauer.

[27]Two recent studies have demonstrated this in slightly different ways. D. Rensberger, *As the Apostle Teaches,* analyzes the primary sources taking account of genre and chronology; A. Lindemann, *Paulus im ältesten Christentum: Das Bild des Apostels und die Rezeption der paulinischen Theologie in der frühchristlichen Literatur bis Marcion,* BHT 58 (Tübingen: Mohr [Siebeck], 1979), has less interest in chronology. See also Rensberger's review of Lindemann in *JBL* 101 (1982) 287-289.

[28]E.g., Nos. 2, 27, 28.

[29]See especially his use of Rom (e.g., Nos. 45, 71, 73).

[30]E.g., Nos. 5, 6, 16, and possibly his Adam-Christ typologies.

(almost to the exclusion of specifically Christian texts) to Christian interpretation of writings that would become part of the New Testament. The gospel of John has pronoundly influenced GTr: its theological motifs are developed beyond their use in John. Matt has been used frequently, but its particular theology has not made such a large impact on Valentinus' thought. Paul is sometimes used in much the same way as Matt; GTr shows thorough familiarity with the Pauline literature but is not influenced by some of the major Pauline theological concepts, such as grace. At other times, Paul is used in much the same way as John; Pauline theological motifs are developed, although the influence of Paul on GTr is not as thoroughgoing as that of John. Indeed, Valentinus uses Matt, the Pauline literature, and even the Johannine literature to develop his own theology, his own understanding of the gospel, and in so doing shows remarkable exegetical skill. By the time of Clement of Alexandria, exegetical methods such as allegory were used with the New Testament material,[31] but GTr, if the attribution to Valentinus is correct, is the earliest surviving example of a Christian writing that integrates material from writings that would become part of the New Testament into its thought by using an interpretive process. What this interpretive process does to the texts and traditions that are used therein is the subject of the final chapter.

---

[31]Campenhausen, p. 303.

4
Valentinus' Interpretation: His Presuppositions and Method

The detailed analyses presented earlier in this study raise certain questions which focus on the nature of Valentinus' interpretation of the texts that he has used. In general, has he been faithful to these texts?

On one level the answer is obviously no. Characteristic changes, such as a shift of topic from Christ to Father, demonstrate the degree of liberty which Valentinus has taken with texts. Thus, the nature of the changes made by Valentinus precludes a faithful understanding of the intentions of their authors. For example, when Valentinus changes the subject of a reference from Christ to Father, he alters the theology of the biblical text by reassigning a function from Christ to the Father. The case is analogous wherever he has changed the subject to Father in passages that originally gave words of Jesus. Moreover, there is a frequent disregard for the context of the source in its incorporation into Valentinus' understanding of the gospel; this suggests that Valentinus' understanding of these texts is not based on the original context.

On another level Valentinus has remained faithful to the texts he has used. He has presented a detailed and careful interpretation of these texts, although it is one based on his own presuppositions and aims. Chief among his presuppositions is that of an all-encompassing Father who is removed from the sphere of human activity. Valentinus' chief aim is to focus upon an epistemological apprehension of salvation. Although basing one's interpretation on one's presuppositions and aims is not considered an acceptable method in "objective" exegesis, the way that Valentinus alludes to texts does not even hint that his aim was objectivity. In short, the question of whether Valentinus has been faithful to the texts that he has used is rather a question of determining his *tendenz*, that is, what types of changes he has made and why.

Valentinus' interpretation seems almost everywhere to be guided by his interest in epistemology, which frequently shifts the level of discussion from the concrete to the abstract, as in Nos. 17 and 30. Also included in this process is a general neglect of spatial categories (e.g., Nos. 9, 38). Underlying this process is Valentinus' presupposition of an all-encompassing Father in whom all that is real has its existence.[1] Reality has been redefined thereby to include only Gnostics. Thus, only those who have knowledge that their origin is within the all-encompassing Father can attain their destiny in him as well. Such knowledge was brought by Christ in his crucifixion, which set in action the salvation of those predestined to it. Thus, Valentinus' emphasis on an abstract, epistemological approach to salvation influences his interpretation of texts and traditions throughout GTr.

Evaluation of Valentinus' interpretations of texts and traditions in GTr falls naturally into two categories: exegetical changes and methods of exegesis. The first primarily concerns the types of changes Valentinus makes in the texts he interprets in order to achieve the desired effect upon the readers. The second concerns established methods of exegesis which are used in GTr, such as allegory and typology, and also the distinctiveness of Valentinus' overall exegetical method.

Exegetical Changes

Changes characteristically made by Valentinus give insight not only into his presuppositions but also into the significance of the changes themselves. These changes include the following:

1. Denaturing of imagery
   (e.g., Nos. 2, 3, 25, 34, 68)
2. Change in aspect of deity from Christ (Jesus, etc.) to Father
   (e.g., Nos. 2, 5, 6, 18, 26, [27], 36, 37)
3. Change from God to Father
   (e.g., Nos. 2, 19, 36, 55, 66, 71)
4. Bringing of Father and Son into closer relationship
   (e.g., Nos. 4, 20, 48, 64, 65, 66, 68)
5. Shift in emphasis away from the eschatological
   (e.g., Nos. 16, 18, 19, 28, 30, 53, 62 (?), 72)
6. Increased focus on predestination
   (e.g., Nos. 10, 11, 12, 32, 50, 62)

---

[1] See the discussions of Nos. 5 and 6 in Chapter 2.

7. Shift from ethical to intellectual plane
   (e.g., Nos. 1, 38, 45, 52 (?), 58, 71)
8. Redefinition of salvation in terms of one's origin
   (e.g., Nos. 5, 6, 22, 23, 48, 49, 55, 60, 71, 72)

There is considerable overlapping among these groups, and neither the list of changes nor the lists of examples are exhaustive. Yet, examination of these types of changes facilitates an understanding of how Valentinus has worked with the texts that he uses in order to present his interpretation of the Christian message.

1. Denaturing of imagery. One interpretive move frequently made by Valentinus is the denaturing of imagery which figures prominently in the texts being used (i.e., "strong" imagery). In this case the imagery from the text which is being interpreted is generally either a feature peculiar to that text or is an image which would not coincide with the images and thought of GTr. A good example is No. 2. In Col 1:25-27, "hidden mystery" is a rich image which refers both to God's plan to admit Jews and Gentiles to salvation and also to Christ's presence among the community. In GTr, it has been denatured so that it is merely an epithet of Jesus ("the hidden mystery, Jesus Christ"). Another excellent example of Valentinus' denaturing of imagery is No. 3, where Jesus' strong statement from John 14:6, "I am the way," is changed to a more bland, "he gave a way." Thus, a striking phrase which is typical of the Johannine Jesus is incorporated into GTr as merely a narrative description of Jesus' work as a teacher. In No. 34, the almost shocking description of the Word as "flesh" from John is replaced in GTr by a reference to the Word as a body ("It [the Word] is not a sound alone, but it became a body"). The two images have completely different connotations even though "body" and "flesh" can in many cases be used interchangeably.

Occasionally, images which appear in the context of the original passage are not retained in GTr. These images contribute a richness of detail in their original context but do not appear at all in GTr. Examples are Nos. 25 and 68. In No. 25, the context of John 10:4 contains the image of a shepherd who is then identified with Jesus. GTr, however, contains no reference to a shepherd, nor is it even clear whether the pronoun "he" which is used refers to Jesus or to someone else, such as the Father ("He has gone before them to their paths"). Again, in No. 68, the context of Rev 19:12 refers to a rider on a white horse (= Jesus), but GTr refers only to "Lord" and gives a string of ambiguous pronouns. These underscore the unity between Father and Son, but they do not retain the vivid image of

Jesus as a rider on a white horse ("But this one who exists exists with his name also . . ."). In the process of denaturing images Valentinus has achieved an implicit goal of clarifying his own perspective to the reader while keeping only those images which enable the reader to recognize the source or which further his own thought.

2. *Change in aspect of deity from Christ (Jesus, etc.) to Father.* The next group of changes may well be the most telling. By altering the focus from Christ, Jesus, or Son to Father, Valentinus does not simply change the meaning of the passages which he incorporates into GTr but, more important, he demonstrates the centrality of the Father in his thought. This is evident even from the opening lines of GTr (16:31-35: "The gospel of truth is a joy for those who have received favor from the Father of truth so that they should know him by means of the power of the Word, who came forth from the fullness") and is even clearer upon examination of the way Valentinus has changed certain texts that he has used in GTr. The focus is frequently shifted from Christ (or Jesus or the Son) to the Father, while Christ's importance as an agent of revelation generally is retained. This is especially clear in No. 2, where the text that Valentinus uses (Col 1:25-27) understands the content of the gospel as Christ. GTr, in contrast, understands the content of the gospel as knowledge of the Father; Christ's work is to disseminate that knowledge. The work of Christ is not thereby negated, but a shift in emphasis has clearly occurred. The same sort of change occurs in No. 36: the content of the mystery spoken of in Col is the Son, whereas in GTr it is the Father. Moreover, in Nos. 5 and 6 the focus is changed from Christ as the agent of creation (Col) to the Father as the creator of all.

All of the preceding examples were from Col, but a similar change in focus occurs when Valentinus uses other texts as well. For example, in No. 26, the text (John 1:18) has Son as the agent who makes the Father known,[2] whereas the interpretation speaks of the Father as manifesting the Son. Similarly in No. 37 (also John 1:18), the text says that the Son explains the Father, whereas GTr presents the Father as explaining himself. Outright substitutions of one aspect of deity for another can also be made. No. 18 shows how Valentinus has interpreted John 12:32 so that emphasis is placed on the Father as the one who draws to himself all those

---

[2]So in No. 27: in the biblical source (Eph 3:9-10) the church is the agent of revelation, whereas the Father's innermost parts are said to be the agent of revelation in GTr.

Valentinus' Interpretation   193

who have received knowledge; John's emphasis is on the future role of Jesus in the gathering of the saved. Moreover, the clear statement that the Father draws people to himself "as < each > person gains knowledge" (GTr 21:11-12) enables Valentinus to preserve the transcendence of the Father by implying that this drawing is not dependent upon the Father's initiative. In summary, one of the chief interpretive moves that Valentinus makes is a shift of focus from Christ or the Son to the Father, which functions in part to show the close relationship between Father and Son but which also underscores the overriding importance of the Father for the theology of GTr.

3. *Change from God to Father.* Another type of change which Valentinus regularly makes is from God to Father. These changes may be motivated by acquaintance with popular Platonism, which had absorbed certain tenets of Stoicism. Thus, Valentinus would feel comfortable with a Middle Platonic concept of a transcendent deity which had absorbed some of the features of an originally Stoic all-encompassing God.[3] The Platonic connection is made particularly clear by Valentinus' practice of referring to this all-encompassing deity as "Father"[4] and also, of course by the several times the transcendence of the Father is underscored (e.g., GTr 17:5-6, 18:31-32: "the inconceivably incomprehensible one"). In one significant instance (see No. 48), a passage in GTr describes the normally inactive Father's intervention into the affairs of humanity by initiating the process of salvation. The instances listed above in which God is changed to Father may show an interaction between popular Middle Platonism and the Johannine literature. In other words, while "Father" was a common designation for the deity in some circles of Middle Platonism, the gospel of John also prefers this designation for God.[5] Thus, Valentinus may have

---

[3]See the discussion of No. 5 in Chapter 2; Stoics might prefer to refer to Nature rather than to God, as M. Aurelius does in 4,23,2. See also Dillon, pp. 45-49, who outlines the adaptation of Stoic concepts into Middle Platonism.

[4]As was a common practice in other hellenistic literature influenced by popular Platonism, e.g., *Corp. Herm.* 1:24-26.

[5]This statement does not imply that John himself could not have been influenced by Middle Platonism; John, however, probably refers to God as Father as a means of underscoring the unity between Father and Son. Of course, GTr also does this (see section 4), but GTr shows other points of contact (those discussed above) with Middle Platonism which John does not have.

drawn upon an affinity for certain elements of Middle Platonism and on his knowledge of John in his use of "Father."

4. *Bringing of Father and Son into closer relationship.* The gospel of John may also have influenced the way the particularly close relationship between Father and Son is understood in GTr. Frequently texts are interpreted so that they underscore the unity between Father and Son. In fact, GTr sometimes fails to make a distinction between Son and Father. This is particularly clear in the latter pages of GTr (e.g., Nos. 64 [Heb 1:5], 65 [John 17:11], 66 [Phil 2:9, 11], and 68 [Rev 19:12]). A particularly good example is No. 65: "He (Father) gave him (Son) his name which is his." In all of these passages, one could almost understand that the interpretation of GTr is determined by Jesus' statement in John 10:30: "I and the Father are one."[6] The lack of differentiation between the two is evident even in the early pages of GTr. In the context of No. 4 (Gen 2:17, 3:7), the fruit of the tree of knowledge of the Father is said to bring discovery of Jesus Christ (GTr 18:27-30) while a little later the Father is said to be discovered within those who eat of the fruit (GTr 18:32-33). Moreover, it is just possible that the interpretation given to John 10:3 in No. 20 presupposes the unity between Jesus and the Father, if indeed both Jesus and the Father are identified with the shepherd.[7]

Finally, one of the most intriguing instances in which the distinction between Father and Son is blurred is in No. 48 (Matt 12:11). This passage follows an interpretation of Matt 18:12-13 in which the beloved Son[8] has been identified with the shepherd in the parable of the lost sheep. Since No. 48 is also about a sheep one would expect the subject of the action regarding the sheep to remain the same, but in fact a close examination of the Coptic suggests that in No. 48 the Father is the subject rather than the beloved Son. Moreover, Valentinus cross-refers to the sheep of the

---

[6]As Standaert, *NTS*, p. 272 has observed, although no direct use of this verse can be shown (e.g., No. 69, where Valentinus' use of John 10:30 was shown to be dubious).

[7]The problem arises because of the passive in the phrase: "if his name has not been called." GTr clearly implies that the Father calls the names of those who are to go to him, but the passage in John refers to Jesus. Thus, this reference could also be understood as another example of the type of change discussed in section 2.

[8]Strictly speaking, the subject of the parable in No. 47 is not stated and might also be the Father, but the discussion of No. 46 in Chapter 2 establishes that the Son is the subject in both No. 46 and 47.

preceding parable ("the sheep which he found") and thereby implicitly identifies the two shepherds with one another. It would be imprecise to label this feature "monarchianism" because monarchianism implies the existence of a distinct group which held this theology. There is evidence for such a group,[9] which is generally associated with Theodotus of Byzantium, but it is not attested before the late second century. Early Christian theology can be characterized by its constant state of flux; this is nowhere more true than in passages which hint at the nature of the relationship between Father and Son. Moreover, GTr may simply demonstrate the profound influence of Valentinus' understanding of the gospel of John in this feature of its theology.

5. *Shift in emphasis away from the eschatological.* The fifth group of examples illustrates a typical shift away from any eschatological character of the text used. The eschatology of GTr is so realized that, even when GTr refers to judgment (e.g., Nos. 32, 33), it appears that the judgment has already occurred and has been brought into effect by the appearance of the Word. The shift away from eschatological expectation is subtle, however, and bears further investigation. Nos. 16 and 30 are excellent examples. In both, the text which is interpreted is from Paul (1 Cor 15:53-54 and 2 Cor 5:4 respectively). In the former example GTr speaks of Jesus, who is understood to have already had eternal life in his earthly life, whereas Paul speaks of the coming eschaton, when all Christians will be changed. Thus by changing the topic, Valentinus is able to shift the emphasis away from eschatology. The latter example refers to Gnostics, for whom the concept "death" is irrelevant, whereas again the original context was eschatological. In No. 18, the text which is being interpreted (John 12:32) refers to the death of Jesus and his eventual drawing of humanity to himself. Valentinus has interpreted the passage to refer to the Gnostic's return to the Father upon his or her acquisition of knowledge. There is no hint that a later judgment is to occur or in fact that any lapse in time occurs before the Gnostic goes to the Father. In the subsequent interpretation of Rom 8:29-30 in No. 19, Valentinus has added a phrase, "at the end," which suggests, not that the end is expected someday, but that the end has in fact already arrived for those who have knowledge that their origin and destiny are with the Father.

---

[9]E.g., Ps-Tertullian, *Adv. Omnes Haer.* 8; Filast., *Haer.* 50.1; Epiphanius, *Pan.* 53, 3-7; Hippolytus, *Ref.* VII 35; and the "Little Labyrinth" in Eusebius, *H. E.* V 28.

Valentinus' interpretation of 1 Cor 7:31 (No. 28) is particularly illustrative. Paul's statement ("For the form of this world is passing away") is clearly eschatological; he expects the end of the world imminently and for that reason can offer certain advice to the unmarried. There is no hint of the original context in GTr; rather one phrase is excerpted almost exactly and applied to the activity of the Son. All eschatological expectation is gone, and the passage now speaks of the Son's role in filling the world's lack through his bringing knowledge of the Father. No. 53 (Eph 4:27) gives a more straightforward indication that the end of the world is no longer expected. After his admonition concerning the role of the devil (or evil), Valentinus adds a phrase, "for you have already brought him to naught," thereby precluding any notion of a forthcoming eschatological event. Finally, both Nos. 62 (Gen 2:15) and 73 (Rom 5:5) indicate that those who are a part of the Father have already joined the Father.[10] The shift in focus away from the eschatological in fact can be understood to underlie all of GTr because of the emphasis in GTr on intellectual apprehension of salvation through knowledge of one's origin and destiny.

6. *Increased focus on predestination.* Along with the shift in emphasis away from eschatological concerns is an increased focus on predestination. This is particularly clear in those sections which deal specifically with the salvific role of Jesus' death (Nos. 10 [Rev 5:3, 6-7], 11 [Heb 2:17-18], and 12 [Matt 20:28]). In these passages, there is a heightened emphasis on predestination owing to the emphasis given in the interpretation of the living book of the living. Although the book was held to be available from before the foundation of all, Jesus does not take it until his death. Central to these interpretations is Jesus' foreknowledge of his death, which was predestined. The interpretation of Matt 20:28 is particularly telling in that Matt's phrase "for many," which refers to the salvific nature of Jesus' death, is taken in a restrictive sense, namely, that Jesus' death "for many" is salvific for those predestined to salvation.

A similar interpretation prevails in No. 50 (Matt 11:28: "Come to me, all who labor and are heavy laden, and I will give you rest"). Here Matt's "all" has been omitted; the implication of GTr is that only those

---

[10] E.g., No. 62: "He (the Father) knows his plantings for it is he who planted them in his paradise." Paradise is then immediately equated with the Father's place of rest (36:38-39) in which Gnostics have been "planted." This passage also, of course, illustrates the focus on predestination in GTr.

predestined to salvation can receive "rest." This interpretation occurs within allegorical paraenesis; the readers of GTr are urged to convert others but not "all" others. GTr does not say how these potential converts are to be identified. In No. 32, John 3:19 is interpreted to imply that people have been subject to an absolute judgment without regard to their own choice or actions. No. 62 (Gen 2:15) supports such an assertion by stating that the Father knows those who belong to him because he "planted" them, i.e., was responsible for their coming into existence. In summary, even though determination of the precise stance of GTr toward predestination is difficult, it is nonetheless the case that GTr occasionally interprets texts so that the focus on predestination is increased.[11]

7. *Shift from ethical to intellectual plane.* In a number of passages, the texts that are interpreted originally had ethical implications. In such cases, Valentinus consistently shifts his interpretation to an intellectual plane. This is evident almost from the beginning of GTr, namely, in No. 1 (Rom 1:21, 23, 25, 27). Here, unlike later examples, some interest in ethics is retained. Both Valentinus and Paul are apparently concerned with the presence of evil in the world. More than Paul, however, Valentinus is concerned with intellectualizing the account of how this world came to be imbued with error and in so doing removes the ethical implications of the presence of evil in the world. Because error is only a lie, a faint substitute for the truth, it somehow is not so much an evil to be eradicated through the doing of good as an unfortunate fact whose consequences are of no concern to the Gnostic, who has only to apprehend that he or she comes from the Father and has nothing to do with error.[12]

An excellent example of Valentinus' lack of interest in ethics is his interpretation of Rom 8:3 in No. 45. He omits Paul's reference to the sinful nature of Jesus' flesh not, in all likelihood, because of a docetic view of Jesus but because the salvific event enabled persons to acquire knowledge. Sin is simply not the issue. Other examples merely underscore this

---

[11] The ambiguity may be deliberate, functioning both to increase group solidarity by strengthening group boundaries and to encourage members to make converts.

[12] Of course, GTr does explain in 18:19-26 that there has been a confrontation between error and Jesus because Jesus taught truth to human beings. The result was Jesus' crucifixion, which brought salvation to all who could partake of its fruit. Nevertheless, this account is so stylized that it is difficult to understand it as a literal description of the human situation.

point. In No. 58 (1 John 1:5), Valentinus has transformed the image of "light," which is an ethical image contrasted with "darkness" in 1 John, into a metaphysical image. Thus, he does not retain a constrast of opposites but rather asserts that there can be no deficiency in the fullness (i.e., light represents what belongs within the deity). In yet another example (No. 71), Valentinus has omitted the reference to sin in his paraphrase of Rom 3:23; this enables him to apply the passage to Gnostics, for whom the category "sin" is not applicable.[13] Finally, in No. 38 (Matt 5:48), Valentinus does not retain Matt's exhortation to imitate the perfection of the heavenly Father but rather makes a theological statement of the Father's perfection. This effectively shifts the reader's attention away from the ethical implications of Matt toward the particular theology of GTr.

8. Redefinition of salvation in terms of one's origin. The last group which is listed above is largely determinative for the soteriology of GTr. All of the examples given demonstrate a basic axiom of GTr, namely, that the Gnostic's origin and destiny are both with the Father. This can be seen most clearly in Nos. 22 (John 3:31) and 23 (John 3:8), where this is discussed explicitly (No. 22: "Thus, if one knows, he is from above"; No. 23: "Whoever knows in this manner understands where he came from and where he is going"), but the motif underlies many other passages in GTr as well. Nos. 5 and 6 (Col 1:16-17) refer primarily to the all-encompassing Father, but the ambiguous "all" in GTr should not be taken only in a cosmological sense as in ps-Paul but also as a reference to the intellectual dwelling place of all those people who have knowledge (see GTr 21:8-14). The interpretation of "sabbath" which is given in No. 48 (Matt 12:11) and 49 (Rev 21:25) applies to the readers (or Gnostics). There it is clear that the perfect light, that is, the light of knowledge, dwells within the

---

[13] One large passage of GTr may be taken to illustrate Valentinus' disinterest in ethics, namely, the section of allegorical paraenesis in 32:35ff. Just how much of the long section that follows should be understood allegorically is not at all clear. It is possible that No. 52 (Matt 6:19) is also to be understood allegorically even though it looks like a straightforward paraenetical injunction. Perhaps the readers are to understand the admonition not to become moth or worm eaten figuratively as an admonition about corruption, or the admonition is to be understood not in an ethical sense but as a reference to something else now unknown. In the latter case GTr would again attest a shift from the ethical plane but not necessarily to the intellectual plane.

Valentinus' Interpretation 199

readers. This light enables them to share in the activity of the Father, who took it upon himself to send his Son to save Gnostics.

No. 55 (2 Cor 2:14) underscores previous statements about the origin and destiny of Gnostics by referring to them as the Father's fragrance. The interpretation makes it clear that the destiny of Gnostics is not dependent upon any response to the gospel but rather upon their origin within the Father (GTr 34:1-3: "it is they [children of the Father] who are his fragrance for they are from the attractiveness of his face"). Moreover, No. 60 (Matt 7:7) explains that the goal of salvation is restoration to the fullness, which entails a return to one's origin within the Father ("those who are disturbed will receive a sending back"). Finally, Nos. 71 (Rom 3:23) and 72 (Rev 21:4) suggest that the Father is comprised of his "parts," that is, Gnostics. Thus, the "parts" of the Father share his (Middle Platonic) attributes and radiate his glory. The fullness is the Father together with all of his "parts," who are finally collected due to their apprehension of their origin and destiny. The knowledge necessary for this intellectual apprehension was brought by Jesus Christ, the Son, whose role was to give all those who have received the knowledge brought through Jesus' crucifixion a way to the Father.

In summary, the types of changes made by Valentinus enable him to shift the reader's attention to the epistemological level. By restricting intellectual reality to events that go on within the deity, Valentinus enables his reader to join the deity as a part of deity. Valentinus does not deny the reality of the material world through his supposition that "all" are in the Father. Moreover, Valentinus does not deny the value of ethical principles for his readers, who of course still live in the material world. Rather, GTr is about salvation through knowledge of one's origin and destiny and as such is not concerned with mundane issues.

Methods of Exegesis

Valentinus uses two exegetical methods which were well-known among Christians in the period of GTr: typology and allegory. Before the time of Valentinus, however, both of these methods were used by Christians in order to interpret Jewish Scriptures, which comprised the Christian Bible. In light of Christian teaching and practice Christians could no longer interpret Jewish Scriptures literally; thus the Scriptures were largely read as a prediction of Christ. This is known as the prophetic-christological exegesis of Scripture and is the primary method used throughout early Christian literature up until around the mid-second century, including most of those writings that were later collected into a New Testament. In the prophetic-christological exegesis, passages of Scripture were seen as predictions or promises that had their fulfillment in Christ. A good example of this method of exegesis is found in Heb 1:5, where Christ is seen to be the fulfillment of Ps 2:7: "You are my son; this day I have begotten you." Valentinus may use this method of exegesis in No. 64 if he does not draw it directly from Heb 1:5. The prophetic-christological exegesis of Scripture is also referred to as the typological method, a term which may be applied more precisely to portions of writings in which the authors have understood a point of Scripture as a "type" which points to Christ. Typological exegesis is found throughout early Christian writings, although perhaps the best examples are to be found in 1 Clem., Barn., and Justin's *Dial*. The dividing line between allegory and typology is indeed thin, but in general allegory is used to interpret portions of Scripture which can no longer be made relevant even with typological exegesis. The best examples are those which concern the Mosaic Law (Barn. 7-8; Justin, *Dial*. 14:29, 19:2, 28:4), which is "spiritualized."[14] Valentinus' method of exegesis for the most part, however, is something very different from either typology or allegory and will be discussed at greater length below.

Instances in which Valentinus employs typology include the following: Nos. 4, 40, 42, 56, 57. In every case but one (No. 57), the passage cited is a typological exegesis of a passage from Gen. Typological exegesis of No. 57 (1 Cor 15:45) is understandable because Valentinus may simply retain Paul's own typology. The pertinent question is whether Valentinus gives an independent typological exegesis of Gen or whether he is following an early Christian traditional Adam-Christ typology based on Paul's use.[15]

---

[14] In the preceding discussion, I must acknowledge a tremendous debt to Campenhausen, pp. 62-102, although the summary given above can in no way be said to encapsulate these pages. The material covered is vast, and the summary above seeks only to set Valentinus' exegetical method within the context of early Christian exegesis of Scripture. The best investigation into Christian attempts to understand Jewish Scripture as Christian Scripture is that of T. Stylianopoulos, *Justin Martyr and the Mosaic Law*, SBLDS 20 (Missoula: Scholars, 1975). Stylianopoulos shows that Justin's attitudes arose in response to those of Gnostics and Marcionites. Because Valentinus does not use Jewish Scripture to a great extent in GTr, Justin's exegesis is only indirectly useful for my study, i.e., for comparison. Yet, it is noteworthy that Justin still feels a need to defend this Scripture.

[15] For an excellent modern treatment of Paul's Adam-Christ typology, see A. Nygren, *Romans* (Philadelphia: Fortress, 1949), pp. 206-229.

Valentinus' Interpretation 201

To what extent is Valentinus influenced by early Christian tradition in his typological exegeses? We know that GTr frequently reflects knowledge of early Christian traditions; this has been noted in the appropriate places in Chapter 2. Moreover, in certain places (e.g. No. 14 [Col 2:14]) GTr shows contact with specific traditional early Christian exegesis.[16] Although it is impossible to be certain, the simplest explanation is to assume that Valentinus' typological exegesis is based on an understanding of the Pauline Adam-Christ typology which Valentinus himself may have extended in the passages he interprets. The treatment of Gen is quite different in Sethian Gnostic literature; see especially HypArch 88:10-89:3 and ApocryJn II 22:3-21:16. Sethian Gnosticism exhibits a very different exegesis of Gen— as a story which must be "corrected" to understand the true meaning. Valentinus' treatment of Gen is much more sympathetic and is in line with most Christian exegesis of Gen from his day.[17]

Instances in which Valentinus employs allegory include the following: 20, 25, 47, 48, 49, 52, 61, 62. In only one place, the double allegorization of sabbath (No. 48 [Matt 12:11]), does the allegory seem forced. In all other places, Valentinus prepares the reader for the allegory, which then seems perfectly natural. Of course, the meaning of an allegorical passage cannot always be recovered by a modern reader because the key to unlock the allegorical passage has not survived. This is especially the case in GTr 32:35ff., where only some of the allegorical meanings (e.g., sleep = ignorance) can be determined from other studies of Gnosticism.[18] Of course, in other cases the allegory is not clear (e.g., No. 47 [Matt 18:12-13], where we at least know that sheep = people = numbers; or the allegory of the vessels in GTr 25:25-35, 26:8-15). These may depend on texts or traditions other than those which were incorporated into Christian scripture, as may large portions of GTr for which no textual source has been proposed in this study. In general, Valentinus' allegory is not arbitrary, as is the exegetical method which Irenaeus accuses later Valentinians of using (e.g., Adv. Haer. I 7.1). In this sense Valentinus is faithful to the texts that he uses, and he differs from later Christians, both gnostic and non-Gnostic (cf. Clement of Alexandria, *Who is that Rich Man?*) in his use of allegory. The reason must lie largely in Valentinus' preparation of his reader for the allegorical interpretations; from the

---

[16] See, for example, the commentary on No. 14 in Chapter 2, where this is discussed.
[17] See the mention of *Diog.* 12 in the discussion of No. 4.
[18] See especially the work of H. Jonas, *The Gnostic Religion*, pp. 68-73.

beginning of GTr one realizes that the action occurs on the epistemological level, and therefore his reader is forced to understand much of GTr figuratively. From there it is a short step to allegorization.

In general, Valentinus' typological exegesis of Gen is not unusual when viewed in the context of contemporaneous Christian exegesis of Scripture. His allegorical exegesis is more unusual because it is used of texts that were to be included in the New Testament, whereas prevailing Christian practice employed allegorical exegesis of Jewish Scripture. Most striking, however, is his general method of incorporating texts into GTr and the concomitant interpretation of these texts. This general method is apparently not used of Christian texts before GTr, although a similar method of incorporating allusions to Jewish Scripture is adopted, for example, by the author of Rev. Valentinus' method of incorporating texts looks very much like midrash in that he has searched and studied the texts in order to understand their meanings. This is especially clear in the way that Valentinus consistently retains enough of a reference to allow a reader to recognize its source while he changes key terms and even ideas. Although such a process enables him to make an entirely different point than that made by the text he interprets, his interpretation remains an interpretation of each specific text (albeit subordinated to Valentinus' Gnostic presuppositions).

Where would Valentinus have come in contact with midrash? It is tempting to suggest a natural source in apocalyptic Judaism.[19] While GTr does interpret certain apocalyptic texts (e.g. Nos. 9 [Rev 13:8], 10 [Rev 5:3, 6-7]), they do not comprise the bulk of the texts that he uses. Moreover, Valentinus occasionally seems to show familiarity with traditions known to us from writings that show continuing influence from Judaism (e.g., No. 14 and those passages about the divine Name). Of course, Valentinus also may have been influenced by Paul's use of midrash (e.g., Rom 10:6-8). There is simply no way to isolate specific groups of people that may have influenced Valentinus, although these suggestions are tantalizing.

Research on midrash in the biblical milieu has shown that the midrashic method was widely used and that its scope is broad. The apocalyptic literature that survives uses the midrashic method almost constantly to

---

[19]R. M. Grant much earlier suggested that Gnosticism arose out of the frustrated hopes of apocalyptic Judaism. See *Gnosticism and Early Christianity* (New York: Columbia University, 1966), pp. 27-38. He later retracted this position.

reinterpret Scripture. This reinterpretation is not arbitrary but results from an intense searching of Scripture to find the meaning in these texts which spoke directly to the apocalypticists' own time. Qumran documents such as the Habakkuk Commentary (pesher) also show affinity with the midrashic method. Moreover, the ancient versions, such as the LXX, show the continuing influence of Jewish exegesis, as does the Palestinian targum. Even the New Testament shows the influence of Jewish midrash.[20]

GTr shares several characteristics with midrash, aside from its general method of incorporating texts. For example, midrash characteristically (1) takes its departure from Scripture and (2) is homiletical. Further, midrash (3) is a study which pays close attention to the text and (4) has, as its goal, adaptation to the present.[21] Each of these characteristics applies to the interpretation of texts in GTr, if one acknowledges that the texts which Valentinus uses must be considered scriptural for him and his readers.[22] Thus, Valentinus takes the texts as a point of departure and throughout pays close attention to the text. For terms that are shocking, such as "flesh" in John 1:14 (No. 34), an interpretive substitute is given ("a body"). Especially in the middle portion of GTr, there are indications that the interpretations have homiletical applications, and hence paraenesis plays a large role in Nos. 49-52. These interpretations may have arisen through homiletical use of the texts interpreted therein, as may all of the interpretations in GTr. Further, GTr may show adaptation to the present in its realized eschatology. As it became clear to Christians that the eschaton may not arrive immediately (or at all), one logical response might be that represented in GTr: a shift onto an epistemological plane in understanding the scriptural texts.

The foregoing suggestions give only a preliminary indication of how further study on GTr might proceed. They do, however, reinforce the view that Valentinus is faithful to the texts that he interprets, although of

---

[20]This discussion is based on the insightful article by R. Bloch, "Midrash," in *Approaches to Ancient Judaism: Theory and Practice*, ed. by W. S. Green, Brown Judaic Studies 1 (Missoula: Scholars, 1978), pp. 44-49.

[21]These are R. Bloch's characteristics which she discusses on pp. 31-33. The following discussion is not intended to be understood as a claim that the method of interpretation used in GTr *is* midrash but that it shares similar characteristics with midrash. The whole question of midrash as an interpretive method (including its history of use by various groups), though interesting, is not apposite to the present study.

[22]This does not mean that the texts were canonical in a strict sense; cf. the discussion of this in Chap. 1.

course his method influences the results of his exegesis. Just as there was Jewish Scripture long before there was a Jewish canon, the process of canonization in Christianity was lengthy. Nevertheless, Christians could not forever retain Jewish Scriptures as their own, and hence the notion of Christian Scripture apart from Jewish Scripture gradually developed. GTr attests a formative stage in that development.

* * * * *

This study has shown GTr to be the product of a creative Gnostic exegete whose work is steeped in early Christian tradition. There is no clear indication that a developed Gnostic system is presupposed; it is more likely that such a system arose from further consideration of some of the tenets of GTr, such as an all-encompassing Father whose "thoughts" could have attributes of their own. Precise identification of the stage of development of a Gnostic myth represented by GTr, however, is not necessary for understanding the interpretation of texts and traditions therein. Rather, the interpretations given to specific texts demonstrate the author's tremendous insight into those texts. It is this insight and the author's search for the meanings of Christian texts that place GTr in a prominent position in the history of early Christian thought.

Appendix

VALENTINUS IN A LETTER (frg. 2) PRESERVED IN CLEMENT OF ALEXANDRIA, STROM. II 114.6 ~ MATT 5:8

Probable.

καὶ οὕτω μακαρίζεται ὁ ἔχων τὴν τοιαύτην καρδίαν ὅτι ὄψεται τὸν θεόν	⁸μακάριοι οἱ καθαροὶ τῇ καρδίᾳ ὅτι (cf. ὄψονται below) τὸν θεὸν ὄψονται

A. Context

Matt 5:3-12 (the Beatitudes). In a series of exhortations, Jesus explains who the blessed are: they are people who have fine moral qualities, such as mercy, purity, and righteousness.

Clement of Alex., Strom. II, 114, 3-6 (letter concerning appendages). One can become pure only by the Father in his manifestation of the Son. When one becomes pure, that person shines with the light of sanctification and is blessed.

B. Elements of Comparison

(1) μακαρίζεται ≅ μακάροι —Both words come from the same root. Matt uses a noun, while Valentinus uses a verb.

(2) ὁ . . . καρδίαν ≅ οἱ . . . καρδίᾳ —Only the grammatical construction differs.

(3) ὅτι = ὅτι —verbatim.

(4) ὄψεται ≅ ὄψονται —verbatim, except for number (singular in Valentinus and plural in Matt).

(5) τὸν θεόν = τὸν θεόν —verbatim.

C. Evaluation of the Parallel

Although the contexts are similar to the extent that both concern purity and blessedness, the forms differ (exhortation in Matt, exposition in Valentinus). Of the five elements of comparison, two are verbatim (3, 5), and one other (4) is nearly so. The other two either contain the same root or differ in grammatical construction. The weight of the evidence suggests that Valentinus almost certainly used Matt here.

D. Interpretation

Valentinus has changed a passage from Matt, which promises that the pure in heart are blessed and will see God, by incorporating it into an illustration about the Father, who purifies evil hearts. A person whose heart is purified is blessed and will see God. Allegorical elements may be present in the passage. Clement says that the passage is about the appendages (προσάρτημα), i.e., unnecessary hindrances to salvation. These may be evil spirits, as the passage says, but they may also apply to hindrances to salvation of any sort, such as evil deeds or even ignorance.

Comparison with GTr

The technique used in this passage is strikingly similar to that used in GTr. Some differences do exist. Valentinus here retains Matt's reference to God, although he speaks of the Father in the passage also. The passage may also center on ethical concerns, unlike GTr, although this is not certain because the context is philosophical (on appendages). Overall, however, the method of interpretation used in this fragment is very similar to that used in GTr.

Bibliography

Arai, S. *Die Christologie des Evangelium Veritatis.* Leiden: Brill, 1964.

Attridge, H. W. "The Gospel of Truth as an Exoteric Text." Typescript of paper to be published in the proceedings of a conference on Gnosticism held at Southwestern Missouri State University, in March 1983.

_____. "Greek and Latin Apocalypses," *Semeia* 14 (1979) 159-186.

Bardy, G. "Les Ecoles romaines au second siècle." *RHE* 28 (1932) 501-532.

_____. "L'Eglise romaine sous le pontificat de saint Anicet (154-155)." *RSR* 17 (1927) 481-511.

Barrett, C. K. "The Gospel of Truth. The Editio Princeps of an Ancient Gnostic Text." *ExpTim* 69 (1958) 167-70.

_____. "The Theological Vocabulary of the Fourth Gospel and of the Gospel of Truth." *Current Issues in New Testament Interpretation: Essays in Honor of Otto A. Piper,* eds. W. Klassen and G. F. Snyder. New York: Harper & Row, 1961, 210-23, 297-98.

Barns, J. W. B., G. M. Browne and J. C. Shelton, eds. *Nag Hammadi Codices: Greek and Coptic Papyri from the Cartonnage of the Covers.* NHS 16. Leiden: Brill, 1981.

Bauer, W., W. F. Arndt and F. W. Gingrich. *A Greek-English Lexicon of the New Testament and Other Early Christian Literature.* 2nd ed. Chicago: University of Chicago, 1974.

Bauer, W. *Orthodoxy and Heresy in Earliest Christianity.* Philadelphia: Fortress, 1971.

Bellet, P. "Analecta Coptica: 4. An Etymological Speculation in the *Gospel of Truth.*" *CBQ* 40 (1978) 49-52.

Blanchette, O. "Does the *Cheirographon* of Col 2, 14 Represent Christ Himself?" *CBQ* 23 (1961) 306-312.

Bloch, R. "Midrash." In *Approaches to Ancient Judaism*, ed. W. S. Green, 29-50. Brown Judaic Studies 1. Missoula: Scholars, 1978.

Böhlig, A. "Zur Ursprache des Evangelium Veritatis." *Muséon* 79 (1966) 317-333.

Braun, F.-M. "L'Enigme des Odes de Salomon." *RevThom* 57 (1957) 597-625.

Campenhausen, H. von. *The Formation of the Christian Bible.* Philadelphia: Fortress, 1972.

Cerfaux, L. "De Saint Paul à 'L'Evangile de la Vérité.'" *NTS* 5 (1958/59) 103-112.

Charlesworth, J. H. *The Odes of Solomon.* SBLTT 13, Pseudepigrapha Series 7. Missoula: Scholars, 1977.

_____. "The Odes of Solomon—Not Gnostic." *CBQ* 31 (1969) 357-69.

Christensen, C. R. "John's Christology and the 'Gospel of Truth.'" *Gordon Review* 10 (1966) 22-31.

Collins, A. Y. *The Combat Myth in the Book of Revelation.* HDR 9. Missoula: Scholars, 1976.

Collins, J. J. "Introduction: Towards the Morphology of a Genre." *Semeia* 14 (1979) 1-20.

Conzelmann, H. *1 Corinthians.* Hermeneia. Philadelphia: Fortress, 1975.

Crum, W. E. *A Coptic Dictionary.* Oxford: Clarendon, 1939 (reprinted 1972).

Daniélou, J. *The Theology of Jewish Christianity.* London: Darton, Longman & Todd, 1964.

Davies, W. D. *The Setting of the Sermon on the Mount.* Cambridge: University, 1966.

de Faye, E. *Gnostiques et Gnosticisme.* 2nd ed. Paris: Librairie Orientalist Paul Geuthner, 1925.

Department of Antiquities of the United Arab Republic, and the United Nations Educational, Scientific and Cultural Organization. *The Facsimile Edition of the Nag Hammadi Codices.* Leiden: Brill, Codex I: 1977; Codices XI, XII, XIII: 1973; Cartonnage: 1979.

Dillon, J. *The Middle Platonists.* London: Duckworth, 1977.

Dubois, J.-D. "Le contexte judaïque du 'nom' dans l'Evangile de Vérité." *RTP* Ser. 3 24 (1974) 198-216.

_____. "Remarques sur le texte de l'Evangile de Vérité (CG I, 2)." *VC* 29 (1975) 138-140.

Dunn, J. W. E. "What Does 'Gospel of Truth' Mean?" *VC* 15 (1961) 160-164.

Elze, M. *Tatian und seine Theologie.* Göttingen: Vandenhoeck & Ruprecht, 1960.

Evangelium Veritatis: Codex Jung f. VIIIv - XVIv, f. XIXr - XXIIr, ed. and tr. M. Malinine, H.-C. Puech, and G. Quispel. Zurich: Rascher, 1956.

Evangelium Veritatis: Codex Jung f. XVIIr - XVIIIv, ed. and tr. M. Malinine, H.-C. Puech, G. Quispel, and W. Till. Zurich: Rascher, 1956.

Fecht, G. "Der erste 'Teil' des sogenannten Evangelium Veritatis." *Or* 30 (1961) 371-90; 31 (1962) 85-119; 32 (1963) 298-335.

Festugière, A.-J. "Notes sur les Extraits de Théodote de Clément d'Alexandrie et sur les fragments de Valentin." *VC* 3 (1949) 193-207.

Ford, J. M. *Revelation.* AB 38. Garden City: Doubleday, 1975.

Förster, W. *Von Valentin zu Herakleon.* BZNW 7. Giessen: A. Töpelmann, 1928.

Giversen, S. "Evangelium Veritatis and the Epistle to the Hebrews." *ST* 13 (1959) 87-96.

Grant, R. M. *Gnosticism and Early Christianity.* New York: Columbia University, 1966.

_____. "Notes on Gnosis." *VC* 11 (1957) 145-51.

_____. Review of *The Gnostic Paul*, and of *The Johannine Gospel in Gnostic Exegesis: Heracleon's Commentary on John*, both by E. H. Pagels. *RelSRev* 34 (1977) 30-35.

Grobel, K. *The Gospel of Truth. A Valentinian Meditation on the Gospel.* New York: Abingdon, 1960.

Haardt, T. "Zur Struktur des Planē-Myths in Evangelium Veritatis des Codex Jung." *Wiener Zeitschrift für die Kunde des Morgenlandes* 58 (1962) 24-38.

Haenchen, E. "Literatur zum Codex Jung." *TRu* 30 (1964) 39-82.

Hamilton, E. and H. Cairns. *Plato: Collected Dialogues.* Bollingen Series 71. Princeton: University, 1961 (reprinted 1978).

Hill, D. *The Gospel of Matthew.* New Century Bible. Greenwood: Attic, 1972.

Jonas, H. "*Evangelium Veritatis* and the Valentinian Speculation." *Studia Patristica* 6 (= TU 81). Berlin: Akademie (1962) 96-111.

_____. *The Gnostic Religion.* 2nd ed., revised. Boston: Beacon, 1963.

Kittel, G. and G. Friedrich, eds. *Theological Dictionary of the New Testament.* Grand Rapids: Eerdmans, 1964-74.

Klauser, T., ed. *Reallexicon für Antike und Christentum.* Stuttgart: Anton Hiersemann, 1978.

Koep, L. *Das himmlische Buch in Antike und Christentum.* Bonn: Peter Hanstein, 1952.

Koester, H. "One Jesus and Four Primitive Gospels." In *Trajectories through Early Christianity.* Philadelphia: Fortress, 1971.

_____. *Synoptische Überlieferung bei den apostolischen Vätern.* TU 65. Berlin: Akademie, 1957.

Lampe, G. W. H. *A Patristic Greek Lexicon.* Oxford: Clarendon, 1961.

Langerbeck, H. "Die Anthropologie der Alexandrinischen Gnosis." *Aufsätze zur Gnosis*, ed. H. Dörrie. Göttingen: Vandenhoeck & Ruprecht, 1967, 38-82.

LaPiana, G. "The Roman Church at the End of the Second Century." *HTR* 17 (1925) 201-277.

Layton, B. Review of *The Facsimile Edition of the Nag Hammadi Codices, Cartonnage; The Facsimile Edition of the Nag Hammadi Codices IX and X; Nag Hammadi Codices, Greek and Coptic Papyri from the Cartonnage of the Covers*, eds. J. W. B. Barns, G. M. Browne and J. C. Shelton; and *Nag Hammadi Codices IX and X*, ed. B. A. Pearson. *JOAS* 102 (1982) 397-398.

_____. *The Gnostic Treatise on Resurrection from Nag Hammadi.* HDR 12. Missoula: Scholars, 1979.

_____. "The Recovery of Gnosticism: The Philologist's task in the Investigation of Nag Hammadi." *Second Century* 1 (1981) 85-99.

Leipoldt, J. "Das 'Evangelium der Wahrheit.'" *TLZ* 82 (1957) 825-34.

Leloir, L. *Ephrem de Nisibe: Commentaire de L'Evangile concordant ou Diatessaron.* SC 121. Paris: le Cerf, 1966.

Liddell, H. G., R. Scott, H. S. Jones and R. McKenzie. *A Greek-English Lexicon.* Oxford: Clarendon, 1940 (reprinted 1976).

Lieu, J. M. "'Authority to Become Children of God': A Study in 1 John." *NovT* 23 (1981) 210-228.

Lindemann, A. *Paulus im ältesten Christentum: Das Bild des Apostels und die Rezeption der paulinischen Theologie in der frühchristlichen Literatur bis Marcion.* Tübingen: Mohr (Siebeck), 1979.

Lohse, E. *Colossians and Philemon.* Hermeneia. Philadelphia: Fortress, 1971.

Lucchesi, E. "Un Terme inconnu de l'Evangile de Vérité." *Or* 47 (1978) 483-484.

Lüdemann, G. "Zur Geschichte des ältesten Christentums in Rom. I. Valentin und Marcion. II. Ptolemäus und Justin." *ZNW* 70 (1979) 86-114.

Ludin, J. H. "Der Begriff ⲡⲧⲏⲣϥ 'das All' im Evangelium Veritatis." *Acta Orientalia* (Copenhagen) 31 (1968) 115-118.

MacRae, G. "Sleep and Awakening in Gnostic Texts." in U. Bianchi, ed. *Le Origini dello Gnosticismo.* Leiden: Brill, 1967, 496-507.

Marrou, H.-I. "L'Evangile de vérité et la diffusion du comput digital dans l'antiquité." *VC* 12 (1958) 98-103.

Massaux, E. *Influence de L'Evangile de saint Matthieu sur la littérature chrétienne avant saint Irénée.* Gembloux: Duculot, 1950.

_____. "L'Influence littéraire de l'Evangile de saint Matthieu sur la Didachè." *EphLov* 25 (1949) 5-41.

Meeks, W. A. "The Image of the Androgyne: Some Uses of a Symbol in Earliest Christianity." *HR* 13 (1974) 165-208.

_____. "The Man from Heaven in Johannine Sectarianism." *JBL* 91 (1972) 44-72.

Meeks, W. A., ed. *The Writings of Saint Paul.* New York: Norton, 1972.

Ménard, J.-E. *L'Evangile de Vérité: Rétroversion grecque et commentaire.* Paris: Letouzey & Ané, 1962.

_____. "La 'Connaissance' dans l'Evangile de Vérité." *RevScRel* 41 (1967) 1-28.

_____. "La structure et la langue originale de l'Evangile de Vérité." *RevScRel* 44 (1970) 128-137.

_____. "'Evangile de Vérité' et le Dieu caché des littératures antiques." *RevScRel* 45 (1971) 146-161.

_____. *L'Evangile de Vérité*. NHS 2. Leiden: Brill, 1972.

_____. "La fonction sotériologique de la memoire chez les Gnostiques." *RevScRel* 54 (1980) 298-310.

Munck, J. "Evangelium Veritatis and Greek Usage as to Book Titles." *ST* 17 (1963) 133-138.

Nagel, P. "Die Herkunft des Evangelium Veritatis in sprachlicher Sicht." *OLZ* 61 (1966) 5-14.

Neyrey, J. H. "John III—A Debate over Johannine Epistemology and Christology." *NovT* 23 (1981) 115-127.

Norden, E. *Die antike Kunstprosa vom VI Jahrhundert v. Chr. bis in die Zeit der Renaissance*, I. Leipzig: Teubner, 1898.

Novum Testamentum Graecae. E. Nestle and K. Aland, eds. 26th ed. Stuttgart: Deutsche Bibelstiftung, 1979.

Nygren, A. *Commentary on Romans*. Philadelphia: Fortress, 1949.

O'Neill, J. C. "The Source of the Christology in Colossians." *NTS* 26 (1979-80) 87-100.

Orbe, A. *Christología Gnóstica*, I, II. Madrid: Biblioteca Autores Cristianos, 1976.

Osborn, E. F. "The Gospel of Truth." *Australian Biblical Review* 10 (1962) 32-41.

Pagels, E. H. *The Gnostic Paul*. Philadelphia: Fortress, 1975.

Palmer, R. E. *Hermeneutics*. Evanston: Northwestern University, 1969.

Pearson, B. A. "Did the Gnostics Curse Jesus?" *JBL* 86 (1967) 301-305.

Piper, O. A. "Change of Perspective, Gnostic and Canonical Gospels." *Int* 16 (1962) 402-417.

Poirier, P.-H. "*L'Evangile de Vérité*, Ephrem le Syrien et le comput digital." *RevEtudAug* 25 (1979) 27-34.

Puech, H.-Ch. and G. Quispel. "Les Ecrits gnostiques du Codex Jung," *VC* 8 (1954) 1-51.

Quecke, H. "Eine missbräuchliche Verwendung des Qualitativs im Koptischen," *Muséon* 75 (1962) 291-300.

Quispel, G. "The Original Doctrine of Valentine," *VC* 1 (1947) 43-73.

_____. "Qumran, John and Jewish Christianity," *John and Qumran*, ed. J. H. Charlesworth, London: Chapman, 1972, 137-155.

Rensberger, D. K. *As the Apostle Teaches*. Ph.D. Dissertation, Yale, 1981.

_____. Review of *Paulus im ältesten Christentum: Das Bild des Apostels und die Reception der paulinischer Theologie in der frühchristlichen Literatur bis Marcion*, by A. Lindemann. *JBL* 101 (1982) 287-289.

Resch, A. *Agrapha: Aussercanonische Schriftfragmente*. Leipzig: Hinrichs, 1906.

Ringgren, H. "Der umgekehrte Baum und das Leben als Traum (Evangelium Veritatis, 28, 16-21)." in *Hommages à G. Dumézil*. Collection *Latomus* 45. Brussels: 1960, 172-176.

_____. "The Gospel of Truth and Valentinian Gnosticism." *ST* 18 (1964) 51-65.

Robinson, J. M. "*Logoi Sophon:* On the Gattung of Q." In *Trajectories through Early Christianity*, by J. M. Robinson and H. Koester, Philadelphia: Fortress, 1971.

_____. "The Discovery of the Nag Hammadi Codices." *BA* 42 (1979) 206-224.

Robinson, J. M., ed. *The Nag Hammadi Library in English*. San Francisco: Harper & Row, 1977.

Robison, A. C. "The *Evangelium Veritatis:* Its Doctrine, Character and Origin." *JR* 43 (1963) 234-243.

Rudolph, K. "Gnosis and Gnostizismus, ein Forschungsbericht." *TRu* n.s. 34 (1969) 121-175, 181-231, 358-361.

Sagnard, F. *La Gnose valentienne et le témoignage de saint Irénée*. Etudes de philosophie médiévale 36. Paris: Librairie Philosophique J. Vrin, 1947.

Sanders, J. N. *The Fourth Gospel in the Early Church*. Cambridge: University, 1943.

Sanders, J. T. "On the Coptic Gnostic Literature from Nag Hammadi." Chapter 7 in *The New Testament Christological Hymns: Their His-*

torical Religious Background. SNTS Monograph Series 15. Cambridge: University, 1971, 121-132.

Schelkle, K. H. "Das Evangelium Veritatis als kanongeschichtliches Zeugnis." BZ 5 (1961) 90-91.

Schenke, H.-M. Die Herkunft des sogenannten Evangelium Veritatis. Göttingen: Vandenhoeck & Ruprecht, 1959.

Schmidtke, F. "Zum Evangelium Veritatis 36, 17 ff." TLZ 85 (1960) 713-714.

Schoedel, W. R. "Gnostic Monism and the Gospel of Truth." In The Rediscovery of Gnosticism I, ed. B. Layton. Leiden: Brill, 1980, 379-390.

Segelberg, E. "Evangelium Veritatis—A Confirmation Homily and its Relation to the Odes of Solomon." Orientalia Suecana, 8 (1959). Uppsala 1960, 1-42.

_____. "The Baptismal Rite According to Some of the Coptic-Gnostic Texts of Nag Hammadi." Studia Patristica 5 (= TU 80). Berlin: Akademie, 1962, 117-128.

Septuaginta. A. Rahlfs, ed. 2 vols. Stuttgart: Wurttembergische Bibelanstalt, 1935.

Smith, J. D. Gaius and the Controversy over the Johannine Literature. Ph.D. Dissertation, Yale, 1979.

Smith, J. Z. "The Garments of Shame." HR 5 (1965-66) 217-239.

Standaert, B. "'Evangelium Veritatis' et 'Veritatis Evangelium.' La question du titre et les témoins patristiques." VC 30 (1976) 138-150.

_____. "'L'Evangile de Vérité': Critique et Lecture." NTS 22 (1976) 243-275.

Staniforth, M. Early Christian Writings. New York: Penguin, 1968 (reprinted 1981).

Stanton, G. N. "5 Ezra and Matthean Christianity in the Second Century." JTS n.s. 28 (1977) 67-83.

Stead, G. C. "In Search of Valentinus." In The Rediscovery of Gnosticism I, ed. B. Layton. Leiden: Brill, 1980, 75-95.

_____. "The Valentinian Myth of Sophia." JTS n.s. 20 (1969) 75-104.

Story, C. I. K. The Nature of Truth in the Gospel of Truth and the Writings of Justin Martyr. Leiden: Brill, 1970.

Stroker, W. D. *The Formation of Secondary Sayings of Jesus*. Ph.D. Dissertation, Yale, 1970.

Stylianopoulos, T. *Justin Martyr and the Mosaic Law*. SBLDS 20. Missoula: Scholars, 1975.

Tardieu, M. "'Comme à travers un tuyau', Quelques remarques sur le mythe valentinien de la chair céleste du Christ." *Colloque International sur les Textes de Nag Hammadi, I*, ed. B. Barc. Quebec: Les Presses de l'Université Laval, 1981, 150-177.

Till, W. "Bemerkungen zur Erstausgabe des 'Evangelium Veritatis.'" *Orientalia* 27 (1958) 269-286.

_____. "Das Evangelium der Wahrheit." *ZNTW* 50 (1959) 165-185.

Turner, J. D. *The Book of Thomas the Contender*. SBLDS 23. Missoula: Scholars, 1975.

van Unnik, W. C. "The 'Gospel of Truth' and the New Testament." In *The Jung Codex*, tr. and ed. F. L. Cross. London: Mowbray, 1955, 79-129.

_____. "'Worthy is the Lamb.' The Background of Apoc 5." *Melanges bibliques en hommage au R. P. Béda Rigaux*, ed. A. Descamps and A. de Halleaux. Gembloux: Duculot, 1970, 445-461.

_____. "Der Neid in der Paradiesgeschichte nach einigen gnostischen Texten." *Essays on the Nag Hammadi Texts in Honour of Alexander Böhlig*, ed. M. Krause. Leiden: Brill, 1972, 120-132.

Voelker, W. *Quellen zur Geschichte der christlichen Gnosis*. Tübingen: Mohr (Siebeck), 1932.

Walker, W. O., Jr., ed. *The Relationships among the Gospels*. San Antonio: Trinity University, 1978.

Wettstein, J. *Novum Testamentum Graecum*. Amsterdam, 1751-1752. Repr. Graz: Akademischer Druck, 1962.

Wilson, R. McL. "A Note on the Gospel of Truth (33.8-9)." *NTS* 9 (1962) 295-298.

_____. "Valentinianism and the Gospel of Truth." *The Rediscovery of Gnosticism*, I, ed. B. Layton. Leiden: Brill, 1980, 133-141.

Index of Modern Authors

Attridge, H., 2, 6
Barns, J. W. B., 2
Barrett, C. K., 9, 114
Blanchette, O., 52, 53
Bloch, R., 203
Browne, G. M., 2
Campenhausen, H. von, 8, 176, 177, 187, 200
Cerfaux, L., 7, 16
Charlesworth, J. H., 25, 139
Conzelmann, H., 57
Cross, F., 5, 7
Daniélou, J., 7, 53, 159
Davies, W. D., 184
Dillon, J., 171, 193
Dubois, J.-D., 7, 159
Dunn, J. W. E., 6
Elze, M., 148
Emmel, S., 15
Giversen, S., 91, 92
Grant, R. M., 10, 202
Green, W. S., 203
Grobel, K., 3, 6, 10, 26, 54, 58, 66, 77, 82, 83, 84, 89, 90, 95, 97, 117, 121, 122, 126, 128, 133, 134, 136, 138, 143, 144, 148, 150, 151, 152, 153, 167
Hill, D., 102, 137
Jonas, H., 5, 201
Kennedy, G., 177
Klassen, W., 9
Koep, L., 39
Koester, H., 6, 8, 12, 175
Layton, B., 1, 2, 4, 22, 31, 81
Leloir, L., 146, 148
Lieu, J. M., 107

Lindemann, A., 186
Lohse, E., 30, 51
Lucchesi, E., 30
Lüdemann, G., 5
Malinine, M., 2, 23, 33, 36, 67, 70, 75, 87, 127, 130, 132, 158, 159, 163, 169
Marrou, H.-I., 7, 122
Massaux, E., 12, 101, 184
Meeks, W. A., 57, 183
Ménard, J.-E., 1, 7, 10, 11
Munck, J., 3
Norden, E., 175
Nygren, A., 200
Pagels, E. H., 10
Pearson, B., 5
Piper, O. A., 6, 7
Poirier, P.-H., 7
Puech, H.-Ch., 2
Quispel, G., 2
Rensberger, D. K., 186
Resch, A., 146
Robinson, J. M., 1, 6, 175
Schenke, H.-M., 113, 115, 121
Schmidtke, F., 151
Schoedel, W. R., 31
Segelberg, E., 151
Shelton, J. C., 2
Smith, J. D., 183
Smith, J. Z., 57
Snyder, E. F., 9
Standaert, B., 3, 4, 7, 104, 111, 112, 165, 177, 194
Stanton, G. N., 184
Stead, G. C., 4
Story, C. I. K., 7, 122

Stroker, W. D., 135
Stylianopoulos, T., 200
Till, W., 2
Turner, J. D., 139
Unnik, W. C. van, 3, 7, 8, 20, 29, 37, 41, 44, 45, 46, 48, 50, 55, 62, 64, 71, 73, 77, 80, 82, 84, 91, 93, 99, 100, 103, 105, 106, 111, 115, 119, 122, 123, 154, 156, 158, 162, 168, 171
Voelker, W., 4
Walker, W. O., Jr., 177
Wilson, R. McL., 16
Yarbro Collins, A., 38

www.ingramcontent.com/pod-product-compliance
Lightning Source LLC
Chambersburg PA
CBHW022058160426
43198CB00008B/270